Talk back to your doctor

Also by Arthur Levin

THE SATISFICERS

Talk back to your doctor

How to demand (and recognize) high-quality health care

By Arthur Levin, M.D.

Doubleday & Company, Inc.
Garden City, New York

Copyright © 1975 by Arthur Levin
All Rights Reserved
Printed in the United States of America

Library of Congress Cataloging in Publication Data

Levin, Arthur.
    Talk back to your doctor.

    Bibliography: p. 231.
    Includes index.
    1. Physician and patient.   2. Medical care.   I. Title.
R727.3.L38   362.1'0973
ISBN 0-385-03455-5
Library of Congress Catalog Card Number 74–12696

To the many workers and teachers in public health, preventive and community medicine—today's leaders in the struggle for better health care for all Americans.

Acknowledgments

Many persons have aided me in writing this book. I would like to thank Professor Osler Peterson and his colleagues at the Harvard Department of Preventive Medicine, John Bunker, Duncan Neuhauser, and Nancy Jones, all of whom were kind enough to share their ideas and knowledge with me. Dr. Norman Simon read and commented upon an early draft manuscript. Professor Mildred Morehead and Gerald Sparer were most helpful, as was Dr. Edward F. X. Hughes. Joseph Terenzio, president of the United Hospital Fund of New York, and Louise Heinze, the Fund's librarian, kindly made available invaluable library facilities. Finally, I should like to thank Professor George Silver, who first spurred my interest in the problems of health care, and Professor Robert Connery, who has been a friend and sounding board for many of my ideas.

A note to the reader

This book was written with one thought uppermost in my mind: How would I behave if I were to need medical care? How would I go about finding the best doctor? The most competent surgeon? The safest hospital? What methods would I use to judge the caliber of the care I had received?

I have tried to imagine myself in a variety of situations, not as a physician, but as a consumer of health and medical care. I have attempted to analyze how I would act in such a role.

How, for instance, would I respond to a doctor who told me I had a rare disease? To one who said my symptoms were of no consequence? To a recommendation that I enter the hospital or undergo surgery?

I have tried to predict how I would respond to these sorts of crises—and how I would go about making sure I was obtaining the best possible advice.

In writing this sort of book, some doctors may say that I have been irresponsible. They may assert that I have sought to undermine public confidence in the health system. Or that I have unjustly "written off" as unsatisfactory large numbers of doctors or hospitals.

My intent, however, is quite different.

I have attempted to offer consumers a guide to finding the *best* health care. I have attempted to share with them knowledge already widely known to doctors, but not to the general public.

Where I have advised against using certain doctors or hospitals it is only because—unfortunately—there exists evidence that they do not provide the best-caliber care. It is because they are doctors or hospitals I myself—and, I believe, most physicians—would avoid, if at all possible.

Some doctors may say that this book is dangerous in that it will encourage people to diagnose or treat their own health problems.

A person who knows something about a physical examination, they might say, might be tempted to try to perform one on himself or on a friend.

I do not share this apprehension. Most people, I feel confident, do not wish to be their own doctors. They are more than happy to let a physician do a physician's job. They would, however, like to be able to judge how well that job is being done.

It is a fact of life—whether doctors like it or not—that people are fast becoming more sophisticated when it comes to health care. They are "shopping around" more for the best care. They are more aware of their options in obtaining services. They are earnestly trying to identify "good" and "not so good" care.

Even the sophisticated consumer, however, faces severe handicaps when it comes to seeking health care. He is at a serious disadvantage. He lacks many of the basic facts and principles which are second nature to most doctors.

This volume will try to supply some of these basic facts.

Over the years, a small band of researchers has examined the quality of health care in the United States. I know many of these researchers. They are men and women dedicated to improving the caliber of our health services. They are dedicated to the prevention of illness and disability.

All too often, however, their work has been ignored by the medical profession as a whole. In many instances it has been actively suppressed, and denied to the public. I hope that this volume, in a small way, will redress the balance and give these studies and research the exposure they deserve. (A list of some of the more important studies on the quality of U.S. health care may be found in the Appendix.)

In addition, there is a great deal that is known about the quality of health care that is not to be found in any studies. Where relevant, I have made use of my own experiences, or those of other physicians and patients, in buttressing the "principles" in this book.

A brief word should be said about some aspects of medical care not emphasized in the book. I have not attempted to deal with dentists and dental health. Mental health services are mentioned only in passing, as are the services of osteopaths, podiatrists, and chiropractors. Various other types of health workers are doubtless not given the attention their proponents would have wanted.

This, however, is not a book about types of health workers, but about health care. It is a book for people who wish to know how health can be preserved and how illness is diagnosed and treated. This is thus, unavoidably, a book primarily about doctors, and about the places they use to care for their patients.

I would encourage the reader—whether consumer or health professional—to be critical of this book. I encourage him to try to think of exceptions to its rules of thumb. Indeed, nothing would please me more than to see the day when many of these rules no longer apply, the day when top-notch care is found in every doctor's office and in every health facility.

If statements in this volume inflame the medical profession, and if their anger spurs them to an all-out investigation of the quality of U.S. health care—so much the better. Such an investigation is long overdue.

Indeed, if the profession had done its job, there would be no need for this kind of a book. If the AMA, medical societies, and other professional groups had exercised proper vigilance, there would be no need to tell the public how to detect and avoid substandard care.

But these groups have not done their job. They have failed to maintain a superior standard of care. They have refused to censure—or in some instances even to criticize—the practices of incompetent doctors. They have failed to close even the worst hospitals or nursing homes.

Someday soon the medical profession will, I hope, take steps to police itself. In the meantime, however, the public must deal as best they can with today's uneven health care system. People must decide whether to go to Doctor A or Doctor B. Whether to use a public or a private hospital, and which one. Whether or not to place an aged relative in a nursing home.

These are the kinds of decisions which face people in today's world. They need better information now to help them make these choices. They need assistance to help them use the health system, to deal on a more equal footing with doctors and the institutions which provide health services in this less than perfect world.

Contents

phasic screening"? Which tests are most important in detecting common causes of death and disability?

How dangerous are prescription drugs? What is the most serious drug prescribing error? What is an "indicated" drug? How can you determine if a drug is indicated? How many drugs should your doctor use? What about doctors who use drug "combinations" or give drugs by injection? What should your drug prescription say? What are generic and brand-name drugs?

How often do doctors seek a second opinion? The doctor who cannot make a correct diagnosis. The doctor who tells you your problem is emotional. Who diagnoses a disease with a bad "prognosis." Should you switch doctors if you think your doctor dislikes you? A second opinion: Where should you go? Should you refer yourself to a specialist?

How good are U.S. hospitals? Is it possible to identify "good" and "bad" hospitals? What should you look for in choosing a hospital? Are large hospitals better than small ones? What services should a hospital provide? Should you—or your doctor—choose your hospital? How to avoid unnecessary hospitalization and minimize your stay. How is the hospital teaching service organized? What are your rights as a hospital patient? Should you take part in a research project? Home care, rehabilitation, and nursing homes.

How dangerous is surgery? Which operations are most often done —and overdone? How can you avoid unneeded surgery? What should you know about surgical anesthesia? Which operations carry the most risk? What tests should your surgeon do before surgery? Is it safe to be operated on by an intern or resident? How long should you stay in the hospital for surgery? How crucial is postoperative care?

Do women receive poorer health care than men? Are they intimidated by doctors? Are doctors too quick to diagnose "emotional" illness in women? To perform surgery? Should a woman use a

woman doctor? Should a woman practice "self-examination"?
Family planning, abortion, and sterilization. What is recommended
prenatal care? What is a "high-risk" pregnancy? Labor and delivery. What is "perinatal" care? What kind of care should your
infant get at birth? The pediatric physical exam. What is recommended well-child care? Which provider should you rely on for
pediatric care?

Are doctors concerned about the quality of medical care? Do official bodies really police quality? Have facts about quality been
suppressed? What can government do about the quality of care?
Consumer groups? In which official agencies should consumers demand a voice? What can individual consumers do?

*Talk back
to your doctor*

Talking back: the consumer and health care

A friend of mine recently visited an orthopedist because of pain in her knee. After her visit, she telephoned me in a state of some agitation. The doctor, she said, had told her she might have a torn cartilage. He wanted to do an "arthrogram" to find out.

My friend's questions came thick and fast. What was an arthrogram? Was it dangerous? Would it tell for sure if she had a damaged cartilage? Would she require surgery?

I listened patiently. Finally, I asked her a question.

"Why didn't you ask your doctor all this?"

"I don't know," she confessed. "I just wanted to get out of there."

This is not an isolated incident. I have seen it happen time and again. I meet a middle-aged friend on the street. He has just come from his yearly checkup. He wants to know if his doctor did everything he should have. Should the doctor have ordered more lab tests? Should he have referred him to another specialist for a possible urinary problem?

"Incompetent." That's the unflattering way that Herbert Klarman, an economist and public health professor, describes the average health care consumer. Buying health care, Klarman explains, is a little like buying a new car. Because it is done infrequently, most people are at a severe disadvantage. They do not know what to expect. The patient has little idea whether, in a particular situation, the care provided is "excellent," "fair," or "poor."

How good is the health care we receive?

"Health," Emerson once said, "is the first wealth." Each year we Americans spend more than $70 billion—more than 7 per cent of our Gross National Product—to purchase that "first wealth." Yet we are a long way from getting our money's worth. Citizens in several nations which spend far less enjoy a longer span of life. The death rate in the United States is essentially unchanged from what it was twenty years ago!

A few years ago, two government statisticians, Lillian Guralnick and Ann Jackson, made an interesting discovery. They found that there were wide gaps in death rates among U.S. states. Middle-aged Americans, it seemed, were dying at twice the rate in some states as in others. In Texas, for instance, Guralnick and Jackson found an almost 25 per cent higher death rate than in the "best" states—or, in other words, some 36,000 excess deaths each year! In that state, moreover, the biggest single cause of these excess deaths was a disease which medical science has known how to treat for decades—tuberculosis!

The Guralnick and Jackson study of excess deaths is a classic. It vividly points out that there are thousands—possibly millions—of Americans, in the prime of life, who die needlessly each year. These people die from conditions which are preventable or treatable by decent-quality health care. And for each person who dies, there are doubtless many others who suffer disability.

This grave situation still exists. Wide discrepancies in health levels between the various states continue. What's more, the worst states are frequently those with the greatest abundance of doctors, hospitals, and other health resources! (Table 1)

These poor health levels, in places with an abundance of doctors and other resources, suggest that something is seriously awry. They suggest that—despite the assurances of many health professionals—there is a great deal of substandard, ineffective, and perhaps even downright harmful care being dispensed.

Every so often, truly bad medical care makes front-page news. Recently, a courageous woman reporter discovered—by posing as a patient—several New York doctors who were injecting large doses of amphetamines to cure everything from headaches to back pain. One of these doctors—dubbed "Doctor Feelgood"—freely admitted using the addicting drugs to treat many of his patients, who included celebrities and prominent political leaders.

Such blatantly poor medicine, experts have always assumed, is the exception and not the rule. Only about 5 per cent of all doctors, estimates New York's health commissioner, provide truly poor quality care.

TABLE 1 Length of Life in the United States and Each State

State	Life Expectancy (years)	State	Life Expectancy (years)
Nebraska	71.95	Maine	70.02
Iowa	71.91	Wyoming	69.90
Kansas	71.90	Florida	69.84
Minnesota	71.84	New Jersey	69.80
North Dakota	71.72	Kentucky	69.66
Utah	71.61	Illinois	69.64
Hawaii	71.55	New York	69.61
Wisconsin	71.22	West Virginia	69.53
Idaho	71.13	Montana	69.49
Connecticut	71.02	New Mexico	69.48
Washington	70.95	Pennsylvania	69.47
South Dakota	70.94	Tennessee	69.43
Oklahoma	70.89	Delaware	69.38
Oregon	70.85	Arizona	68.91
California	70.82	Virginia	68.80
Colorado	70.79	Maryland	68.72
Massachusetts	70.61	North Carolina	68.40
Rhode Island	70.60	Louisiana	68.13
New Hampshire	70.41	Alabama	68.11
Missouri	70.40	Georgia	67.91
Indiana	70.37	Mississippi	67.70
Vermont	70.35	Alaska	67.51
Ohio	70.18	Nevada	67.42
Arkansas	70.16	South Carolina	66.41
Michigan	70.13	(District of Columbia	66.62)
Texas	70.12	United States	69.89

SOURCE: National Center for Health Statistics, Department of Health, Education and Welfare.

This low estimate, however, may be wishful thinking. Over the years there have been several careful surveys of the quality of physician practice in the United States. These surveys paint a far from reassuring picture. Some of the unpleasant—and unpublicized—details:

In North Carolina, some 40 per cent of GPs studied were found to be delivering less than adequate care. Only 8 per cent were practicing at the highest level.

Less than one third of patients seeing a group of rural "solo" doctors were given a rectal exam; less than 30 per cent of women received a Pap smear to check for cervical cancer.

Of California women dying during pregnancy, in half the deaths a physician error in judgment or technique was found. A study of deaths in early infancy called nearly half the deaths preventable—and found medical errors in three quarters of these.

Among children seen by Washington, D.C., physicians 80 per cent had no record of any vision test. In the same study, one in five children with ear infections received "inappropriate" antibiotic treatment.

In a study of hospital patients, 40 per cent received "less than optimal" care—and 15 per cent did not require hospitalization at all!

One third of all patients, in a national sample, whose appendices were removed at surgery, were found to have no evidence of appendicitis.

In a study of Connecticut nursing homes, "well under 30 per cent" of patients surveyed received an annual physical exam.

The evidence from these, and other, studies points to a single, clear conclusion. Substandard care is not limited to a few doctors or hospitals. It is much more pervasive.

"There is much evidence," says Avedis Donabedian, a University of Michigan professor, "to indicate that the quality of care available *under many circumstances* falls far below acceptable levels" (italics mine).

"The quality of the product being dispensed," notes a recent New York State governor's report, "varies greatly."

"Even when people do get care," says Cornell health expert Roger Battistella, "the care they receive is, in many instances . . . below prevailing acceptable medical standards."

Battistella makes a vital point. As we all know, many people have great difficulty obtaining medical care. But even when they manage to obtain it, there is no guarantee that it will be of satisfactory quality.

Poor-quality health care is a real hazard for everyone.

The study of hospital patients cited above was carried out in one of our most affluent, most medically advanced areas—New York City. The examples of patient mismanagement found involved all types of hospitals. They involved "ward" as well as private patients. Indeed, the study's authors called it "discouraging" to find so many examples of what they kindly termed "poor clinical judgment" in a city with so many prestige hospitals and supposedly well-trained physicians.

Poor-quality care knows no boundaries—social, economic, or geographic. Its victims are Americans of all ages, men and women, rich and poor. We are all, in a very real sense, a single population at risk.

Is it possible to define high-quality care?

Everyone agrees that high-quality health care involves more than simply treating illness, or acute health problems. There is general agreement that it also involves other things.

Principle: High-quality health care is care which (1) maintains or improves your health through preventive medicine, (2) correctly diagnoses and treats illness, and (3) rehabilitates to as high a health level as possible.

These are the basic triad of high-caliber care. They are the three things which you, as a consumer, have a right to demand whenever you seek care.

When I began writing this book, I spoke with several doctors. Most were not especially warm to the idea of a book which sought to aid consumers in judging the caliber of their care. Some, in fact, were openly skeptical.

"I must confess," one specialist told me, "that I am having a considerable amount of difficulty in this sphere myself, even after many years of practice."

Is it really so difficult to judge the quality of health care? Need the consumer be helpless when it comes to spotting inadequate doctors? Unacceptable medical practices? Poor hospitals or other facilities?

The medical profession has, for the most part, sought to foster the idea that quality in health care is a concept which defies definition.

"No two patients are the same," I have heard doctors say. Or, "Every case is unique." These phrases are often used to convey the impression that it is impossible to set rules or standards for good-quality care.

This myth is so pervasive it has been swallowed by people who should know better. Here, for instance, is a writer for *Woman's Day* magazine:

> Medicine . . . contains vast gray areas in which honest doctors differ. Some treat the flue [*sic*] with aspirin; others give a shot of penicillin. One doctor removes a child's tonsils at the first sign of trouble; another calls this unnecessary surgery . . .

This writer leaves us with the feeling that there are as many ways to practice good medicine as there are doctors! She leaves us with the impression that every doctor is entitled to set his own standards.

Fortunately, such is not the case.

There are far fewer ways to practice good medicine than the *Woman's Day* writer—and many doctors—would have us believe. In fact, the two examples cited prove the point. The doctor who gives a shot of penicillin for influenza, a viral disease, is providing a worthless treatment and, thus, substandard care. So, likewise, is the physician who removes a child's tonsils "at the first sign of trouble."

These are both such blatant examples of poor care, I am amazed that anyone would use them as illustrative of "gray areas in which honest doctors differ."

Principle: It is possible to set standards for good medical care, and to identify doctors (hospitals, etc.) who adhere to these standards.

There are, naturally, instances where even the most knowledgeable doctors will disagree on what constitutes optimal care. More often than not, however, it is possible to agree on standards. More important, it is also possible for people *who are not physicians* to learn how to use these standards to evaluate the quality of their own care.

To be sure, there are limits. None of us, regardless of how much we know, will be able to tell if our surgeon has dropped a stitch during our gallbladder operation. But there are plenty of things we can detect. And not only after—but *while* we are receiving care.

Why should consumers learn to judge their care?

The object of this book is to give you, the health consumer, the basic facts you need to judge the quality of your care. As we have seen, there is a good deal wrong with the quality of such care. Most experts believe that the solution to these deficiencies is "peer review"—doctors checking up on other doctors, the profession policing itself.

Peer review is important. But I think there is another—and thus far neglected—weapon in the fight to improve quality. This weapon is the informed consumer.

The consumer can be, I am confident, the most powerful force for bettering the caliber of health care. But, first, he must learn to play a more active role in that care. He must begin intelligently to question and assess what his doctor does.

The consumer, in other words, must start to "talk back."

Why is "talking back" so important?

Doctors, like everyone else, perform better when their performance is being scrutinized. A doctor doing an exam in the presence of a medical student is more apt to do a complete exam, and not to cut corners, than the physician who is unobserved.

Most physicians, sadly, *are* unobserved. There is no one looking over their shoulder. They work in the isolation of their offices, alone except for one person—the patient. Thus the more informed a consumer the patient is, the better his doctor is apt to perform.

Talking back keeps the doctor honest. "Doctor," I have heard a sophisticated patient say, "shouldn't I have a blood test for anemia?" And the physician, who might otherwise have been tempted to cut corners and avoid the test, will not do so.

Talking back is not, of course, limited to the patient. I have seen patients languish in a hospital bed until an angry relative comes in and lambastes the doctor-in-charge. Then, as if by magic, things happen. Tests which could not be scheduled are done. Consulting physicians who were unavailable appear at the bedside. A diagnosis is made, and treatment instituted.

And all because someone spoke up! Because someone decided it was time to talk back.

What makes patients reluctant to "talk back"?

I have spent a great deal of time talking with people who have sought medical care. Time and again, I have been struck by their reluctance to ask their doctor questions I thought were obvious ones—questions about their diagnosis, their drug prescription, their hospital stay, about any of the dozens of facets of their care.

Most of these people, like my friend with the sore knee, mentioned at the start of this chapter, offer unconvincing reasons for their reluctance to talk back:

"The doctor seemed so busy."

"I thought my question might seem foolish."

"Before I knew it, I was out of the office."

All too often the result is the same: the patient seems perfectly willing to accept whatever the doctor says or does, without a murmur. The patient seems, in a word, intimidated.

Many doctors, I am sure, encourage this intimidation. They employ a variety of methods to keep the patient at a safe distance—and to discourage talking back.

Some doctors rely on medical mystification to accomplish this end. They use medical jargon to puzzle their patients. (The doctor who uses the term "rhinorrhea" stands a better chance of confusing you than if he had said "runny nose.") They write their prescriptions in Latin, or almost illegibly.

A doctor may conduct his office visits in a way which works against any form of doctor-patient dialogue. Such a doctor will be busily writing at his desk when you enter. He may murmur a disinterested "Good morning." He will ask his questions in a quick, dry fashion which encourages only the briefest replies.

Such a doctor's message to you, the patient, is clear: no questions, no interruptions or detours in the routine will be tolerated. The doctor is in control.

I have seen and heard of doctors responding to a patient's questions with outright hostility. In one extreme case, a gynecologist operated upon a woman for a fibroid—a benign tumor—of the uterus. The doctor, ominously, did not come to see his patient in the hospital before surgery. Afterwards, she had to request to see him. When the physician did finally appear, he reacted to his patient's pent-up questions with outright anger.

"I took it out," he snapped, "so what more do you need to know?"

It is easy to see how a patient—faced with such a physician—might be intimidated.

Luckily, not all doctors respond this way to patients' requests for information. I have seen the finest—and busiest—cardiac surgeons sit at a patient's bedside and draw meticulous diagrams to explain a forthcoming operation. I have seen the most eminent professors of medicine postpone lectures or conferences to sit and talk to a distraught family.

Doctors *are* busy people. And the best are apt to be the busiest. But in my experience, these are the doctors who are also able, somehow, to find the most time to talk to their patients—and to let them talk back.

I only wish people appreciated this fact—and kept it in mind when they were faced with a physician unwilling to carry on a dialogue with them about their care. I only wish—if I could do one thing— that I could convince people that *they need not stick with a physician who is too busy to talk with them.*

Do consumers have a choice when it comes to health care?

What's the point, someone asked me, in telling people to talk back? In telling them to be more critical of their doctors, and of the quality of their care? Most people, after all, are lucky to get any care at all. Therefore, they can hardly afford to be too critical of the care they do receive.

I cannot agree with this argument.

The United States, as a nation, has more health resources than any other nation in the world. We have more doctors for our population than almost any other country. We have more hospital beds—so many that about 20 per cent of them are empty on any given day!

I am often amazed at how little most people know about the different places they can obtain care. Usually, they have limited their experience to one or two private "solo" physicians. They have never thought of enrolling in a prepaid group practice plan. They have never considered trying a hospital outpatient clinic. They are unaware of the public health or other low-cost clinics in their locale.

There are, of course, places where care is in such short supply that the doctors who provide it are in the driver's seat. There are still towns with only a single physician. But, fortunately, the situation is different in most parts of the country. In most places, even rural areas, there are alternative sources of care. Consumers need not put up with doctors or hospitals who are not responsive to their needs.

You, the health consumer, do have a choice!

And you can begin to exercise that choice right now—with the selection of a personal physician.

2

Choosing doctors: good, better, best

"Go see Doctor X. He has all kinds of famous people for his patients."

"Doctor Y must be good. It takes two months to get an appointment to see him."

"I'm telling you—I was feeling terrible and this guy saved my life."

Good advice? Or a bum steer?

Most people, studies show, select a doctor with about as much forethought as they select an automobile. Often they rely on the casual advice of their neighbors, business associates, even their barber or hairdresser. Sometimes their choice works out. Just as frequently, however, it proves to be a disaster.

Choosing a doctor is your first step in entering the health system. It is a step that can have far-reaching consequences. It is too important a choice to make solely on the advice of a friend, however well intentioned.

I recall once sending a friend to another doctor. Her ailment was a minor one. I knew that the man to whom I sent her was adequate to deal with the problem, though I had a strong suspicion that he was not a top-quality physician. My friend, however, had no such suspicion. She, in turn, sent one of her co-workers—a woman with a far more complex diagnostic problem—to the same doctor. To my horror he failed utterly to make a correct diagnosis, and the second woman nearly died as a result.

Many people have a good sense of what is a grave problem and what is a trivial one. I can remember, time and again, as a resident, asking patients why they had chosen to come to the teaching hospital for a particular problem rather than consulting their own doctor.

"I bring him to the doctor for most things," said one black woman, talking about her son. "But this time I knew he had to come here."

If you are the type of person who can sense—as this mother did—when an illness is a serious one, you are fortunate. You will know when it is absolutely essential to find a top-notch doctor.

But this "sixth sense" is not possessed by everyone, not even by every physician. And many times what begins as a trivial illness turns into a major one.

For these reasons, it is useful to know how to select the best doctor. It is useful to know how good a doctor is likely to be *before*—and not after—you set foot in his office.

What things predict how well a doctor will perform?

There are five things which you can use to predict how well any physician will perform. These five are:

(1) the doctor's training
(2) his age
(3) his credentials
(4) his practice environment
(5) his continuing education

While these five factors won't absolutely assure that your doctor will perform well, they can go a long way towards minimizing the risk of a poor choice.

Let's discuss each of the five in detail.

The doctor's training

A doctor's training is a long process. It starts with medical school —usually four years in length. Then comes a year of hospital internship followed by two or more years of residency training. Usually two or more years of military service are interspersed, somewhere along the line.

All this adds up to some ten years before a doctor is ready to practice. Often the period is longer. I know many doctors who are thirty-five or older before they finally start their private practice. They have seen literally thousands of patients before opening their own offices.

Of all this training, at what should you look in choosing a doctor? Medical school is *not*—contrary to popular opinion—very important. Where a doctor went to medical school, or even his class standing, are not very good guides to his future performance.

Why is this?

One reason is that while there are certain "prestige" medical schools, most schools are more alike than they are different. Most teach the same things at the same times. Another reason is that most medical students are far from decided on their future careers. They have yet to make the all-important choice of a medical specialty.

Internship, too, is not a very good guide to a doctor's quality. Many doctors are still undecided about their future specialty. I have friends who began their careers as surgical interns only to wind up as cardiologists. And vice versa.

I do not mean that medical school and internship are unimportant in a doctor's training. I mean only that they are not likely to be very useful *to you* in predicting a doctor's caliber.

What *is* useful?

Principle: Knowing the facts about a doctor's residency training is a good way to predict how well he will perform.

Residency training *is* important as a guide to a doctor's caliber. Residency training is specialty oriented. A doctor takes a residency in medicine, surgery, pediatrics, etc. Often the residency becomes more specialized as it goes along—from general surgery to chest surgery to heart surgery, for example.

Also, a residency lasts a long time. The shortest type is at least two years. Some areas of surgery have residency programs that last five years or more.

A decent residency program will enable a doctor to overcome even a lackluster record in medical school. It can make up for even a bad internship. The residency years leave their lasting mark on a doctor—on how well he performs in later life.

Most other doctors know this.

"Where did he train?" a physician will often be heard to ask about a colleague. The training he is usually asking about is the other's residency.

You can get an answer to the same question. Consult the *Directory of Medical Specialists*. This volume is published by Marquis Publishers (Chicago)—the same folks who publish *Who's Who*. It can be found in most public libraries.

The *Directory* contains the names of every U.S. "specialist" (see below). It will tell you where each of these doctors went to medical school. It will tell you where he did his internship. And, most important, it will tell you where he did his residency.

Sadly, not all residencies are equal. Some are better than others. The best are in those hospitals which are affiliated with medical schools. Next best are residency programs which—while not in medical school-affiliated hospitals—are approved by the AMA. Worst are programs which are not approved.

Another volume, the AMA *Directory of Approved Internships and Residencies** will tell you if your prospective doctor's residency took place at a medical school-affiliated hospital, and if it was AMA-approved. (If your doctor did his residency several years ago, the status of the hospital or program may have changed. This is not a serious problem for doctors who have completed their training recently.)

Principle: In general, the longer a doctor's training period, the better he will perform.

Everyone knows about the "perennial student." There are such people in medicine too—doctors who prolong their training for years because they can't bear the thought of finishing. I remember vividly one gray-haired surgeon who told me—with no distaste—that he might well be a resident until he was 40!

Excepting these people, however, the longer a doctor trains the better he will perform in later life. If I were selecting a family or "primary care" physician (see below), I would want one with at least two years of residency—and preferably three or even more.

The *Directory of Medical Specialists* will tell you how many years your doctor has trained. (Many states also publish directories of physicians with the same information contained.)

If you do not have access to a library, you can find out about your doctor's training in other ways. One source is your local county medical society. Simply call the society and say: "I am considering using Doctor X. I would like to know some facts about his training." Then inquire about the kind of residency he has done (obviously, you don't want a family physician who did a surgical residency). Ask about the length of the residency program and whether or not the doctor completed it. Ask whether or not the hospital was medical school-affiliated and the residency AMA-approved.

* The AMA *Directory* may be obtained from: Order Dept., OP-378, American Medical Association, 535 N. Dearborn St., Chicago, Ill. 60610.

You may want to make still further inquiries into your doctor's training. You may wish to know, for instance, if he ever served as chief resident. This is a person selected by the chief of the service (chief of medicine, surgery, etc.) at the hospital. The chief resident usually serves for one year. It is his job to supervise all the other residents. As a result, a doctor who has been a chief resident is usually a person of higher-than-average ability.

You can find out if your doctor was a chief resident (or any other outstanding aspects of his training—fellowships, research papers published, etc.) by calling the hospital where he trained. Ask for the relevant department chief. His secretary will probably be able to provide you with the facts.

The doctor's age

There is a persistent myth about doctors: namely, that older ones are better. Older doctors, the reasoning goes, have more experience. This, in turn, makes them better than the physician who has just completed training.

Experience is, of course, important. But there are other things —up-to-date knowledge, alertness, stamina—which are far more vital when it comes to providing high-caliber care.

Osler Peterson, now a Harvard professor of public health, did one of the very few studies of how age affects physician performance. Peterson studied nearly 100 North Carolina doctors. Younger doctors, he found, made a greater effort to keep their recently acquired medical knowledge up-to-date. They read more medical journals. As the doctors grew older, the caliber of their performance grew less good.

"The decades beyond age 45," concluded Peterson, "are accompanied by a gradual decline in the quality of work."

Though this study is not a recent one, I believe its results still hold true: age does not help physician performance.

High-quality physician performance requires great stamina. A doctor's job is a twenty-four-hour one. There is no "slow season." My own family's personal physician, an internist, was forced to give up his practice before age fifty—simply because he found it was too arduous. He was forced to switch to a less demanding nine-to-five salaried post, much to his patients' sorrow.

A younger doctor—besides having more recent training and more sheer stamina—is also, I believe, more alert mentally. His mind is more likely to be open to the unusual, the peculiar.

I recall one evening, as a resident, getting a call from the medical student on duty in the emergency room. When I arrived he showed me a two-month-old child whose mother had brought him in with a "cold."

"There's something funny," said the student, "about his urine."

I looked at the sample he held in a test tube. The urine was clear, almost colorless. It looked exactly like water.

"He does pass his water a lot," volunteered the child's mother.

"It's funny, isn't it?" the student asked.

It *was* funny. The child was admitted to the hospital. He underwent a series of diagnostic tests. He was found to have a rare condition known as diabetes insipidus, in which, due to a lack of a pituitary hormone, the patient loses excessive amounts of urine. Undetected, the condition would surely have been fatal.

But the disease was detected. And all because an alert medical student noticed "something funny."

I have seen this sort of thing happen too many times to be a coincidence. I have seen younger doctors or doctors-in-training—medical students, interns, residents—make diagnoses that older, more experienced physicians have missed.

I recall a saying we were told as students: When you hear hoofbeats, think of zebras. The younger doctor, I think, is more likely to be alert to the "zebras"—the unusual sign, the rare diagnosis.

These days it is not uncommon for a physician to be thirty years of age when he or she completes training. The "prime" of a doctor's professional life, therefore, may be only some fifteen years. You should look for a physician in this "prime" period.

Principle: You should, if possible, choose a younger doctor—preferably one in the age range thirty to forty-five years.

There are, of course, many exceptions to this rule. Some physicians continue to perform well, even at an advanced age. I myself know a few doctors who, though in their seventies, continue to deliver high-caliber care. This is particularly true of doctors who work in an academic setting—a large medical school hospital—where younger doctors are available to perform much of the "legwork."

In general, however, you would do well to seek a younger physician—one in the prime of his career, his early years.

The doctor's credentials

Credentials *are* important in choosing a doctor—if only to assure yourself a *minimum level of competence*. There are at least four types of credentials that count:

(1) the M.D. degree
(2) a state license to practice
(3) hospital appointment(s)
(4) Board certification

The M.D. degree is least important. It tells you only that its possessor is a graduate of a school of medicine. All U.S. schools are approved by the AMA and, as we have said, all are substantially the same. The only value of the M.D., then, is that it allows you to distinguish a doctor of medicine from other "doctors."†

Having an M.D. alone does not mean a doctor can legally practice medicine. To do this he must have a state license. A doctor may not practice legally in any state in which he is not licensed. (There are various arrangements by which doctors may work temporarily without a regular license, as a hospital intern, for example.)

You may find out if any doctor is legally qualified to practice medicine *in your state* by checking with the state health or (in some states) education departments. The state or county medical societies can also provide you with this information.

The *American Medical Directory,* published by the AMA, lists all of the nation's legally qualified M.D.s.

A doctor's *hospital appointment* is an important credential. It means that a doctor has been appointed to the staff of a particular hospital. This means that he can admit patients to that hospital.

"If you want to know how good a doctor is," says one New York specialist, "just look in the New York State Physicians Directory for his hospital appointments."

The *Directory of Medical Specialists* contains this information for all U.S. specialists.

Principle: You should, if possible, choose a doctor who holds at least one appointment to a medical school-affiliated hospital.

† Dentists use the initials D.D.S. Doctors of osteopathy use D.O. Podiatrists and chiropractors may use D.P.M. and D.C., respectively.

Many doctors, particularly in large cities, hold several hospital appointments. The number of appointments held is of no value in choosing a doctor. But the caliber of the hospitals is. A doctor who can admit patients to at least one medical school-affiliated hospital is more likely to be a good doctor.

The last important credential is your doctor's *specialty status*. The term "specialist" has long been abused by American doctors. A GP who spends a lot of his time treating children with runny noses may call himself a "specialist in child care." A doctor who does a lot of surgery (or even a little surgery) may call himself a surgeon.‡
Needless to say, such doctors are not true specialists.
The term "specialist" should be used to mean a physician who has passed his specialty "Boards." The Board requirements differ in each specialty. They include a certain number of years of training and also various examinations, both written and oral.
Physicians who have passed these requirements are known as "Board-certified" or "Board-qualified." Those who have done everything except take a final (usually oral) exam may be known as "Board-eligible."

Principle: You should, whenever possible, choose a doctor who is Board-certified or Board-eligible.

This is your only way of making sure you have a true specialist. Let's say, for instance, that a physician has informed you that you have a heart problem. You want to go to a specialist in cardiology. If you simply select a doctor who calls himself a "cardiologist," chances are 50–50 that you will not get a specialist. You must specify that you wish a doctor who is Board-certified (or eligible). This means you will want a doctor who has at least passed his Boards in internal medicine and, preferably, his subsidiary Boards in cardiovascular disease as well.

Why go to all this trouble? Do specialists really provide that much better care than non-specialists?
The answer is "yes!" In the Columbia hospital studies, patients of non-specialists were found to have *a 50 per cent greater chance*

‡ I have always found it curious that the AMA, which gets so exercised over doctors who "advertise" finds it so easy to ignore this blatant sort of "false advertising" by so many physicians.

of getting substandard care. Harvard's Osler Peterson compared
GPs with Board-certified internists. He scored both groups on their
diagnostic and treatment skills. The internists, on average, scored
twice as high as the GPs. One third of the internists scored in the
top fifth, while only a single GP did!

TABLE 2   Office Performance of GPs and Internists

Score in the:	GPs (%)	INTERNISTS (%)
Top fifth	1	36
2nd fifth	15	32
3rd fifth	19	27
4th fifth	49	5
Bottom fifth	16	0
	100	100
Average score (out of a total of 100 points)	37.3	71.0

SOURCE: Peterson, O. L., unpublished data. For a complete description of the
method used and the results in the GPs, see the *Journal of Medical Education*,
vol. 31, no. 12, part 2.

In still another study, this time of health centers all caring for similar health problems, those centers staffed by specialists scored *25
per cent higher* in quality than non-specialist centers.

"Tell me the truth," I have asked various physicians. "Would you
yourself go to a physician who was not Board-certified?"

Every doctor to whom I have yet posed this question has said that
he or she would avoid consulting a non-specialist, if at all possible.
Most have qualified this statement by saying that they would accept
a physician who was Board-eligible.

There was one doctor who said something else.

"Put in a good word for GPs," said this physician, who himself
had been a dedicated GP in a small New England town for many
years.

Yet, in the next breath, this physician informed me—with no
small pride—that he had "studied up" and had just passed his
Boards in Family Practice!*

* Family Practice is a relatively new specialty. It was designed to supplant general practice and includes training in internal medicine, plus pediatrics, obstetrics, and gynecology. An increasing number of older GPs have updated their
knowledge and have become Board-certified in this specialty—needless to say, a
most salutary trend.

You can easily determine whether or not any doctor is a bona fide specialist. Here are some ways:

(1) Look him up in the *Directory of Medical Specialists*.
(2) Call the state or local department of health.
(3) Call the state or local county medical society.
(4) Ask him—or his secretary.

(The correct question, in all these instances, should be: "Is Doctor X Board-certified in internal medicine [pediatrics, family practice, etc.]?" Or: "In what specialties does Doctor Y hold specialty Boards?")

In addition, all Board-certified doctors will have a certificate, like a diploma. This certificate will have the name of the specialty Board across the top. You can look for this document in your physician's office. Also, doctors usually indicate their specialty status on their cards and letterheads. Examples are: William Smith, M.D., F.A.A.P. (for Fellow, American Academy of Pediatrics). Or: John Phillips, F.A.C.P. (Fellow, American College of Physicians).

Interns and residents are a special class of doctors. Because they are not fully trained specialists they have been accused of providing "second-class" care—care which is inferior to that provided by fully trained specialists.

Principle: Interns and residents usually provide care which is as good as that provided by fully trained specialists.

The Columbia hospital studies found—contrary to what most people think—that interns and residents do deliver high-quality care. In fact, their care was found to be considerably better than that of all except the best specialists!

Why is this so?

One reason is that interns and residents work in hospitals—usually larger hospitals—where their work is checked by many other doctors (see Chapter 8 for more on the organization of teaching hospitals). Interns and residents, in other words, work in a practice environment which helps produce high-caliber care.

The practice environment

Most people do not realize how much their doctor's practice environment influences his performance. This strong influence is one of the best-kept secrets of American health professionals.

Principle: Doctors who work with other doctors—and whose performance is checked by others—provide better care than doctors who work alone.

This should not seem so surprising. Yet, for years, the AMA and other medical societies have inundated Americans with the myth that "solo" doctors provide the best medical care. Private "solo" physicians have perpetuated this myth by statements such as this one, from Michael Halberstam, a Washington, D.C. internist:

> So far, prepaid [group] practice has been like Kentucky Fried Chicken—never very good or very bad.

Regardless of statements like this, the facts are clear. Every study has shown the same results: private "solo" doctors provide the poorest-quality medical care.

Mildred Morehead, professor of community health at Albert Einstein College of Medicine, compared the care of "solo" non-specialists with that of other physicians. In all areas, the "solo" doctors came out worst. The records of these "solo" physicians were called "deplorable." Dr. Morehead concluded that their care was *"unacceptable by any standards"* (Italics mine).

Studies of prepaid group practice plans have shown, time after time, that their patients have lower death rates and spend less time in the hospital than people who get their care from "solo" physicians. In one such study, the care provided by the group doctors was better than that provided by "solo" specialists.

Tables 3 and 4 show how much your doctor's practice environment can influence the caliber of his care.

TABLE 3   Quality of Care—Different Health Providers
(Adult Medical Care Only)

PROVIDER	HISTORY	PHYSICAL EXAM	LAB/ X-RAY
Medical school-affiliated hospital outpatient depts.	good	fair	good
Federal Neighborhood Health Centers	good	good	excellent
Group practices	excellent	good	fair
Private solo non-specialists	poor	poor	poor

SOURCE: Adapted from Morehead, M., et al., *American Journal of Public Health,* July 1971.

TABLE 4 Comparison of Health Status of Persons Cared for by Group vs. "Solo" Physicians

MEASURE OF HEALTH STATUS	RESULTS
Newborn death rate (perinatal mortality)	lower for Group patients by 20% (white infants) and 30% (non-whites)[a]
Over-65 death rate	lower for Group patients by 14%[b]
Hospital admissions per 100 enrollees	lower for Group patients by 33%[c]

[a] Shapiro, S., et al., *American Journal of Public Health,* September 1960.

[b] Shapiro, S., et al., *American Journal of Public Health,* May 1967.

[c] Ellwood, P., and Herbert, M., *The Harvard Business Review,* July–August 1973. (See also Chapter 8 for discussion.)

Continuing education

Continuing education—in some form—is vital to any doctor who wants to provide high-caliber care. A shelf of medical books—according to the IRS—will depreciate to zero value in ten years. A doctor's medical knowledge will do the same—unless he takes pains to keep it up-to-date.

Principle: You should choose a physician who makes a continuing effort to keep his knowledge current.

There are several ways you can assess any doctor's efforts at continuing education. Here are a few of the questions you should ask:

(1) Does he teach? Doctors who teach others (medical students, interns, residents, etc.) will be better doctors. Their students will keep them on their toes. A doctor may hold a teaching appointment at a medical school (this may be checked through the school). Or he may supervise interns and residents in a local hospital. Regardless of how he does it, any doctor who spends several hours each week teaching, will provide better care.

(2) Does he read medical journals? You may have to wait until your first visit to determine this (unless you can get the doctor or his secretary to tell you in advance). Count the different journals you see. (Many doctors have them bound, in their office.) As a

rule, doctors who read three to five journals regularly will be better than those who read less. (A doctor who has some dozen journals may be trying to impress his patients—or himself.)

Some doctors keep their journals at home. If you see none in the office, you can easily find a tactful way to ask the doctor himself about his reading habits: "You must have to read a good deal in order to keep up with things . . ."

Not all journals, incidentally, are equal. You should not count, in your estimate, the "throwaways" that often litter doctors' waiting rooms and which contain articles on how to invest in stocks, etc. A few of the best general medical journals are: *The New England Journal of Medicine* (N.E.J.M.), *American Journal of Medicine, Annals of Internal Medicine, G.P., Journal of Clinical Investigation* (J.C.I.), *The Lancet* (British), and *The British Medical Journal*. (Of these, *The New England Journal of Medicine* is often called the most prestigious American journal.)

(3) Does the doctor participate in other self-education activities? He may be enrolled in a series of lectures at the local hospital or medical school. He may attend hospital grand rounds each week, or go to hospital conferences. (Do not, however, give him much credit for going to Las Vegas for a medical convention, or taking a "medical cruise." These are usually gimmicks for tax write-off purposes—not genuine educational efforts.)

Again, the best source here will be the doctor himself. You can usually get the facts if you ask in a casual, non-threatening way. You might do this as a follow-up to your question about reading habits: "And what else do you do to keep up? . . ." Or: "Does the medical school (any of the medical schools, the hospitals, etc.) have any meetings to help you keep up?"

Some other considerations in choosing a doctor

There are several items which—while they don't have much (or anything) to do with the quality of a doctor's care—are of importance to most people. Here are a few:

Office hours—Most people want a doctor who has office hours that are convenient for them. Many physicians have hours on Saturdays or evenings for the benefit of people who cannot easily take time from work.

House calls—A "medical luxury" is the way most doctors describe house calls. They point out—and rightly—that there is not much a doctor can do to diagnose an illness in the patient's home. You will have to pay more for a house call. And there is a limit to its usefulness. Nevertheless, for certain people—the aged or disabled—the doctor's willingness to make house calls may be a valid concern.

Fees—Fees are important to most everyone. But *how much a doctor charges is no indication of his quality.* I know many professors of medicine at "prestige" medical schools—the best doctors in their fields—who charge only ten dollars a visit (excluding lab tests, etc.). You should ask your doctor's secretary about fees, in advance. Ask what the doctor's fee includes. If it seems too high, you may be able to check with your local Medicare office or medical society to find out what are "reasonable and customary" charges in your locale.

You may wish to compare charges at a few hospital outpatient departments with those charged by private physicians. Most hospital OPDs adjust fees according to your ability to pay.

A word should be said about *prepaid group practice plans* (now often called Health Maintenance Organizations, or HMOs). These plans offer a range of medical services for a set yearly premium, like an insurance plan. Usually an HMO will provide better coverage for less money than will Blue Cross-Blue Shield. The savings in your total yearly bill may be as much as 30 per cent.

To find an HMO near you, contact: Group Health Association of America, 1321 14th St., Washington, D.C. 20005.

Appointment system—You are better off with a doctor who encourages his patients to make appointments. Such a physician will, in general, be more organized and deliver better care as a result.

Use of assistants—Again, the better doctors will use assistants, including nurses and/or a physician's assistant. These doctors will deliver better, more efficient care. (See Chapter 4 for more on such assistants.)

Foreign language ability—While it is not essential that a doctor speak your language, it certainly helps. Most large hospitals and physician groups employ interpreters, or have physicians who can speak foreign languages. If you have trouble with English, you should check on this aspect of care in advance. If necessary, be prepared to bring your own interpreter—it can be a great help.

Office location—This may be important to you if it is hard, or costly, for you to get around. Many of the federal Neighborhood Health

Centers have minibuses to pick up and deposit patients. The Harvard Community Health Plan, an HMO, also has such an arrangement.

It is not wise, though, to choose a doctor solely because he lives on your block, without any thought to his caliber. (After all, you wouldn't purchase moldy pears or bad vegetables simply because the supermarket was nearby, would you?)

A few "red herrings"

There are a few bad reasons for choosing a doctor. These are "red herrings"—things that have nothing to do with either quality or convenience. Some examples:

(1) the social status of the doctor
(2) the social status of the doctor's patients
(3) the size of the doctor's practice (it may be very large because he never succeeds in solving his patients' problems, or does not refer enough patients)
(4) the time the doctor makes you wait for an appointment (the best doctors can usually fit you in within a few weeks—and promptly for true emergencies)
(5) the time he makes you wait in his office
(6) his membership in medical societies, or social clubs (with few exceptions, these are not based on merit)

Finding a "primary care" physician

Everyone should have a "primary care" physician. This is what used to be called a "family doctor." It is the physician you consult first and who can, if necessary, refer you for more specialized care.

There are essentially three types† (if we exclude non-Board-certified GPs) of primary care physicians:

internists
pediatricians (for infants and children)
family practice physicians

Principle: Start looking for a primary care physician when you are well—not sick.

† Many women use their obstetrician-gynecologist as a primary care physician—probably an unwise practice (see Chapter 10).

This seems such an obvious rule, I am almost embarrassed to write it. Yet surprisingly few people do it. Most people wait until they are ill before they start to look for a primary care doctor—obviously not the best situation in which to begin.

It is nearly impossible to be totally rational when you are "under the gun" of illness. You want to believe that the doctor you have selected is a good doctor—that he is doing the correct thing.

Probably the best way to find a good primary care doctor is to select one—using the principles in this chapter—*for a routine checkup*. This will allow you to judge the doctor's performance in a relaxed, unworried frame of mind.

Principle: Enrolling in a prepaid plan (HMO) is one easy way of finding a primary care physician.

When you join such a plan, you will be assigned to a medical group, and to a specific doctor within that group. (This should, for adults, be an internist.) Most plans will let you switch doctors—or even groups—if you wish. You can also obtain care, at any time, from a doctor outside the plan—although your yearly premium will not cover such care (you will have to pay for it yourself).

Principle: Hospital residents are an excellent source of information on high-caliber physicians.

A young man, a psychologist, tells how he used this principle to find a primary care physician for himself:

I went to the Mass. General [Hospital], walked into the medicine clinic and struck up a conversation with the residents there. I spoke to three of them in all. I told them who I was and that I was looking for a competent internist. I asked them who on the staff they would recommend. When I'd finished I had three names to check out further . . .

This is one of the best ways to find a doctor. A resident in medicine will know who are the best internists on the staff of his hospital.‡ After all, he works with these men every day, if they teach. Or he sees their patients who are admitted to the hospital.

When I was a resident, we knew—myself and the others—which staff physicians were most competent and which were the "PR guys"

‡ You should, obviously, try a pediatric resident if you want a pediatrician, an obstetrics resident for an obstetrician, etc.

—the doctors who gave their patients a nice smile but who didn't know how to treat a case of diabetic coma.

The psychologist above went to a large medical school-affiliated hospital—in fact, one of the best—for his advice. You should try to do the same, if you can. The psychologist also went to the hospital in person. If this is inconvenient, you might try calling the hospital instead. Residents are often hard to reach by phone, but your chances are better if you ask for someone specific, either by name or by title ("May I have the chief resident in medicine", "Could you connect me with the senior resident in the pediatric outpatient department", etc.)

Another method for finding a primary care physician is to call the Department of Medicine (Pediatrics, etc.). Many departments keep the names of a few of their staff members for just such calls. This is also a good way to get hold of a resident, since the departmental secretary usually knows where all the residents are at any time.

Principle: If you have one good doctor, he may be a source for another.

Good doctors tend to know others of like caliber, in different parts of the country. If you are moving from Baltimore to Los Angeles, and already have a competent doctor, don't forget to get some names from him. He may have served his residency, or his military service, with another physician who is now in L.A. Or he may know of someone by reputation, or by a scientific paper he has read.

Principle: The chief of service at a good teaching hospital is another source.

Many chiefs—in addition to their teaching duties—also see patients. Some do this even though they are on a salaried basis at their hospital (if the hospital rules permit).

In general, a doctor who is chief of medicine (sometimes called the department chairman, etc.) will be a capable internist. Or will be able to suggest one.

You can find the name of every chief of every specialty service in the United States by consulting the AMA's *Directory of Approved Internships and Residencies* (see above for order address). Then simply call the department office, and talk with the physician or his secretary. (Ask: "Does Doctor X see private patients?") Incidentally, since all department chiefs will be specialists, you may find out any chief's training, age, etc. Just look under his name in the *Directory of Medical Specialists*.

Finding a doctor in an emergency

This is the worst possible situation. You awaken in the middle of the night with that excruciating pain in your belly. Or you return from that first summer weekend with a severe sunburn. Or you suddenly start having fever and chills.

I invariably advise friends with such emergencies—if they have no primary care doctor—to go to the outpatient department of a large medical school-affiliated hospital. This, I feel, is by far a safer course than trying to pick a decent physician out of the Yellow Pages. It is probably safer than trusting to the advice of a friend, whom you have woken in the middle of the night.

Remember, in at least one study, interns and residents—the doctors who will see you in the emergency ward—provided better care than most other physicians. And if worse comes to worst and you need hospital care, you will be admitted directly to the hospital's teaching service (see Chapter 8 for more on which hospitals are best and on being a "teaching case.")

An emergency situation is no time to "test" doctors. Faced with such a situation, I myself would go at once to the emergency room of a large, high-grade hospital. You should probably do the same.

With the foregoing in mind, you are now ready to visit the doctor whom you have chosen. Regardless of his training, his age, how many journals he reads—the true test is about to come. How well he performs will depend on what he says and does after you have walked through his office door.

The following chapters will help you judge this performance.

3

The process of diagnosis

I recall one of my first cases as a medical student: a fifty-year-old woman who came to the hospital complaining of fatigue. Her hobby, she explained, was swimming. She had done it every day, all her life. Only lately she found herself unable to swim as long as she used to.

"How much," she was asked, "do you normally swim?"

"Fifty laps a day," was the reply.

"And how much can you swim now?"

"Only thirty."

The woman had been to other doctors. They had not been very impressed with her story. One had told her that, in all probability, she was simply getting old. Another had laughed and said that he himself would be quite happy being able to swim even thirty laps!

But the woman would not be content. She felt certain that something was awry. She was sure, she told us, that something was sapping her energy.

Those of us who saw her were impressed by her story. She was admitted to the medical service for metabolic tests. She bravely put up with the inconvenience of having an intravenous needle in her arm for several days. She put up with the indignity of having her urine constantly collected, of being poked and prodded several times daily.

Her stoicism had its reward. We were able to discover that her parathyroid glands—four pea-sized glands in the neck—were not functioning properly. They were not secreting enough parathyroid hormone, a substance that influences muscle strength, into her blood.

The woman had hypoparathyroidism. This rare condition was the cause of her symptoms. Given daily supplements of the hormone, her strength returned. Soon she was back in the swimming pool, doing her customary fifty laps a day.

Why do people seek medical care?

Most people visit a doctor—if we exclude regular checkups—because they believe something is "not right." Because they have one or more *symptoms.* They may have a persistent cough. Or pain during urination. Or headaches. Or simply a vague feeling of fatigue, or unease.

All these symptoms are equally valid ones. All could mean significant illness—or something trivial. All are perfectly valid reasons for seeking medical care.

Principle: You are the best judge of your own health status—of when something is "not right."

The woman swimmer's symptoms were not dramatic ones. Nor were they unusual. They could have been dismissed as part of the normal process of "getting old." But her symptoms *were* unusual, as far as she was concerned. She refused to accept them as normal. And her conviction led her to persist until a diagnosis was made.

What is your doctor's first job?

Your doctor's first, and most important, job is to determine what your symptoms mean. It is his job to determine if they indicate the presence of significant illness or disease.

It is your doctor's job, in other words, to distinguish those patients who are truly sick from those who are what one health expert has called the "worried well."

Principle: It is just as crucial for your doctor to rule out the presence of significant disease as it is for him to diagnose it.

Some people are willing to go to great lengths to assure themselves that a particular condition has been "ruled out." Here is an example:

Case 3–1: A Madison Avenue executive in his mid-thirties began to experience bouts of chest pain. A relative had died at an early age of a heart attack. Another had angina (cardiac pain due to narrowed coronary arteries).

The executive went to his internist. The doctor listened to his story, examined him, and did an electrocardiogram. He told his patient that he did not suffer from heart disease.

But the man was not satisfied. He knew that an ordinary electrocardiogram was a poor way to detect coronary artery disease. He did not feel his doctor had done enough to rule out the possibility.

He purchased a plane ticket to Arizona, where he entered the Arizona Heart Institute, a facility for the diagnosis and treatment of heart ailments. There he underwent a complete cardiac work-up, which included a "stress EKG" (an electrocardiogram done while the patient exercises), and other tests.

The cardiac work-up was completely negative. The patient, reassured that he did not have heart disease, returned to his work. His symptoms, which might have been psychological, abated.

Not all of us, obviously, have the time or money to go to such great lengths to "rule out" a particular condition we might be worried about. But the Madison Avenue man's story makes an important point: If you are still worried over whether or not you have a significant illness, your doctor has not done his job. And you should seriously consider seeing another doctor.

The Madison Avenue executive was a sophisticated health consumer. He knew that his physician had not done an adequate job of ruling out possible heart disease. He knew that better diagnostic methods were available.

You may or may not be so sophisticated. But, in any case, you should not be afraid to trust your instincts. If something leads you to suspect that your doctor has not adequately ruled out significant illness, you should take steps to find one who will.

How well do doctors diagnose?

Not very much is known about how well most doctors diagnose. But there are a few hints. In one study, some 20 per cent of physicians' diagnoses were deemed "not justified" by any of the facts the doctors had ascertained. In another study, a "smart" computer—one which had been programmed by expert physicians—was better at diagnosis than about 85 per cent of other doctors.

One computer expert, Columbia professor Allen Ginsberg, summarizes the doctor's diagnostic skills this way:

> The medical literature is replete with evidence of cases in which the decisions of experienced physicians have been far from optimal, both in the sense of committing diagnostic error and in the selection of diagnostic tests . . .

What are common errors in diagnosis?

There are three basic types of errors a doctor can make in diagnosis. These are:

(1) *diagnosing a condition which is not present*
(2) *"missing" a diagnosis*
(3) *mistaking one condition for another*

Diagnosing a condition which is not there

This is not at all an unusual occurrence. A few years ago an article in *The New England Journal of Medicine* discussed what it called the diagnosis of "non-disease"—disease that was not really present. The practice, the article concluded, was quite common.

In another study, nearly one third of schoolchildren diagnosed as "cardiacs" were later found to have no evidence of heart disease. These children had been told they were sick and, in some cases, they had been forced to take drugs or forgo exercise, for no reason whatsoever.

Sometimes it is truly amazing to see how a doctor can make a diagnosis when there is no evidence of disease. Here is a case from my own personal knowledge:

Case 3–2: A two-year-old girl was taken to a pediatrician because her mother was concerned about the child's growth. She thought her little girl might be too short for her age and a bit overweight. The pediatrician examined the child. He took her height and weight. Both were within normal limits for age. The child was alert and active and showed no sign of thyroid disease. A blood test for thyroid hormone was also normal. Nevertheless, the doctor thought the child might still be suffering from hidden, or "subclinical," thyroid disease. He proposed treatment with thyroid hormone. The mother refused treatment, and the child has continued to grow and develop normally.

This case is a striking example of a doctor diagnosing a non-existent disease, hypothyroidism, despite the fact that there was no evidence for its presence. This physician would have subjected a two-year-old child to treatment with thyroid hormone, for no reason whatsoever.

Every condition has certain criteria which are more or less necessary for its diagnosis. No competent doctor, for instance, would diagnose active tuberculosis without at least a positive TB skin test. No one, hopefully, would diagnose a "strep" throat, without a positive throat culture.

Yet some doctors persist in diagnosing non-disease. Sometimes they rationalize such diagnoses by telling the patient that the disease is still in its early stage, before it shows any physical or laboratory signs.

Principle: You should be suspicious of a doctor who makes a diagnosis in the absence of any positive physical or laboratory findings.

The term "subclinical disease" is often used. Subclinical disease is disease which is too mild or early in its course to offer any physical signs. In infectious hepatitis, for instance, there may be no jaundice (yellow skin color) visible, but lab tests of liver function may be abnormal, and the virus may be present in body fluids.

In other words, if a doctor calls your disease "subclinical," he should mean only that there are no physical signs of its presence. Needless to say, he should still be prepared to prove that the disease is present—before making a final diagnosis—by laboratory tests or procedures.

Which conditions are often "over-diagnosed" by doctors?

Certain conditions are undoubtedly diagnosed more often than they should be. This means they are diagnosed by doctors on the basis of insufficient or wrong evidence. While there are few studies of this phenomenon, there is little doubt that it is a real one.

We know, for instance, that thyroid hormone is one of the most often prescribed drugs—far in excess of the known incidence of hypothyroidism. It is fair to conclude, then, that hypothyroidism is one condition which doctors often diagnose when it is not really present. Congenital heart disease in children, studies show, is another example.

There is also little doubt that bacterial infections of all types are over-diagnosed. The huge amounts of antibiotics prescribed far exceed the known incidence of bacterial illness.*

Finally, it is my impression—with all the hazards of such guesswork—that so-called psychoneuroses are often over-diagnosed. I

---

* For more on drug-prescribing habits, see Chapter 6.

have encountered many patients whose problem was termed neurotic ("nerves," etc.) by one doctor, only to turn out to be a nonemotional one.

Table 5 lists the diagnoses most often made in everyday practice by a group of internists.

TABLE 5 The Most Common Diagnoses of Non-hospitalized Adults
Made by Internists

DIAGNOSIS	RATE PER 1,000 PATIENT VISITS
Arteriosclerotic heart disease (including coronary disease)	71.9
Hypertension	66.2
Psychoneurosis	61.4
Diabetes	28.3
Vincent's infection (infection of gums)	24.2
Asthma	22.6
Strokes (cerebrovascular accidents)	20.2
Acute upper respiratory infection	17.8
Gastroenteritis and colitis (except ulcerative colitis)	15.3
Infections of uterus, vagina, and vulva	14.5
Acute bronchitis	13.7
Osteoarthritis and allied conditions	12.9
Acute pharyngitis	11.3
Acute tonsillitis	11.3
Psychosis	11.3
Synovitis, bursitis, and tenosynovitis	10.5

NOTE: All diagnoses made more often than 10 per 1,000 patient visits. Excludes medical checkups, vaccinations, and other well-person care.

SOURCE: Spain, R. S., et al., "The Quality of Patient Care Given by Internists," paper submitted for publication.

"Missing" a diagnosis

Missing a condition which is present is, sadly, an all too common event. The woman swimmer with hypoparathyroidism is an example of how several doctors can miss a diagnosis. Here are two others:

Case 3–3: A woman graduate student suffered from headaches and a vague sensation of "feeling tired all the time." She went to several physicians and underwent a variety of tests. One doctor said her problem was due to "nerves" and prescribed a tranquilizer. Her symptoms continued. Studying became difficult. She had fears of having to drop out of school. During this period she tried another physician. This doctor performed a glucose tolerance test and determined that the woman was unable to absorb adequate amounts of sugar from her intestine. This, in turn, caused hypoglycemia, or a low blood sugar. The doctor treated the patient with a high-protein diet and her symptoms gradually abated.

Case 3–4: A businessman suffered from what he described as "indigestion." He had been to several doctors. He had had x-rays of his gastrointestinal tract which were normal. Anti-ulcer medications had been prescribed without relief. Finally, he visited an internist whose special interest was parasitic diseases. This physician obtained a stool specimen and examined it under the microscope. He made a diagnosis of schistosomiasis. Treated for this infection, the patient made a rapid and uneventful recovery.

These two cases have a good deal in common. In both, the patients had unusual—but by no means rare—conditions. Yet both visited several doctors before a correct diagnosis was made. In both cases, several physicians missed a diagnosis which could have been made with little difficulty.

Fortunately, though both patients had significant illnesses, neither had a life-threatening disease. A delay of a few months in the detection of a malignant tumor, for instance, can mean the difference between death and survival. So can a missed case of high blood pressure, or a urinary tract infection.

Both of the above patients suspected that their correct diagnoses had been missed for a simple reason: their symptoms failed to improve despite treatment. After a short period of time both sought another doctor.

Principle: You should suspect a missed diagnosis if, after a reasonable period of time (a few weeks), your symptoms do not improve, despite treatment.

There are, of course, exceptions to the above rule. We all know that there are conditions which are not amenable to any treatment. Needless to say, you should ask your doctor if your condition is treatable (see Chapter 6).

And another warning: simply because your symptoms improve at first, does not necessarily mean your doctor has made a correct diagnosis. There are numerous conditions which will improve temporarily, even if the wrong diagnosis is made and the wrong treatment administered.

Finally, one more thing to bear in mind. Sometimes the symptoms which led you to seek medical care may not be as significant to your doctor as something else. Thus he may simply neglect to try to relieve them, despite the fact that he has made a correct diagnosis.

I have seen, for instance, patients with kidney failure who were bothered by intense itching—an extremely unpleasant symptom, and a hard one to relieve. Their doctors were giving them good care for their serious basic condition, while neglecting the thing that caused them the most misery. This did not mean, however, that their diagnosis had been missed.

With all these caveats to remember, the above rule is still, I believe, useful: improvement in your symptoms—the reasons you sought care in the first place—is still the best guide to whether or not your doctor has made a correct diagnosis.

Which conditions are most often missed by doctors?

This is not an easy question to answer. To my knowledge, there has never been a study of missed diagnoses. We can draw some conclusions, however, from indirect evidence. We know, for instance, that some two thirds of men seeing a doctor do not receive a rectal exam—a procedure which will detect 75 per cent of colon-rectum cancer. It is safe to assume, then, that many such cases are missed each year. The same holds true for cervical cancer—detectable by the Pap test—in women.

Few physicians routinely test for visual and hearing acuity. Yet we know, from special surveys, that some 15 per cent of persons suffer from conditions which impair these senses. Anemia and urinary infections—conditions present in 2–3 per cent of people—are two more examples.

Many of the leading causes of death and disability are frequently not diagnosed before the patient winds up in the hospital. Examples are emphysema, cirrhosis of the liver, and kidney diseases of all types.

Table 6 lists several fairly common conditions which, in all likelihood, are frequently missed, or under-diagnosed, by doctors. (Note, however, that I have listed only broad groups of conditions and not specific diagnostic categories.)

TABLE 6   Conditions Probably Under-diagnosed by Doctors

Condition	How Common?
Anemia	10–15% of population
Cancer	2nd leading cause of death; various special detection programs always turn up previously undetected cases
Deafness and related ear disease	about 1 in 10 people
Emphysema	8th most common cause of death and fastest rising common cause; a common autopsy finding
Epilepsy (seizure disorders)	about 2% of U.S. population
Gallbladder disease	11th most common cause of hospitalization; a common autopsy finding
Kidney disease (nephritis or nephrosis)	12th leading cause of death (higher if high blood pressure due to kidney damage is included)
Liver disease (cirrhosis)	7th leading cause of death; often associated with alcoholism
Mental retardation, mild (includes learning disabilities)	estimates vary from 1% to 10% of persons under age 18
Neuromuscular diseases (muscular dystrophy, multiple sclerosis, Parkinsonism, etc.)	about 1 in 500 has MD; about 1 in 400 has MS or a related disease; about 1 in 200 has Parkinsonism
Nutritional deficiency	may be as high as 15%
Parasitic infestation	no precise estimates, but probably quite common
Peptic ulcer	13th leading cause of death; a common autopsy finding
Tuberculosis	about 1–3% of persons screened will have present or prior infection
Urinary tract infections	about 1–2% of all women screened
Vision loss and related eye diseases	about 2% of U.S. population; 2–3% over age 40 have glaucoma

Why do doctors make diagnostic errors?

From what we have said, it should be clear that there may be many reasons why doctors make errors in diagnosis. A doctor may misinterpret a piece of information—an x-ray, for example. He may mistake one symptom for another—cardiac pain for skeletal pain. Or he may simply fail to think of a particular disease.

Invariably, though, when a diagnostic error is re-examined it becomes clear that the doctor omitted certain vital items in the diagnostic process. He may have failed to ask enough questions, or to press the patient for adequate answers. He may have left out certain parts of the physical exam, or failed to order certain lab tests.

Principle: Failure to do a complete diagnostic work-up is the most common reason for diagnostic error.

What is a complete work-up?

A complete diagnostic work-up consists of three parts. These are:

    (1) the history (the question-and-answer part)
    (2) the physical examination
    (3) diagnostic tests and procedures

Surprisingly often, doctors fail to perform these three parts of the work-up in adequate detail. Some give short shrift to the history, asking only a few general questions. Others gloss over the physical exam, or do without any lab tests.

Chapters 4 and 5 discuss, in detail, these three aspects of the diagnostic work-up.

How does your doctor think of you and your body?

The diagnostic process is an extremely complex one. Most doctors themselves, when asked, cannot explain how they make a correct diagnosis. They are at a loss to describe the thought processes which are involved.

When your doctor does his diagnostic work-up, he gathers a large amount of information. Some of this information is in the form of your replies to his questions. Other information comes from his physical exam or various tests and procedures.

Your doctor has been trained to organize this information in several ways. While none is "ideal," each of these ways serves a purpose. Each is a "handle" by which the physician seeks to arrive at a correct diagnosis. They are the ways in which he thinks of you, your symptoms, and your body.

Your doctor thinks of you, first, as a collection of *organ systems*. He will try to localize your symptoms—and his own findings—to one or more of these systems. If you have symptoms of chest pain and shortness of breath, for example, he should immediately think of the heart and lungs—your cardiopulmonary system—as the possible locus. Vomiting and diarrhea will suggest the gastrointestinal system.

The doctor must, of course, frequently think of more than one organ system. Vomiting, for instance, may be the presenting symptom in diseases of the brain (central nervous system) as well as the gastrointestinal system. As he gathers more data, however, the physician should be able to make the distinction.

Your doctor thinks of you, next, as a *disease process*. He should ask himself, "What kind of a disease is going on in this patient?" He may consider an infectious process, where there is invasion of various body organs by an infectious organism. He may consider a metabolic disease such as diabetes, in which there is a disorder of carbohydrate and fat metabolism which affects virtually all organ systems. He may think of a purely structural process—a broken bone or a herniated intestine. Or he may think of some combination of processes—a metabolic disease such as gout causing a structural problem such as kidney stones, for instance.

The disease process—admittedly not a completely satisfactory way of thinking about disease—is often called the *pathology* or *pathophysiology* of the disease.

Finally, your doctor will think of you in terms of the *cause* of your problem. The medical word for this is *etiology*. Doctors will often speak of an etiologic agent or factor responsible for a disease. The tubercle bacillus, for example, is thought of as the etiologic agent of tuberculosis. (Sometimes environmental conditions such as overcrowding are called etiologic factors in this disease.) The lead in lead paint may be thought of as the etiologic agent in lead poisoning.

Sometimes you may hear a doctor refer to a condition as *idiopathic*. This simply means that there is no readily identifiable cause for the condition. Use of this term, of course, implies that all known causes have been ruled out.†

These are the major ways—untidy as they may be—in which your doctor should think about you and your diagnosis. They are ways in which he should try to organize the information he obtains in his diagnostic work-up.

† The "cause" of any disease, naturally, has endless ramifications. The cause of sickle-cell anemia, for instance, was first said to be over-fast destruction of red blood cells, due to their abnormal sickled shape. Now, however, it is known that this abnormal shape is, in turn, caused by a genetic variation in the hemoglobin molecule. Eventually, still more will be known about what caused this variation in the first place.

Your doctor should, naturally, be willing and able to share his thinking about your diagnosis with you, the patient.

Principle: Your doctor should be able to discuss your health problem in terms of (1) the body system(s) involved, (2) the disease process at work, and (3) the etiology, or cause.

What is meant by the term "differential diagnosis"?

As your doctor gathers the information from his diagnostic work-up, another very important process should be taking place. As he first hears your symptoms and takes his medical history, a list of possible diagnoses should flash in his mind. Some of these diagnoses will be more likely than others. As the doctor continues his work-up, this list should change. Some conditions should stand out as the most likely diagnostic possibilities. Others should drop way down, as very improbable. This process of narrowing down all the possible diagnoses to the correct one is sometimes called *differential diagnosis*.

Differential diagnosis is where mistakes are often made. Some doctors will jump too quickly to a particular diagnosis, without adequately ruling out all the others. Other physicians may be unable to narrow down the list; the more tests and procedures they do, the more diagnoses suggest themselves.

Let us look at some more brief case histories, to see how the diagnostic process might actually work:

Case 3–5: A thirty-year-old construction worker presents with symptoms of fever, cough, and chest pain. These have been present for two days. Before that time, he was completely well. The history is otherwise unremarkable. On the physical exam, the doctor hears crackling noises over the left side of the chest. He orders a chest x-ray, which shows a "pneumonic infiltrate" in the left lower lobe of the lung. A TB skin test is negative. The man's sputum is cultured and pneumococci grow out. The doctor makes a diagnosis of pneumococcal pneumonia.

In this case, several items are significant. First, the man has been sick for two days. This suggests a condition such as pneumonia, rather than a heart attack, in which the symptoms would be much more acute.

Secondly, the physical exam reveals a key positive finding: crackles (the medical term is "rales") heard in the lung. This enables the doctor to localize the disease to a specific organ system.

The chest film, also positive for pneumonia, further helps in the diagnosis. The alert physician will make sure that the chest film truly looks like pneumonia, and not like a more unusual problem, such as a pulmonary embolism (blood clot in the lung).

Finally, the positive sputum culture enables the physician to nail down the etiologic agent which is causing the pneumonia, the pneumococci. (This also enables him to be more precise in his treatment—see Chapter 6.)

Note that, in this abbreviated diagnosis, there are both *significant positives* and *significant negatives*. The presence of "rales," for instance, is a significant positive finding. The negative TB skin test, which virtually rules out tuberculosis, is a significant negative.

Principle: Your doctor should be able to summarize the significant positives and negatives in your diagnostic work-up, and what they mean.

He should, in other words, be able to tell you which findings (or absence thereof) he has used to arrive at your final diagnosis.

Case 3–6: A twenty-six-year-old graduate student comes to the doctor because she thinks she "looks funny." Further history reveals her symptom is of recent onset. On examination, the doctor observes that she is slightly jaundiced (yellow color to the skin and eyes). She also has several large, tender lymph glands. A blood test for mononucleosis is reported as "positive."

Case 3–7: A twenty-six-year-old graduate student comes to the doctor because she thinks she "looks funny." Her symptom is of recent onset. On examination, the doctor notes that she is slightly jaundiced. Further history elicits the fact that she has had several bouts of acute abdominal pain during the last few years. The doctor orders an abdominal x-ray which reveals the presence of several large gallstones. No other metabolic abnormalities are found.

In these two cases, both women presented with exactly the same initial complaint. And both had the same key physical finding: jaundice. Yet their diagnoses were quite different. There were other, less obvious differences as well. The first woman had a few swollen lymph nodes, which a less observant doctor might have overlooked. These are a clue that she might have a disease such as mononucleosis. The second woman recalled her bouts of abdominal pain (a thorough doctor would be sure to ask her specifically about this). This added symptom was the clue that suggested to the doctor that he order an abdominal x-ray (a gallbladder series might also have been ordered).

In both these cases, it was the doctor's meticulous history and physical exam that enabled him to come to the correct diagnosis.

Doctors who fail to make a complete diagnosis

This is a not uncommon phenomenon in modern medical practice. Poor doctors will often fail to make what I call a complete diagnosis. Such doctors mistake your symptoms and physical or lab findings for the disease process itself.

Let us take an example.

Anemia is a condition where there are not enough red blood cells. The presence of anemia can be determined by either of two simple tests—a hemoglobin or a hematocrit determination. (The first measures the amount of red cell pigment, the second the red cell volume, as a proportion of total blood.)

But "anemia" itself is not a complete diagnosis. There are numerous different types of anemias. There are numerous causes of each type. A complete diagnosis might be "iron-deficiency anemia secondary to blood loss from gastric ulcer." Or "anemia secondary to vitamin B_{12} deficiency." Or "hemolytic anemia secondary to sickle-cell crisis." Or a number of others.

Sadly, many doctors do not make complete diagnoses when it comes to the lab finding of anemia. In fact, this is probably the most common example of incomplete diagnosis.

"The majority of physicians," one study found, "failed to make a definitive diagnosis in the case of anemia." In this study, most doctors considered "anemia" (a low hemoglobin or hematocrit) their final diagnosis. They made no attempt at further elucidation.

"Hypertension" is another common incomplete diagnosis. Hypertension is a physical finding. It means that your blood pressure is above normal. This finding may have any of several causes. (If all known causes have been ruled out, the hypertension is usually called "essential hypertension.")

Yet many doctors (exact figures are hard to come by) never go beyond a diagnosis of "hypertension." They fail to make a complete diagnosis.

Other examples of incomplete diagnoses are "jaundice" (see Cases 3-6 and 3-7, above), "heart failure," and "epilepsy." Complete diagnoses, in each case, might be "jaundice secondary to infectious hepatitis," "heart failure secondary to myocardial infarction," or "petit mal epilepsy of idiopathic origin (cause unknown)."

A doctor who makes a diagnosis of "pneumonia" is, in effect, making an incomplete diagnosis. He should at least make an effort to distinguish between bacterial, viral, and other types of pneumonia, as in Case 3–5.

Doctors who use out-of-date or "invented" diagnoses

Some doctors, particularly those whose training is no longer up-to-date, rely on diagnoses which are obsolete and have long since been made meaningless by advances in medical science. "Rheumatism" is an example. "Walking pneumonia," "double pneumonia," and "fat around the heart" are others.

Needless to say, doctors who use such outmoded terms are best avoided.

Certain doctors have been known to invent diagnoses—their own conditions that no one else has ever heard of! Frequently, these "unique" conditions have equally unique cures which only their inventor knows about.

Fortunately, there are several ways in which the consumer can check up on his doctor's "diagnosis." One way, obviously, is to call another physician and ask him if he has ever heard of the diagnosis in question. You may also try the person in charge of the record room at any large hospital, or the vital statistics office of your local health department.

Or you can check the diagnosis yourself.

If you suspect your doctor of inventing a diagnosis or of using an outmoded one, a *disease classification* is one place to look. The one most often used by health experts is called the *International Classification of Diseases Adapted* (ICDA). The ICDA may be purchased from the U. S. Government Printing Office or found in most libraries. It lists recognized diagnoses under more than a dozen major headings ("Infective and Parasitic Diseases," "Neoplasms," "Diseases of the Blood," etc.).

Another useful reference in checking a diagnosis is *Current Medical Information and Terminology* (CMIT). CMIT is a computer-designed system for naming and describing diseases, based on the various body organ systems. CMIT—unlike the ICDA—contains brief paragraphs on the etiology, symptoms, physical signs, and laboratory findings for each disease. (See Appendix, p. 236.) CMIT is available for eight dollars from the American Medical Association, 535 N. Dearborn Street, Chicago, Ill. 60610.

You might also need a *medical dictionary*. There are several on the market (Dorland's is the one I use) to help you decipher your doctor's diagnosis.

Doctors who try to conceal their ignorance of your diagnosis

Some doctors may attempt to conceal the fact that they are unable to make a proper and complete diagnosis. One way of doing this is to substitute one of your symptoms or physical signs for a diagnosis. For instance, as we have already seen, a doctor may make a "diagnosis" of anemia or jaundice. Or he may use one of a variety of medical terms which sound like diagnoses but aren't. Some examples are: hyperpyrexia (fever), dyspnea (difficulty breathing), rhinorrhea (clear fluid discharge, or runny nose), hematemesis (vomiting blood), etc.

You will usually be able to sense when a doctor is engaging in this form of obscurantism. The best remedy is simply to ask him the meaning of whatever term he uses. Or look it up in the ICDA, CMIT, or medical dictionary. It should be readily apparent when your doctor is trying to hide his inability to make a diagnosis behind medical jargon.

Principle: You should insist that your doctor tell you his diagnosis in medical terms.

This is a crucial point. Some physicians never tell their patients their diagnoses in anything but "lay" language. This practice is as bad as that of doctors who invent a phony diagnosis or hide behind medical jargon.

"Your child has a hole in his heart," I have heard doctors say. Others tell their patients with anemia that they suffer from "low blood."

This kind of explanation is worse than no explanation at all. It is usually the resort of doctors who do not wish to take the trouble to explain their diagnosis fully.

If you do not know your "official" medical diagnosis, you will not be able to use the ICDA or any other medical reference. More important, you will not be able to tell it to another doctor whom you might consult. Believe me, there is nothing more frustrating than to see a patient who has just been to another physician, yet who has not been told his medical diagnosis.

If need be, ask your doctor to write your diagnosis *legibly* on one of his own prescription pads. This should make him think twice before writing anything but the most precise, medically accurate diagnosis he can determine. This written diagnosis is, moreover, the very least you should demand for your money and time. And it is a bare minimal necessity if you decide to seek a second medical opinion (for more, see Chapter 7).

In this chapter I have tried to deal with the overall process of diagnosis. In the next few chapters, we will look at the specific things your doctor does during the diagnostic work-up.

4

The physician visit: what to expect

What happened during your last visit to a physician?

Did the doctor ask about your heart? About your bowel habits? Did he check your blood pressure? Your gait? Your skin temperature?

You may know the answers to these questions. But if you do, you are in a distinct minority. Most people, I have found, have little memory of what happened during their doctor's visit—even when that visit occurred only hours before. They have little idea of what the doctor said or did.

This inability to recall what happened is, I believe, due to the fact that most people do not know what to expect when they visit their doctor. They have little idea of what *ought to happen*—of how the physician ought to go about working up their health problem.

In the previous chapter we spoke about the diagnostic process in general terms. In this one we shall consider the specifics—what your doctor should do during your initial visit, for any health problem.

How long should your doctor's visit be?

A few years ago, a group of medical experts met in Washington to help plan a national program for child health. During their meeting the question arose as to how many patients a competent physician could see during a working day. Most of the expert physicians agreed that, so far as children were concerned, the doctor should spend *at least one half hour with each new patient.*

Adults, certainly, should require at least as much time as children, if not more. Since they are older, their medical history is longer. And while children usually suffer from only a single condition, many adults have two or even more.

Principle: During an initial office visit, the doctor should spend at least one half hour with you.

Many doctors spend more time, during a first visit. Some routinely "block out" an entire hour for all their new patients. These physicians feel that this time is needed, regardless of the patient's presenting complaint.

On the other hand, many doctors spend considerably less time. I have been told of physicians seeing new patients in as little as ten minutes, or even less. Incredible as it may seem, there are physicians who see several hundred patients, many for the first time, each day.*

Clearly, this kind of "assembly line" medicine is not conducive to high-caliber care. As an informed consumer, you would do well to guard against it. One simple way to do so is to ask your doctor's secretary, when you call for an initial appointment, how long the physician will spend with you. Answers such as "That depends on how busy he is" or "That depends on your problem" are not adequate. The best answer should be "The doctor is prepared to spend at least ——— minutes with each new patient."

If the reply seems vague or otherwise unsatisfactory, you might do well to try to clarify it, or to try another physician.

What is the medical history?

The medical history is the talking part of your doctor's visit. It is the story of your recent, and previous, health problems. It is also, virtually all experts agree, the single most important part of any diagnostic work-up.

What makes the history so important?

Done properly, the history provides your doctor with a great deal of information. It enables him to narrow down his list of possible diagnoses considerably—often to only a few. It thus eliminates the need for many costly diagnostic tests and procedures. It means that,

---

* A law, recently proposed in New York City, would make it illegal for any physician to see more than fifty patients a day. Even this many, I think, would stretch the physician's ability to provide high caliber care to the limit.

in searching for a correct diagnosis, your doctor is not simply "shooting in the dark."

Surprisingly, many doctors fail to allot the history the importance it deserves. Some take histories which last only a few seconds. Their questions, if any, are limited to the patient's immediate complaint. A few physicians ask no questions whatsoever!

The history is not a social chat. It is the detailed record of your health problems. It is your doctor's job to take his history in a methodical, organized way. We shall say more, below, about how the history should be organized.

What kinds of history questions should your doctor ask?

To begin, the best doctors will let you "tell your own story." They will usually ask one or two "open-ended" questions, such as "What brings you here today?" or "What kind of a problem have you been having?" Then, after you have had a chance at least to begin the story in your own words, the doctor will ask his questions.

You can tell a lot about a doctor from the questions he asks. The best doctors ask many, very specific questions. They take nothing for granted. They never assume you have recalled everything of importance.

Poorer doctors, on the other hand, ask few questions. And the ones they do ask are vague, or ambiguous.

Here are some examples of poor and better ways to ask questions:

Poor: "Do you have trouble breathing?"
Better: "Do you get short of breath when you climb stairs? How many flights can you climb?"

Poor: "Have you had any pain?"
Better: "Do you ever have abdominal pain before meals? In the middle of the night? After eating? etc."

Poor: "How are your sleep habits?"
Better: "How many hours a night do you sleep? Do you ever awaken during the night? How often? etc."

Poor: "Have you noticed any trouble with your bowels?"
Better: "Have you had any recent diarrhea (blood in your stools, constipation, etc.)?"

The good doctor—like a good detective—will relentlessly pursue every "lead." If you suggest any symptom, the good physician will follow up on it. Here is an example:

PATIENT: Doctor, I've noticed some pains in my chest.
DOCTOR: What kind of pains?
PATIENT: Short, sharp ones.
DOCTOR: What seems to bring them on?
PATIENT: They come after eating.
DOCTOR: Are they associated with exercise (cold weather, deep breathing, irregular heartbeats, etc.)?

How much time should the history require?

The best doctors will exhaust each symptom, before moving on to another. This process takes time. This is particularly true if it is your initial visit.

Principle: A complete initial history should require at least fifteen minutes, and, preferably, longer. (One half hour has been suggested as an "ideal" time.)

The less "well focused" your symptoms are, the longer it may take for the doctor to get to the bottom of them. A complaint such as "I feel tired all the time" obviously needs more elucidation than does "I hit my thumb with a hammer."

This *does not* mean that your complaints or symptoms have to be well focused! If you have come to the doctor because you "feel tired all the time," you should not feel guilty for saying so—in those words. It is your doctor's job to get to the bottom of your problems, no matter how vague or non-specific they may first appear. It is, of course, better if you can describe your symptoms clearly and in detail. But it is not a necessity. (And it is certainly not a reason to avoid visiting a doctor, if you are unable to do so.)

The best doctor, then, will take adequate time to elucidate fully the nature of your health problem, through his history.

Here are some other general rules:

(1) *The history should be taken in private.* No third party, no matter how well meaning, has any right to intrude upon the story you tell your doctor. You should have no qualms about asking a relative—even a husband or wife—to leave the room, if their pres-

ence might exert an inhibiting effect on what you say. On the other hand, you may *want* another person present. This, too, is your privilege. You may also wish to allow the doctor to talk with relatives or friends, in order to add to his history.

(2) *The history should be thoroughly recorded.* Observe your doctor as he takes your history. He should make notes, *as he obtains it.* (Some doctors use checklists or other aids.) I, for one, would have my doubts about any doctor who claims that he can recall the details of a complete history, after his patient has left the office.

(3) *The history should be done uninterrupted.* It is as much a medical procedure as taking your temperature. The doctor should do it all at once, not in bits and pieces. He should give it his undivided attention. The practice of taking a history while getting a head start on your physical exam, while often done, is less than optimal.

How is the history organized?

The history has several parts. Most doctors who take a complete history will take it in the following order:

(1) chief complaint
(2) present illness
(3) past history
(4) family history
(5) social and occupational history
(6) review of systems

Principle: An initial history is not complete unless it includes each of the above parts.

Let us look at each of these parts of the history in more detail.

The chief complaint—This is the reason, *in the patient's own words,* why he or she is seeking care. When the doctor asks a question like "What brings you here today?" or "What seems to be the problem?", your answer becomes the chief complaint. The doctor should write it at the top of his notes. He should include your *age, sex, race* or *national origin* (if relevant), and the *duration* of the complaint.

Here are some examples:

"A fifty-two-year-old white male with the CC 'Can't catch my breath' —three weeks duration."

"33-year-old housewife with complaint 'Tired all the time'—recent onset."

"19 y.o. cauc. male—CC fever, vomiting, and 'pain behind my eyes' of 72 hrs. duration."

The chief complaint, then, is your doctor's reminder of why you sought medical care. Often, it is incidental to your real problem. Generally, however, it provides the doctor with a starting point, an important clue to be pursued.

The present illness—Using the chief complaint as his starting point, the doctor will now ask you more about your illness. He may encourage you to tell him the story in your own words with a question like "Tell me how all this began" or "Tell me about the first time you had this problem." Or he may ask you his own specific questions.

The method used is not too important. What is important is that your doctor explore your presenting symptoms as thoroughly as possible. Here are some of the things your doctor should ask about your presenting symptoms:

(1) precisely when and under what circumstances they began (you first noticed them)
(2) their location in your body
(3) their nature and severity
(4) what, if anything, aggravates them or gives relief
(5) the presence or absence of other symptoms
(6) relation to time of day, or to meals, sleeping, exercise, other activities

Here is how a doctor might ask the questions which would allow him to construct a thorough present illness, starting from the moment Mr. Smith—a thirty-year-old white construction worker—enters his office:

M.D.: Tell me, Mr. Smith. What brings you here today?
SMITH: I've been having these headaches, Doctor.
M.D.: When did they begin?
SMITH: Oh, I'd say about three weeks ago.
   [*Note: at this point the chief complaint has been established—"headaches of three weeks' duration."*]
M.D.: And can you describe the first time you noticed them?
SMITH: Well, I woke up one morning and I had this terrible pain in

my head. Right here [*points to the back of his head*]. I've never had anything like it before.

M.D.: And is it a steady pain or does it come and go?

SMITH: It's pretty steady. And it gets worse as the day goes on.

M.D.: Does anything you take make it better?

SMITH: Not really. Sometimes I can take four aspirins and it's still the same.

M.D.: Does it change after meals? When you lie down or bend over?

SMITH: No.

M.D.: Have you had any recent injury to your head?

SMITH: Not that I can recall.

M.D.: Have you had any vomiting? Blurring of vision? Ringing in your ears? Dizzy spells . . .

This abbreviated dialogue illustrates how the doctor goes about elucidating the patient's present illness. When he has finished, the doctor should have a clear idea of the course of Mr. Smith's problem, from its onset to the present moment.

Past history—The past history is the story of the patient's health from birth to the time the symptoms of the present illness began. Many doctors neglect to take a thorough past history. They assume that the patient's problems begin with his present illness. But such is not always the case. Mr. Smith may have had an attack of sinusitis two years ago, which might be relevant to his present illness. He might have fallen down a flight of stairs four months before his present headaches began.

The past history is an important, and often neglected, portion of the history. Some of the items your doctor should ask about, in this part, are:

(1) previous illnesses, particularly if serious enough to warrant a doctor's care, hospitalization, or surgery
(2) accidental injuries
(3) chronic use of medications, including drug abuse
(4) drug or other allergies
(5) pregnancy history, in women
(6) birth history, growth and development, childhood illnesses, immunizations
(7) foreign travel
(8) recent exposure to communicable disease

Family history—Many health problems tend to run in families. The thorough doctor will take a detailed family history. He will ask you about all your near relatives—living and dead. If dead, he will try to ascertain the cause of death. He will pay special attention to members of your family who have died early in life, or who have had repeated hospitalizations or illnesses.

TABLE 7 A SAMPLE FAMILY PEDIGREE

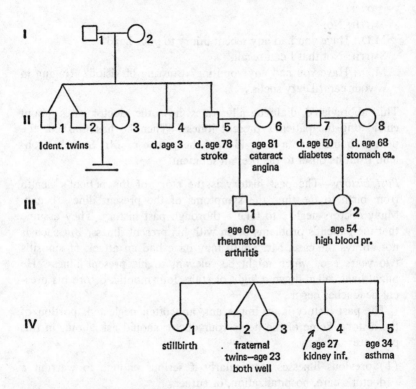

Rules for drawing a pedigree chart:
  (1) Males are shown by squares, females by circles.
  (2) Generations are designated by roman numerals, with the earliest at the top of the chart.
  (3) Individuals within each generation are numbered, in order of birth, from left to right, with arabic numbers.
  (4) The patient for whom the pedigree is being drawn is designated with an arrow.
  (5) Other information may be written beneath each individual, or on separate cards.

The most thorough doctors will frequently draw a pedigree—a diagrammatic representation of your family tree. This is something you may wish to do yourself. A sample pedigree is shown in Table 7.

Finally, the doctor will ask you about the presence or absence of specific conditions in your family. He will explain—if you do not know—the manifestations of each. Here is a list of medical conditions which are asked about on the medical service of a major teaching hospital (you will note that many are really *signs* or groups of conditions):

anemia
allergy
arthritis
bleeding
cancer
diabetes
endocrine (hormonal) disease
epilepsy
gout
heart disease
hypertension
jaundice
kidney disease
mental retardation
migraine
obesity
psychiatric illness
tuberculosis

Social and occupational history—This is another often neglected portion of the history. Some doctors feel that it is not necessary to ask questions which their patients may resent or consider embarrassing. It should be obvious, however, that a complete history must include inquiries about your marital status, your habits (including use of cigarettes, alcohol, other drugs), your living environment (age of dwelling, heat, pets), and your occupational environment. The thorough physician will ask you these things in a tactful way, making clear why the information is needed.

Review of systems—This is usually the last part of the history. In the review of systems, your doctor should ask you several questions about each one of the following body parts or organ systems:

head
eyes (visual system)
ears (auditory system)
respiratory system
lymph glands
breasts
heart and blood vessels (cardiovascular system)
gastrointestinal system
genitourinary system
endocrine system
immunologic system
skin and extremities
neurologic system
emotional-mental health

Sometimes these organ systems are grouped somewhat differently. Nevertheless, each one should be covered—even if it has been dealt with in detail in the Present Illness.

Principle: The history is not complete unless your doctor has asked you questions about each organ system.

This final review is like an airplane pilot's final checklist. Its purpose is to make sure nothing of importance has escaped notice, that nothing has fallen "between the cracks." For this reason, the questions asked should be very specific ones:

"Have you had headaches (dizzy spells, ringing in the ears, spots before your eyes, etc.)?"

"Have you had any recent vomiting (abdominal pains, diarrhea, blood in your stools, etc.)?"

"Have you experienced any pain on urination (increased frequency, abnormal color, etc.)?"

Once the doctor has gone through all your body systems, asking several questions about each, he can be reasonably sure that he has done a thorough job of history taking. He can be reasonably sure that he has done everything possible to prevent overlooking even a minor symptom which might add to his total history.

How should your doctor do a physical exam?

After taking his history, the doctor will turn to the physical exam. As with the history, you can tell a good deal about what kind of a physician he is by the way in which he conducts this part of your diagnostic work-up.

A decent exam requires, first, adequate *time*. It cannot be rushed. I have seen top-notch doctors spend several minutes, with certain patients, merely listening to one area over the heart or feeling the size of the liver. On the other hand, I have also seen doctors do what they considered a complete exam in seconds, literally just "laying on the hands."

Principle: A complete initial physical exam should take at least ten to fifteen minutes.

The second thing the doctor needs for his exam, as for the history, is *privacy*. Nobody likes to be examined, even superficially, in public. Lack of privacy can even affect the patient's reactions to various parts of the exam.

The exam should be done in a *quiet, warm, well-lit room* (natural light is best). There should be an examining table covered by a clean sheet, or paper. If you are female, and the doctor is a male, there should be a "chaperon" (usually a nurse) in attendance.

To perform a complete exam, the doctor needs at least these *items of equipment:*

(1) a scale, with a ruler for measuring height
(2) a blood pressure cuff and gauge
(3) a stethoscope
(4) a thermometer
(5) an ophthalmoscope-otoscope (the flashlight-type instrument for looking into eyes, ears, nose)
(6) a tongue depressor (flat wooden stick) and a penlight (for examining the mouth)
(7) an eye chart
(8) a tuning fork
(9) a tape measure
(10) a pin or feather (for testing skin sensation)
(11) a reflex hammer
(12) rubber gloves, speculum, filter paper, glass slides, etc. (for rectal or vaginal exams)

In doing the exam, your doctor will use *four basic skills:*

(1) observation
(2) palpation (feeling)

(3) percussion ("thumping," as on the chest, abdomen, etc.)
(4) auscultation (listening, usually with stethoscope)

Some doctors tend to rely more on one skill than on another. But all four should be used, in some degree.

In this regard, your doctor should ask that you disrobe for the exam. (In one study, nearly half the physicians tried to examine their patients fully or almost fully clothed!) The doctor should provide female patients with a gown or sheet to be worn during the exam.

Most doctors perform the exam in a "top–down" fashion. That is, they begin at your head and progress down the body towards the feet. Usually "vital signs"—pulse, respiration rate, blood pressure, and temperature—as well as height and weight, will be taken at the very beginning, possibly by a nurse. Rectal and vaginal exams are usually done last.

Some doctors will make the mistake of trying to "cut corners" on the physical exam. If you complain of stomach pains, for instance, the physician may go directly to your belly, neglecting to do an orderly exam. Or if you have a cough, he may immediately listen to your chest. If something abnormal is then found, the physician may neglect to do the remainder of the exam.

This type of "cutting corners" is substandard care. It can be highly dangerous. Many, if not most, diseases affect more than a single part of the body. Moreover, the doctor who goes immediately for the "hot spot" and neglects to do a complete exam runs the risk of missing a serious condition—one of which the patient is totally unaware.

Here is an example:

Case 4–1: A fifty-year-old man is brought to the emergency ward one winter evening. He gives a history of having slipped on the sidewalk and fallen three hours previous. He complains of throbbing pain in the right wrist. The doctor on duty examines the wrist and orders an x-ray. The x-ray films reveal a hairline fracture of a small bone in the wrist. The doctor fits the man with a cast, prescribes a pain-killer (analgesic), and gives him a return appointment to have his cast rechecked.

Did this patient get good care? Not necessarily.

Perhaps, despite his story, the man did not simply "slip" on the ice. If the doctor had taken a more complete history, the patient might have recalled that he has had headaches and dizzy spells, for the past few months. If the doctor had not limited his exam to the man's broken wrist, he might have discovered some small hemorrhages in the retinas of his eyes. He might have found that the patient had some numbness in his fingers and toes.

These findings might alert the physician to the fact that his patient with a wrist fracture also had early diabetes.

Every physician has seen cases such as this.

A housewife cuts her finger on a paring knife. A routine laceration? Maybe not. Maybe she has been getting increasingly "clumsy" lately. Maybe she has had some trouble talking. Or swallowing. Maybe a good neurologic exam might show that she cannot walk without lurching from side to side. Or that she cannot tie her shoes without difficulty.

What began as a simple cut finger has become—after a complete exam—a much more complicated case.

Principle: If your doctor fails to examine all parts of your body, he is providing less than optimal medical care.

Your doctor has a responsibility to conduct a complete physical exam. This holds true, *regardless of the complaint that made you visit him in the first place.*

What are the parts of a complete physical exam?

Like the history, the physical exam is made up of several parts. These parts correspond to parts of the body (head, eyes, ears, etc.) or to organ systems (lymph glands, neurologic exam, etc.). The way in which the parts of the exam are stated is not important. Neither is the order in which they are performed.

What *is* important is that your doctor examine all parts of your body—and all organ systems.

Table 8 presents a basic adult physical exam. This exam is adapted from those in use at several major medical school hospitals. The exam is divided into seventeen parts. Under each part I have listed a number of different items.

TABLE 8   The Basic Adult Physical Examination

I. Vital signs
   (1) pulse rate
   (2) respiratory (breathing) rate

TABLE 8   The Basic Adult Physical Examination

I. Vital Signs
  (3) temperature
  (4) blood pressure—both arms, lying down and sitting

II. Head
  (1) observation and palpation of skull
  (2) observation and palpation of hair
  (3) auscultation over skull and eyes (closed)

III. Eyes
  (1) observation of conjunctival and bulbar sclerae (M.D. pulls down lower
        lids, asks patient to look up, to right, etc.)
  (2) observation (or measurement) of eyeball prominence
  (3) testing of eyeball movements ("follow my finger, the light, etc.")
  (4) testing of vision (eye chart)
  (5) testing of pupil reaction (light shone in each eye; patient asked to follow
        light (finger, etc.) as M.D. moves it toward patient's nose)
  (6) testing of visual fields (patient asked to cover one eye and look at spe-
        cific spot; M.D. then moves light or object slowly into patient's field of
        vision and patient indicates when object first appears)
  (7) exam of eye with ophthalmoscope

IV. Ears
  (1) observation and palpation of ear cartilage, including palpation in front
        and behind cartilage
  (2) testing of hearing (M.D. whispers in ear, holds ticking watch, uses tun-
        ing fork, uses audiometer)
  (3) exam of ear with otoscope

V. Nose
  (1) exam of nasal canals (otoscope used)
  (2) exam of sinuses (M.D. taps above eyebrows with finger, presses with
        thumbs on either side of nose; patient in darkness and light source
        placed in mouth or under eyebrows to "transilluminate" sinus cavi-
        ties)
  (3) smell tested (patient told to close eyes, M.D. places various substances
        under nose)

VI. Mouth
  (1) observation of lips, gums, tongue
  (2) observation and pressure with throat stick on teeth
  (3) observation of palate, tonsils and pharynx
  (4) observation of larynx (vocal chords) with light and head mirror

VII. Neck
  (1) palpation of lymph nodes ("glands")
  (2) palpation of salivary glands
  (3) exam of thyroid (M.D. stands behind patient and palpates thyroid gland
        with both hands; M.D. asks patient to swallow and observes motion
        of gland)

TABLE 8   The Basic Adult Physical Examination

VII. Neck
(4) observation of neck veins (patient lying flat, at thirty degrees, and sitting)
(5) observation, palpation, and auscultation of carotid artery pulses
(6) palpation of trachea ("windpipe")
(7) testing of neck motion—esp. flexion (patient lies on back and M.D. bends head so chin touches chest)

VIII. Breasts (in female)
(1) observation of breasts, nipples, skin
(2) palpation, including up into armpits

IX. Arms and Hands
(1) palpation for lymph nodes in axillae (armpits) and at elbows
(2) testing of range of motion of arms
(3) observation of fingers and nails, including nail-bed pulse

X. Chest
(1) palpation for lymph nodes above and below collarbones
(2) observation of chest shape and breathing movements
(3) percussion of chest
(4) auscultation of chest with stethoscope, front and back, at least three locations each side, as patient breathes in and out, says "E," etc.

XI. Heart
(1) observation of heart impulse
(2) palpation of heart impulse
(3) determination of heart size by percussion (M.D. asks patient to lie on back, taps out heart size)
(4) auscultation of heart sounds with stethoscope, at least five locations, front and left side of chest

XII. Abdomen
(1) observation of size (measurement with tape measure, if enlarged)
(2) percussion, if enlarged
(3) palpation and percussion of liver size (right upper quadrant) and spleen size (left upper quadrant)
(4) palpation of kidneys (M.D.'s fingers pressed deep, both sides of navel; M.D. presses with thumbs, both sides of lower back, patient sitting)
(5) auscultation with stethoscope, all four quadrants
(6) palpation and percussion of bladder (midline, just above pubis)
(7) exam for hernias (M.D. places fingers over groin or up into scrotum [male] and asks patient to cough or bear down)
(8) palpation of groin for lymph nodes

XIII. Genitalia
Male:
(1) palpation of penis, spermatic cords, and testicles
(2) transillumination of testicles with light source, if enlarged
Female:
(1) palpation of vagina, uterus, tubes, and ovaries ("bimanual" exam—

TABLE 8   The Basic Adult Physical Examination

XIII. Genitalia

M.D. places two fingers of gloved hand in vagina and other hand on lower abdomen)

(2) observation of vagina and uterine cervix (M.D. uses light source and speculum; takes Pap smear and stains cervix with dye)

XIV. Rectum

(1) digital palpation of rectum and prostate (male)—M.D. inserts gloved index finger in rectum; usually done as part of bimanual exam in female.

(2) testing of stool for hidden ("occult") blood

XV. Legs and Feet

(1) palpation for pulses behind knees, at inside of ankles, and on top of feet

(2) exam for excess fluid (edema) (M.D. presses with thumb over lower shins)

(3) testing of range of motion of legs

(4) observation and palpation of skin of legs and feet (texture, warmth)

(5) palpation of calves for tenderness or thrombosed veins (cords)

XVI. Neurologic exam

(1) cranial nerves tested (M.D. asks patient to raise eyebrows, move facial muscles, shrug shoulders—see also III, 3–7; IV, 2–3; V, 3; VI, 3–4)

(2) gait tested (patient asked to walk)

(3) balance tested (patient asked to stand on one foot, stand with feet together and eyes closed, hop, etc.)

(4) co-ordination tested (patient asked to touch M.D.'s finger with his own, to do rapid hand and finger movements, write, etc.)

(5) muscle mass palpated

(6) muscle strength tested in arms, hands, legs, feet

(7) tendon reflexes tested (M.D. taps with reflex hammer—elbows, wrists, knees, and ankles)

(8) toe reflexes tested (M.D. runs edge of nail, key, etc., along bottom of patient's foot)

(9) exam for tremor (patient asked to hold out hands)

(10) sensation tested (patient touched with piece of cotton, pin, tuning fork held to ankle, etc.)

XVII. Mental Status

(1) basic orientation tested (M.D. asks patient to identify himself, the location, the date, etc.)

(2) memory tested ("Who is President of U.S.?" "Repeat the following numbers after me . . .", etc.)

(3) intellectual function tested ("psychologic testing"—a variety of tests of problem solving, spatial relations, etc.)

This basic exam is not meant to be necessarily the "best" or only acceptable exam. Many doctors will do more, under each part, than the items I have listed. Some will substitute other items. The purpose of the basic exam is to provide you, the reader, with a sample physical exam—to provide you with one idea of what might constitute a complete exam, and to alert you to areas which your doctor may omit.

If, for instance, your doctor omits entire parts of the body—the head or eyes, let us say—he is not doing a complete exam. If he brushes over other parts, doing only one or two items, he is also providing less than optimal care.

What should you do if this happens?

You should, quite simply, request that the physician examine the neglected part. For instance:

"Doctor, would you please check my eyes (sinuses, abdomen, ankle pulses, etc.)"

"Doctor, I'd appreciate it if you'd give me a rectal (vaginal, neurologic, etc.) exam."

"Doctor, would you test my blood pressure (visual acuity, hearing, muscle strength, etc.)"

"Doctor, would you examine me for hernias (swollen glands, edema fluid, etc.)"

Most doctors, if you ask, will readily comply. Some may take offense. If so, you should merely say that you want a complete exam, regardless of your complaint. The doctor may question you further. If so, you should simply stick to your guns.

Here is a sample exchange:

PATIENT: Doctor, would you please check my hearing?
DOCTOR: Why, have you had any trouble?
PATIENT: No, I'd just like to have it checked. [If the answer is "yes," naturally, say "yes."]

Some doctors may tell you they do not "routinely" do certain parts of the physical exam. "I don't do a neurologic exam in every patient," your doctor may say. Or the doctor may try to tell you that your diagnosis does not warrant a complete exam. ("You have the 'flu.' You don't need a rectal exam.")

As I have noted, the best doctors will do a complete exam for all new patients, regardless of symptoms. You may not wish to put up a fight if your doctor fails to do a complete exam, but you should certainly keep it in mind when judging his overall performance.

Remember: *there is no need to feel apologetic about asking your physician to perform a complete physical exam.* It is your right, as a health consumer.

Which diagnostic tests should be part of your initial visit?

Laboratory tests and procedures will be discussed in Chapter 5. For the present, it will be adequate to note that there are a few tests which probably ought to be done on every new patient. These tests should be, in effect, part and parcel of the physical exam.

Two of these basic tests are noted in Table 8. These are:

(1) stool test for hidden ("occult") blood
(2) Pap smear for cervical cancer (taken during vaginal exam, and sent to diagnostic lab)

There are three other basic tests. These are:

(1) the tuberculin skin test
(2) the complete blood count (CBC)
(3) the urinalysis (UA)

These tests can all be done by the doctor, or by an assistant. They should be a routine part of every first office visit.

Can an assistant (non-physician) do a history or physical exam?

More and more, doctors are using assistants to do certain tasks. For years, of course, nurses have been taking blood pressure and asking patients simple questions. Now, however, non-physicians are being used to do more complex tasks—even taking an entire history or doing a complete physical exam.

Can a non-physician do these kinds of things?

The answer is definitely "yes." There is nothing sacrosanct about the history or physical exam. With special training, a non-physician can learn to do both.

"Special training" are the key words. An ordinary nurse (either a licensed practical nurse or a registered nurse) does not have such special training. Neither does a lab technician, a physical therapist, or most other health workers.

Specially trained persons go under a variety of names. They may be called "physician assistants" or "physician associates." "Medex" is the name given to graduates of a program that trains former military medical corpsmen to be physician assistants. In child care such specially trained persons are called "pediatric nurse assistant" or "pediatric nurse associate."

Whatever the name, these specially trained assistants should all be graduates of a recognized training program, in which they learned their skills. Most of these programs are run by schools of medicine or nursing. Most last two years (Medex, which takes returning military medics, is fifteen months).

If you have any doubts as to your doctor's assistant's training credentials and qualifications, there are several things you can do. First, you can ask your doctor. Or you can contact your state health or education department, which will keep a list of all approved physician assistant programs. Some states already license physician assistants. If your state is one, you should be able to find out if your doctor's assistant is licensed.

Principle: Your doctor's assistant should work under his direct supervision.

This is vital. Regardless of his or her credentials, no physician assistant should work alone. The physician should be on the premises. He should be readily available to supervise his assistant. He should be ready to check, for instance, on any *abnormal findings* in the history or physical exam.

Needless to say, the same standards of completeness which apply to a physician who takes a history or does an exam will also apply to his assistant.

Physician assistants are not yet widely used in most parts of the United States. But their use is increasing. More and more, tasks which were once done by doctors are being done by assistants. In some instances, assistants are trained to make tentative diagnoses and to treat minor conditions.

None of this, however, changes the basic principles in this book. It does not alter the basic elements of a complete history or physical exam. It does not alter the fact that, in the end, your physician is the person responsible for the caliber of your care.

5

Diagnostic technology: which tests and when?

A young woman magazine writer visited her internist. She was in good health and only wanted a checkup. She emerged with a bill for $135 in laboratory tests.

"Were all those tests necessary?" she asks.

Today lab tests and procedures are a vital part of almost every diagnostic work-up. Yet there seems to be a good deal of confusion, on the part of doctors, as to which tests to order and when. Some physicians seem to use no tests at all. Others, like the internist above, order a large battery of tests routinely on every patient.

How many tests should a doctor use? Alvan Feinstein, in his book *Clinical Judgment,* sums up the dilemma this way:

> If he orders too many tests indiscriminately, he wastes everyone's time, effort, and money. . . . too few . . . [and] he runs the risk of making major diagnostic and therapeutic blunders.

Many doctors undoubtedly use more tests than they should. The New York City health department has found, in checking Medicaid records, that many doctors order tests that have no relation to their patients' suspected diagnosis. In another study, doctors who suspected heart disease in children were found to use about five times as many tests as they really needed to make a correct diagnosis.

On the other hand, just as many physicians use too few tests. I have seen patients referred to the hospital by their doctors without any lab tests at all. I have seen, for example, patients referred with the diagnosis of "anemia" who had not had either a hemoglobin or a hematocrit—both tests for anemia which any doctor should be able to do in his office. I have seen patients sent in with the diagnosis of cystitis, or urinary tract infection, who had not had a urinalysis—again, a simple test which every doctor's office should be able to perform.

I have seen patients treated for several days with a diagnosis of pneumonia, whose doctors had never ordered a chest x-ray, or given them a TB skin test.

All these are, in my opinion, clear-cut examples of poor medical care. They are examples of doctors failing to obtain even the most basic tests, when these tests were clearly indicated.

What should your doctor tell you about tests?

There are certain key things your physician should be able to tell you concerning every diagnostic test and procedure. These are things which you should inquire about if your doctor does not volunteer the information.

Principle: Your doctor should tell you the purpose of every diagnostic test.

He should, in other words, tell you what he hopes to learn from the test, and why this information is important in your particular case.

You should not be satisfied with a doctor who tells you that a test is "routine." Or one who says, "I always get a serum calcium on my patients." The doctor should be able to give you a reply that makes sense. Here are a few examples:

"I ordered a serum bilirubin because you appear jaundiced, which suggests liver disease, and bilirubin is a chemical test of liver function."

"Your chest pain suggests pleuritis, and a chest film might show pleural thickening which would corroborate that impression."

"I ordered a blood urea nitrogen because you show signs of heart failure, and the BUN is usually increased in heart failure."

Your doctor may simply tell you he has ordered a test to help him "rule out" or "rule in" a certain diagnosis. This answer, while often used, is not really an adequate one. You should ask him what other information leads him to suspect the diagnosis in the first place.

Principle: Your doctor should tell you the likelihood of any test yielding useful diagnostic information.

Some tests are better than others. They are more likely to yield a "positive" result, for instance, if you have a particular disease. A TB skin test, for example, will be positive in nearly 100 per cent of cases of active tuberculosis. A chest x-ray, by contrast, will be positive in a much lower percentage of cases. If you have pneumococcal pneumonia, a chest film will be positive about 70 per cent of the time. A blood culture, however, will be positive only about 30 per cent of the time.

Your doctor should have some idea how likely it is that any test will provide useful data for your health problem.

Principle: Your doctor should tell you the risks of any test.

Most of the common lab tests involve little or no risk. Tests where blood is drawn for chemical analysis are an example. The amount of blood taken, even in several tubes, is so small that the body can compensate for it easily. The risk of infection, if throwaway needles are used, is nil. Most x-rays, such as those of the chest, extremities, skull, etc., are also essentially harmless, the amounts of radiation involved being slight.

On the other hand, some tests involve somewhat greater risks. A thoracentesis involves removing fluid, which is normally absent, from around the lung. This procedure may be necessary for therapeutic purposes (to allow the patient to breathe more easily) as well as for diagnostic ones (to analyze the fluid). This test is an example of one which entails small, but definite risks. These include bleeding into the lung, collapse of the lung, etc.*

A lumbar puncture—sometimes called a "spinal tap"—is another example of a test which involves some risk. In this test, a contaminated needle can cause meningitis—the very condition the test is usually used to detect. (It should be emphasized, however, that this risk —while theoretically possible—is extremely unlikely, given good sterile technique.)

Finally, there are some tests which involve substantial risks. Often this is true because these tests are performed on patients who are quite ill. Cardiac catheterization is an obvious example. In this procedure a wire catheter is inserted into a vein or artery and threaded up into the heart. The catheter allows the physician to measure the

---

* One study gives the risk of death from thoracentesis as 1:1,000, and that of bleeding and lung collapse as 1:100 and 5:100, respectively.

pressures and oxygen levels within the heart. It can also be used to inject dye for x-rays, or cine-angiograms, showing the heart's action.

Depending on the condition of the patient, this is a test which can have a definite risk of injury or even death.

Principle: Your doctor ought to explain to you why any test which has some element of risk is justified.

Sometimes this justification will be clear. The risks of missing a case of meningitis in a child, for instance, far outweigh the risks of a lumbar puncture. (This is another example of a diagnostic test which is probably done far too little, rather than too much.)

At other times, this benefit-risk balance may be less clear. In small infants with congenital heart disease, for instance, the risks of cardiac catheterization are considerable. If the infant is not gravely ill, there may be no need to make a definite diagnosis early in life. In this case, the test may be safely deferred until the child is older and better able to tolerate it.

Other things you should know about diagnostic tests

You should know something about the *time required* for your test results to be reported. Most results should be available in a few days. I have known people to wait for weeks, however, for results.

Sometimes this time factor can be important. A "strep" throat, for instance, should be treated with penicillin within four or five days, at the most. A throat culture (as is true with most bacterial cultures) should take only twelve to eighteen hours to show some results. Clearly, any doctor who cannot guarantee "next day" throat culture results is doing his patients a disservice.

If the time required seems inordinately long, you should ask your doctor about the likelihood of your condition changing in the interim. You may wish to have your tests done at a hospital outpatient department, where the results might be reported more rapidly.

You should also ask about the *cost* of your tests. Many doctors forget about the high costs of tests. When forced to check on it, they are often surprised that a test costs so much. Not infrequently, a doctor will "re-think" and decide that a particular test is not really necessary, when he discovers how much it costs.

Which tests should every office physician be able to perform?

There are a few tests which are so basic to good medical care that every office physician who provides primary care should be able to do them on the spot, during your initial visit. These tests require little time, are easy to do, and can yield a great deal of useful information about your health problem.

The *complete blood count* (CBC) is really several tests: the hemoglobin (or hematocrit), the white blood cell count, and an examination of the blood smear. The hemoglobin (or hematocrit) is the basic test for anemia. The white cell count is a test for infection or other illness involving the white blood cells. The blood smear exam tells the physician more about both red and white cells.

A CBC can be done by your doctor, or an assistant, in minutes. It requires only a few drops of blood, a microscope, glass slides, and a few other items. Results, if the test is done in the doctor's office, can be ready in minutes.

The *urinalysis* (UA) is the examination of your urine. The urine is tested for its concentration (specific gravity). By dipping a specially treated paper strip into the urine, the presence or absence of certain chemicals (protein, sugar, ketones) is tested. The urine is spun in a tabletop centrifuge and the urine sediment is looked at under the microscope.

Again, all these procedures can be done on a few drops of urine. All can be done in minutes.

Principle: The complete blood count and urinalysis should be part of every diagnostic work-up.

There may be some exceptions to this rule (patients with the common "cold" or other trivial problems). But certainly, for anyone visiting a physician for the first time with any but the most trivial complaint, it will hold true.

The best doctors will be prepared to perform these tests on all such patients. They will have a small room or alcove, for use as a lab. It will contain certain basic equipment: a microscope, a tabletop centrifuge for spinning blood and urine, glass slides and other materials.

Table 9 lists the several parts of the CBC and UA, and their most common uses.

TABLE 9   Basic Blood and Urine Tests

Test	Definition	Commonly used in the diagnosis of
Complete blood count (CBC)		
Hematocrit (Hct.)	volume of red cells (after tube of blood is spun in centrifuge) as a percent of total volume	anemia (defined as Hct. of less than 30–35%) N.B.: does not tell *type* of anemia present
Hemoglobin (Hgb.)	Grams of red cell pigment in 100 cc. of blood	anemia (defined as Hgb. of less than 10–12 grams/100 cc.)
White cell count (WBC)	number of white cells per cubic millimeter of blood	infections (usually elevated)
Blood smear examination		
differential white count (Diff.)	microsopic exam and count of 100 white cells to determine proportions of various types	type of infection (bacterial, viral, fungal, parasitic, etc.)
		allergic disorders (eosinophils usually elevated)
red cell size and shape ("red cell morphology")	microscopic appearance of red cells	type of anemia (example: in iron-deficiency a. red cells are smaller and paler than normal)
platelets	microscopic estimate of number of platelets present	certain blood-clotting conditions (platelets may be decreased in number)
Urinalysis (UA)		
Specific gravity (S.G.)	degree of concentration of urine	urinary tract obstruction with kidney damage (S.G. often low) dehydration (S.G. high)

TABLE 9 Basic Blood and Urine Tests

Test	Definition	Commonly used in the diagnosis of
Urinalysis (UA)		
pH	degree of acidity of urine	kidney, lung or other conditions causing acidosis or alkalosis
Protein	approximate amount of protein present (paper strip dipped in urine and read as 0, 1—4+)	kidney damage of various types ("nephritis," "nephrosis")
Sugar (or "reducing substances")	approximate amount of glucose, fructose, etc. present	diabetes (may be elevated), hypoglycemic conditions (may be low)
Ketones	approximate amount of acetone and other ketone chemicals present	severe diabetes (may be elevated), starvation (elevated), other metabolic disorders
Urine sediment exam	microscopic examination of spun (centrifuged) urine for (1) red cells (2) white cells (3) casts and kidney cells (4) crystals (5) micro- organisms	kidney damage (red cells, casts and kidney cells); urinary tract infection (white cells, micro-organisms); gout (crystals)

What are "cultures" and when should your doctor use them?

A culture is a test that shows the presence or absence of a micro-organism (bacterium, virus, etc.) Your doctor, for instance, may obtain a culture of your sore throat by running a cotton swab over it. He will then run the swab over an agar plate. He then leaves the plate overnight in an incubator. The next morning he can look at ("read") the plate for the presence of abnormal organisms, such as streptococcal bacteria. If he sees such bacterial colonies, he will read the culture as "positive." If not, the culture will be read "negative."

Principle: A culture should be obtained in every case of suspected infection.

There is little doubt that most doctors do not take enough cultures. Many, in fact, do not even own an incubator or keep a supply of agar plates. (In many urban areas even these are not necessary—there are labs which will pick up culture swabs several times a day and report the results the next day.)

It is a simple matter to obtain specimens of the throat, sputum, blood, urine, and stool, as well as secretions from the eye, vagina, skin wounds, etc., for culture. Every primary care physician should be able to obtain such specimens. Doctors who work in rural areas and lack access to a hospital center must also be able to obtain spinal fluid by lumbar puncture ("spinal tap") in suspected cases of meningitis. (Most urban doctors will send such cases to a hospital emergency room for this relatively simple procedure.)

After obtaining the specimen for culture, the doctor—if he does not plate and incubate it himself—will send it to a bacteriology lab.† He will specify on the lab slip the type of specimen (sputum, urine, wound, etc.). He will also specify the type of culture desired (bacterial, fungal, viral, etc.).

Many doctors will not obtain any cultures in the case of a "cold" or other mild viral infection (influenza, measles, etc.). This practice is permissible—if the doctor is sure the infection is viral—since there is no treatment for most viral infections (with a few exceptions).

Needless to say, if a doctor thinks an infection is viral and chooses not to obtain a culture, he should not administer antibiotics. The huge volume of these drugs prescribed each year is ample evidence that many doctors ignore this rule. (See Chapter 6.)

Principle: A culture specimen (or specimens) should always be obtained and sent to the lab before antibiotics are used.

What are "sensitivities"?

Sensitivities tell the doctor what antibiotics will kill a particular organism (what drugs it is sensitive to). For some infections (bacterial "strep" throat is an example) sensitivities are not needed. But for most, such as infections of the urinary tract, bowel, wounds,

---

† The term "bacteriology lab" is misleading. These labs test not only for bacteria, but also for fungi, and often for parasites and even viruses.

eyes, ears, etc., they should be done. Sensitivities are ordered by the doctor at the same time he orders a culture, by simply writing the word "sensitivities" on the lab slip.

How are culture and sensitivity results reported?

Let us suppose you visit your doctor with the complaint of fever and pain on urination. After a history and physical exam he suspects a urinary tract infection. He should then obtain a "clean voided" urine specimen.‡ He should write on the lab slip the words "culture, colony count, and sensitivities."

The results will then be reported by the lab in one to two days. Here is how they might look:

organism: E. Coli [a common urinary pathogen]
colony count: more than 100,000 colonies per cc. [diagnostic of a
    urinary tract infection]
sensitivities:
      penicillin   S [sensitive]
      ampicillin   S
      tetracycline R [resistant]
      sulfadiazine S
      etc.

Not all culture reports will have the same form (a colony count, for instance, is only ordered for urine cultures). But all should state the organism(s) and their sensitivities, if these were ordered.

Here are a few common physician errors in the use of cultures:

(1) diagnosing "strep" throat without a positive throat culture
(2) diagnosing a urinary tract infection without a "clean" urine culture and a colony count "greater then 100,000/cc."
(3) diagnosing pneumonia without determining the type of pneumonia by obtaining sputum (if present) and blood cultures
(4) failing to culture the stool for bacteria, and for ova and parasites, in all cases of diarrhea
(5) failing to obtain blood cultures in any case of severe generalized infection which is not obviously viral.
(6) failing to obtain cultures for a "repeat" infection, particularly urinary tract infections (it is not safe to assume that the repeat infection is due to the same organism as the first one was)

‡ A "clean voided" urine is one obtained after careful anti-bacterial cleansing of the urinary orifice.

How should diagnostic x-rays be done?

Diagnostic x-rays are one of the physician's most valuable tools. Properly taken and read, they can provide a great deal of information. An ordinary chest film, for instance, can provide information about the heart, lungs, lymph glands, blood vessels, and even the bone marrow and blood.

X-rays should, however, be taken only when needed. They should not be done as a "routine" part of every examination.*

Principle: Diagnostic x-rays should be done and interpreted by doctors who are Board-certified (or Board-eligible) radiologists. They should be done using modern equipment.

A surprising number of primary care doctors still take their own x-rays. This practice occurs even in urban areas with ready access to trained radiologists and hospital x-ray departments. Doctors have been found using outmoded x-ray equipment which delivers 100 times as much radiation dose as needed!

Some physicians still do their own *fluoroscopy*. Fluoroscopy is a procedure which utilizes a special x-ray machine (the fluoroscope) that takes a continuous x-ray which in turn allows the doctor to see the movement of internal organs (expansion of the lungs, for example). Fluoroscopy has its valid uses. But it exposes the patient to many times the dose of an ordinary x-ray. For this reason, it should be done only by a Board-certified radiologist, and only when absolutely necessary.

In general, you should steer clear of non-radiologist physicians who do their own x-rays. You should also beware of those who use ancient machines which deliver several times the needed dosage to your body. In theory, all x-ray machines are inspected by public health officials periodically. In practice, many machines—particularly those in doctors' offices—go uninspected.

You can avoid this whole problem if you have your x-rays done in the outpatient department of a medical school hospital. As a second choice, a private non-hospital radiologist may be used.

* There is some disagreement over whether even a chest film ought to be used as a screening tool. Despite its use in multiphasic centers, most public health experts feel it should not be a "routine" part of every examination. Tuberculosis screening, for example, is more safely and more accurately done with the TB skin test than by chest x-ray.

What is the major risk of diagnostic x-rays?

The major risk of x-rays is still the dose of radiation they deliver to your body. High doses of irradiation damage body cells, in particular the chromosomes or genetic material of the cell nuclei. Moderately high doses of x-rays have been linked, in humans, to the later development of cancers of various types and of leukemia.

It is believed that the risks of x-ray dosage are *linear*—that is, the more dosage a person receives during a lifetime, the greater that person's chances of developing cancer or another abnormality. Your body's tolerance to x-rays, then, is a bit like a bank account that can only be drawn down, not replenished. For this reason, it would seem prudent to use x-rays only when necessary, especially when you are young, keeping in mind that you might well need your "bank account" for your older years.

Principle: You should ask your doctor about the need for every x-ray examination. You should ask him the dosage involved.

"Are these x-rays absolutely necessary?" This query, on your part, will convey to your physician your concern about unneeded x-ray examination. It will make him reconsider his decision to obtain x-ray films. It will make him think twice.

Needless to say, the doctor should be able to tell you exactly what he hopes to learn from your x-rays. He should be able to tell you why this added information is important to your diagnosis of treatment.

The doctor should also be able to tell you the approximate dose of any x-ray examination, in millirads or millirems (for x-rays both are the same). He should be able to tell you both the whole-body and gonadal doses. The National Commission on Radiation Protection and Measurement recommends that no person be exposed to more than *five rem each year*. By contrast, a standard chest x-ray involves only 5–10 millirem (.005–.010 rem). On the other hand, some x-ray studies involve much larger amounts, 3–400 millirem (.3–.4 rem) or more.

Table 10 lists several commonly done x-ray examinations and the rough amount of dosage they involve. This table was adapted from *Medical and Dental X-Rays,* an excellent consumer guide. This guide is available, for $2.00, from the Health Research Group, 2000 P Street, Washington, D.C. 20036. I highly recommend it to anyone interested in the subject of diagnostic x-rays.

TABLE 10   Doses of Common X-Ray Procedures

Type of Procedure	Average No. of films per exam	whole-body	Dose[1] gonadal males	females
Abdomen	3	medium	medium	medium
Chest	2	low	low	low
Cholecystogram (gall bladder)	3	high	medium	medium
Dental	1–3	low	low	low
Extremities	2	low	low	low
GI series, upper	fluoroscopy	high	medium	medium
GI series, lower or Barium enema	fluoroscopy	high	high	high
Hip or Upper Femur (upper thigh)	3	medium	high	high
Intravenous pyelogram (IVP)	3	high	high	high
Lumbo-pelvic	3	medium	high	high
Mammography	3	medium	—	low
Shoulder	2	low	low	low
Skull or Sinuses	4	low	low	low
Spine, cervical (neck)	4	low	low	low
Spine, thoracic (middle back)	3	high	medium	medium
Spine, lumbar (lower back)	3	high	high	high

[1] High dose=more than 200 millirads per average examination.
Medium dose=50–200 millirads per average examination.
Low dose=less than 50 millirads per average examination.

SOURCE: Adapted from Laws, P. W., *Medical and Dental X-Rays*, Health Research Group (Washington, D.C.), 1974.

Who is at special risk from x-ray dosage?

Two types of people are at special risk from the dosage of diagnostic x-rays: children and women who are (or might be) pregnant.

In the case of children, who have their whole lives before them, it is obviously important to minimize the use of x-rays. In addition, the cells of children are multiplying rapidly, a fact which renders them more susceptible to the effects of radiation.

This rapid cell multiplication is also characteristic of the fetus. For this reason, women who are (or who might be) pregnant should avoid x-rays, if at all possible. If x-rays must be done, care should be taken to shield the ovaries, in the lower abdomen, with a *lead apron*. Such an apron, in fact, should be used to shield both male and female gonads from scattered radiation in *all* instances, except when the shield will interfere with the examination.

If you are a woman who is, or is trying to become, pregnant, you should be more careful of x-ray exposure. You should try to avoid any x-rays after the first ten days of your menstrual cycle. This is the period during which pregnancy can occur and during which the newly fertilized egg is thought to be especially susceptible to radiation damage. Later, when you know you are pregnant, though the danger may be less, exposure should still be kept to an absolute minimum.† A pregnant woman should not be asked to hold a child for an x-ray exam.

What about doctors who insist that your x-rays be repeated?

Some doctors make a standard practice of taking new x-rays on all their new patients, regardless of what films the patient has already had. This is one of the less desirable practices of some "prestige" hospitals. I have seen hospital radiologists summarily dismiss films taken "on the outside" and subject the patient to new ones, even though the old x-rays were perfectly adequate.

Principle: X-rays are your property. You have a right to demand that they be sent to any doctor or hospital of your choice.

I have seen patients saved from having new x-rays taken because they themselves carried their films from one doctor or hospital to another. On the other hand, there may be valid reasons for retaking x-rays (films not recent, of poor quality, etc.). You should make sure your x-rays are being redone for a valid reason, and not simply because of institutional chauvinism or snobbery. (Warning: in some circumstances this may be a tough fight; best to forgo it in situations where only one or two low-dose films are involved, and to reserve it for situations such as repeat of a gallbladder, GI series, etc.).

What are "contrast" x-rays?

There are essentially two types of diagnostic x-rays. The first are called "plain" films. These are ordinary films of various parts of the

† The National Council on Radiation Protection and Measurement recommends that radiation dose for a fetus during pregnancy not exceed 0.3 rem (300 millirem).

body (chest, skull, abdomen, extremities, etc.). The second type are called "contrast" films. These are films where a foreign substance (a chemical dye, air, etc.) is introduced into the body to contrast with normal body tissues.

Contrast films are now quite commonly done. The upper GI series is an example. In this test, usually done for suspected ulcer disease, a small quantity of contrast material is swallowed. This material then coats the stomach and upper intestine and allows their inner surface to be outlined on the x-ray.

The IVP (intravenous pyelogram) is another example of a contrast x-ray study. In this procedure an amount of dye is injected into an arm vein. This dye is excreted by the kidneys. When x-rays are taken, the dye can be seen outlining the kidneys and the rest of the urinary tract. (Many experts feel that an IVP should be done on every patient who has a first urinary tract infection, and certainly if there is a repeat infection.)

Cardiac catheterization usually includes the injection of a contrast material into the heart. X-rays are then taken in rapid sequence, to show the outline of the heart, its valves and great vessels. Continuous films—called *cine-angiograms* (doctors often refer to them as "cines")—can be done. These films are really x-ray movies. They can be shown on a screen to reveal, in slow motion, the movement of dye through the heart's chambers and its nearby vessels.

Most contrast studies involve little risk, other than that of the material used. (The risk of allergy to the dye can be minimized if the doctor injects a small amount under the skin, as with a skin test, and observes for any rash or other reaction.)

Some contrast studies do, however, involve added risk. Studies of the heart or the brain (cerebral angiography, pneumoencephalography) are examples of high-risk diagnostic x-ray studies.

Principle: For any high-risk diagnostic x-rays you should go to a medical school-affiliated hospital.

In these large hospitals, many dozens of these procedures are done each month. And they are done by teams of physicians and technicians. I spent some time, as a medical student, observing a neuro-radiology team perform cerebral angiography at Boston's Massachusetts General Hospital. In this study contrast dye is injected into arteries in the neck. The dye then goes to the brain, where it outlines the cerebral arteries.

Needless to say, this is a procedure that demands skilled person-

nel. Improperly done it can cause a stroke or other serious complication. Most hospitals do very few numbers of this study, and their
complication rates are substantial. It was not uncommon for the
MGH team, however, to do three or four such studies in a single
morning. During the few months I spent there, I did not observe
a single serious complication.

Table 11 lists many of the contrast studies that can be done, and
indicates those which may be considered high-risk procedures.

TABLE 11   Commonly Done "Contrast" X-ray Studies and Their Uses

TYPE OF STUDY	METHOD	USES
Arteriogram	x-ray dye injected into artery	dye outlines artery and its branches
Arthrogram	dye injected into joint (knee, hip, etc.)	outlines inside of joint, cartilage, etc.
Barium enema	dye given rectally	outlines colon and rectum
Barium swallow	patient swallows dye	outlines upper digestive tract (pharynx, esophagus)
aBronchogram	dye injected into lung bronchi (air passages)	outlines bronchial tree
Cholecystogram	dye given as pills twelve hrs. before films	outlines biliary tract (gallbladder and bile ducts)
aCerebral angiogram (arteriogram)	dye injected into carotid and/or vertebral arteries in neck	outlines blood vessels in neck and brain
aCoronary angiogram (arteriogram)	dye injected into chambers of heart	outlines heart chambers, valves, and surrounding arteries and veins
Cystourethrogram	dye placed in bladder by means of urinary catheter; patient expells dye by voiding	outlines lower urinary tract (bladder and urethra)
GI series	patient swallows dye	outlines stomach, duodenum, and remainder of small intestine

TABLE 11   Commonly Done "Contrast" X-ray Studies and Their Uses

TYPE OF STUDY	METHOD	USES
Hysterogram	dye injected through vaginal catheter into uterus	outlines inside of uterus, Fallopian tubes
Intravenous pyelogram (IVP)	dye injected into arm vein	outlines urinary tract (kidneys, ureters, and bladder)
Myelogram	dye injected by needle (as with lumbar puncture) into fluid surrounding spinal cord	outlines cord and any structures compressing it (slipped disc, tumor, etc.)
aPneumoencephalo-gram (PEG)	air injected (as per myelogram); air rises into brain	outlines chambers and surface of brain
aPulmonary angiogram (arteriogram)	dye injected into pulmonary arteries as they leave heart	outlines blood vessels (arteries and veins) in lungs
Venogram	dye injected into vein	outlines venous system (clots, varicose veins) of leg, arm, etc.

a Indicates high-risk procedure.

What are "chemistries"?

When your doctor speaks of chemistries, he is talking about any of a large number of tests which measure the amount of minerals and other chemical compounds in your body. Serum sodium, potassium, calcium, cholesterol—all are examples of chemistries. The chemistry lab can perform such determinations on blood or serum, urine, sweat, saliva, spinal fluid—in fact, on virtually any body fluid.

Table 12 lists some of the chemistries most often ordered, and some of their uses.

TABLE 12   Common Chemistry Tests and Their Uses

TEST	COMMONLY USED AS A TEST FOR	EXAMPLES
Amylase, serum	pancreatic damage	high in pancreatitis, often in gallbladder

TABLE 12   Common Chemistry Tests and Their Uses

TEST	COMMONLY USED AS A TEST FOR	EXAMPLES
		or biliary tract disease
Bilirubin, serum	liver function	high in hepatitis; also in biliary tract disease
Bromsulfalein, serum	liver function	elevated in liver cell damage
Calcium, serum	parathyroid function	high in hyper-parathyroidism; low in hypopara-thyroidism
Carbon dioxide, serum	acid–base balance	high in respiratory insufficiency; low in diabetic acidosis
Chloride, serum	body water and elec-trolyte balance	often high in acidosis
Cholesterol, serum	lipid metabolism	risk factor for coronary artery disease
Creatinine, serum and urine	kidney function	high where urine formation is diminished
Glucose, serum	carbohydrate metabolism	high in untreated diabetes; low in various "hypo-glycemic" disorders
Latex fixation	"rheumatoid factor"	positive in most cases of rheumatoid arthritis; often in other conditions
Lactic dehydrogenase (LDH), serum	heart muscle integrity	high after most "heart attacks"
Phosphorus, serum	parathyroid function	low in hyper-parathyroidism; high in hypopara-thyroidism

TABLE 12 Common Chemistry Tests and Their Uses

TEST	COMMONLY USED AS A TEST FOR	EXAMPLES
Phosphatase, acid (serum)	prostatic integrity	high in many cases of prostatic cancer
Phosphatase, alkaline (serum)	liver function	high in biliary tract disease
Potassium, serum	body water and electrolyte balance	high in renal failure
Protein bound iodine (PBI)	thyroid function	low in hypothyroidism; high in hyperthyroidism
Protein, serum total	protein metabolism	high in certain "overproducing" disorders; low in certain rare "infection-susceptible" conditions
Protein, serum albumin	liver function	low in liver damage
Prothrombin time, plasma	blood coagulation	lengthened in various coagulation disorders
Sodium, serum	body water and electrolyte balance	high in dehydration
Transaminase (SGOT), serum	liver function	high in liver cell damage, heart attack
Urea nitrogen, serum	kidney function	high when more than 50% of kidney tissue not functioning
Uric acid, serum	nucleic acid metabolism	high in gout, massive cellular destruction

Chemistry results may be reported in "milligrams per cent" (milligrams per 100 cc. of fluid) or in various other ways. For each chemistry test, as for every biologic test, there is a normal range. The normal range may also depend on the laboratory doing the test.

Principle: You should ask your doctor where your test results lie, in relation to the normal range.

Many doctors tell patients their test results in such vague terms as "high-normal," "low-normal," "borderline-normal," etc. Needless to say, you will have a far clearer idea of your results by knowing the actual value and the normal range.

What do "borderline" or abnormal test results mean?

Results which approach or exceed the normal range may mean that you have a health problem. But then again, they may not.

Your doctor, in his eagerness to make a diagnosis, may grasp at a "borderline" test result. He may, for instance, try to convince himself (and you) that your low-normal PBI signifies hypothyroidism. Or that that high-normal serum uric acid value means that you have gout.

But such borderline results do not necessarily mean that any illness is present. They are best repeated, either at once or after a short waiting period.

Even an abnormal result may not mean that anything is wrong. The best chemistry labs can make mistakes. Blood samples can get mixed up. Machines can malfunction. For this reason, an abnormal test result should also be repeated—particularly if it is a major factor in your doctor's diagnosis.

One common error doctors make is failure to recognize that an abnormal test result may be due to medication the patient is taking, or even to something in the diet. I remember quite clearly a woman treated for hypothyroidism on the basis of a low PBI (serum-protein-bound iodide—a test for thyroid hormone). Her doctor failed to recognize, however, that she was taking a diuretic, which, among its side effects, lowered the PBI.

There are many other examples of how drugs or diet can disturb laboratory results—and even mimic certain diseases. Cortisone can elevate your blood sugar, and make it look like you have diabetes. Aspirin prolongs the time it takes blood to clot, as in certain bleeding conditions. A diet overly rich in protein can raise your blood uric acid level, as is found in gout.

Needless to say, these changes do not mean that you have diabetes, or a bleeding disorder, or gout. All are the result of drugs or diet. (For more examples, consult any pharmacology text.)

Principle: Before you accept as valid any abnormal laboratory result, you should ask if it could be caused by medications or diet.

If your doctor has taken a complete history, he should have questioned you about drugs and diet. It never hurts to remind him, however, of this possibility. And to remind yourself, too.

Several other things can affect certain chemistry results. These include things such as the time of day the specimen was collected, the way it was stored, etc. If you have any suspicions, again, ask your physician. If *he* has any doubts, you might suggest he contact the director of the chemistry lab or consult a book on laboratory techniques, of which there are several.

There are, incidentally, unreliable chemistry labs. Doing blood chemistries and other lab tests is a lucrative business, and it has attracted many less than competent operators. The Federal Government's Medicare program certifies some 2,750 so-called "independent" labs (independent of doctor's offices or hospitals)—presumably the better ones. The best labs, however, are those in the biggest hospitals. Independent for-profit labs, with some notable exceptions, often do too few of many kinds of tests to do them accurately.

Principle: You may wish to have an abnormal test result checked by the laboratory of a large hospital or medical center.

What is the most common physician error in dealing with an abnormal test result?

An abnormal test result cannot be ignored. It may not necessarily signify disease. But it cannot, nevertheless, be swept under the rug.

Unfortunately, this too often happens.

I have seen many patients turn up in a hospital emergency room with serious illnesses. On examining their medical records, frequently, an abnormal test result months earlier may be found—a result that should have signaled their physician that something was afoot.

In one recent study of doctors in federal Neighborhood Health Centers, the single most common error of these physicians (who, on the whole, performed far better than private "solo" practitioners) was their failure to follow up on abnormal test results.

Principle: Every patient with an abnormal test result deserves to be followed (1) until a reason for the abnormality is found, or (2) until the test returns to normal.

A man who has had hepatitis may appear completely normal. Yet he may still have an elevated SGOT—a test of liver function —indicating leftover liver damage that has not yet healed. The careful physician will continue to follow his patient, and to repeat the test, every few weeks (or more often) until it has returned to normal.

The same holds true with any kind of test. Consider the following case:

> **Case 5-1:** A middle-aged secretary visited her doctor, complaining of low back pain, of several weeks duration. The rest of her history and physical exam were unremarkable. The doctor ordered x-rays of the lower back and spine. These were reported back to him as showing "osteoporosis" (less than normal bone density). The physician informed the patient of the abnormal finding. He then instructed her to return, if she wished, for another x-ray in about eight months.

This case presents a glaring example of poor care. The doctor ordered an appropriate diagnostic test. The test was reported as abnormal. Yet the physician then failed to follow up adequately on the abnormal result.

In this case, the x-ray finding—osteoporosis—might have been a spurious result due to poor x-ray technique. This possibility could have been checked by repeating the film. Or the osteoporosis might, indeed, have signaled a significant health problem (kidney disease, parathyroid disease, diabetes, etc.) The physician should have taken steps to rule out these possible causes, one by one.

If, having taken these steps, the doctor still had nothing to explain the abnormal x-ray finding, he should have either obtained another physician's opinion, or instructed his patient to return for a repeat film—only in a much shorter time than eight months.

All of this would have constituted a more adequate follow-up of the abnormal test.

What about doctors who "treat the laboratory"?

As we have noted, an abnormal test result is not really what is important. It is what has caused the abnormal test—your diagnosis —that is the crucial thing. Yet some doctors forget this. They wind up treating the laboratory, not the patient's problem.

Let us say, for example, that you have a low serum calcium due to hypoparathyroidism—insufficient parathyroid hormone in the body. The doctor can correct your blood calcium level by giving you oral calcium, but he will not remedy your basic problem—lack of the calcium-regulating hormone. Parathyroid hormone replacement is the correct treatment.

Similarly, if you have a low blood sugar due to a tumor of the pancreas (a rare condition), doses of glucose—though they may temporarily raise your blood sugar—won't solve your basic disease problem.

It may be hard to recognize the doctor who makes this sort of error. But you can suspect it, especially if you discuss matters with him thoroughly. You should try to satisfy yourself that your doctor knows what your diagnosis is, and that he is administering therapy that makes logical sense in terms of your disease process. Otherwise, you may reasonably suspect that he is treating your test results, and not your diagnosis. (Chapter 6 discusses treatment in more detail.)

What about doctors who order tests in batches?

Many private labs have a new gimmick. They offer groups of tests—primarily chemistries—at a special price. These groups are given appealing names such as the "Executive Profile" or the "Geriatric Profile" to encourage doctors to order them.

While this kind of batch testing may save you a few dollars, it is not a particularly good way for your doctor to practice medicine. It encourages him to order tests in a "shotgun" fashion. It discourages him from thinking about the need for each test—or, indeed, about any specific diagnosis at all.

The internist cited at the start of this chapter who racked up $135 worth of tests for a routine checkup was undoubtedly batch testing—ordering the same group of tests on all his patients, regardless of their symptoms or health status. In general, the best doctors will not order tests in this way.

What are the tests of body electrical activity?

Best known of this group is the *electrocardiogram* (EKG, ECG). This test assesses the electrical activity of the heart. It is painless, requires only an EKG machine and a source of electricity, and can be done in a minute or less.

Principle: An EKG should be done as part of a complete physical exam, in every adult aged forty or over.

There may be some who would disagree with this rule. But it is probably a valid one. Heart disease is the nation's number one killer disease. The EKG will detect some of those who are at risk. The "stress EKG," mentioned earlier, will detect an even greater percentage.

Most of these persons will have coronary artery disease—narrowing of the arteries which supply blood to the heart. This condition is the precursor of myocardial infarction, or heart attack, the leading cause of death in middle-aged American males.

It is not only important to detect those persons who might have a heart attack. It is equally important to detect those who have had one. One quarter of persons surviving a first attack will have a second within five years.

Diagnosis, therefore, becomes a matter of some importance. The EKG is the major test used in the immediate diagnosis of heart attack—after the history and physical exam. The EKG will be abnormal in nearly all cases, but often *serial tracings* will have to be taken for several days before the electrical changes become evident. Other tests used in the diagnosis of myocardial infarction include: the white blood count (elevated), red cell sedimentation rate (elevated), heart muscle enzymes (elevated), serum bilirubin (elevated).

The *electroencephalogram* (EEG) is a test of the electrical activity of the outer layers of the brain. It requires costly equipment, but is otherwise easy and painless to perform. Interpretation of the results, however, may be quite difficult, and requires the services of a neurologist specially trained in this art. Unlike an EKG tracing, which can fit on a single sheet of paper, the EEG tracing occupies a sheaf of papers about the size and thickness of a moderate-sized phone book. The EEG's major uses are: to detect seizure activity (epilepsy); to detect brain injury, infection, or tumors; in the diagnosis of congenital brain deformities.

The *electromyogram* (EMG) is a test of the electrical activity of a particular muscle. It is a difficult test to perform and, often, to interpret. EMGs are done only in the largest hospitals, usually by a special technician. The EMG is useful in the diagnosis of neuromuscular disorders, including polio, myasthenia gravis, and the various forms of muscular dystrophy.

What is a "biopsy"?

A biopsy is a test in which a small sample of body tissue is obtained and examined under the microscope. It is most often done for the detection of cancer (malignancy), though it has other uses as well.

An *open biopsy* means that the organ is surgically exposed. An open liver biopsy, for example, involves making an incision in the abdomen to see the liver, before a tissue sample is taken. *Closed* or *needle biopsy* means taking a tissue sample, through the skin, using a special needle.

If possible, it is preferable to use the closed method, which avoids the need for surgery.

All biopsies should be interpreted by a *pathologist*. The pathologist looks at the tissue, and describes its appearance in a written report. At the end of the report he "signs out" the specimen with one or more diagnoses. (He does the same thing, incidentally, with all specimens obtained at surgery.)

In the case of a liver biopsy, for instance, the pathologist might sign out the specimen as "cirrhosis, acute and chronic." Or, if the tissue is undiseased, he will simply sign it out as "normal liver."

Principle: As with any other test, you should ask your doctor for the results of the pathologist's report. You may wish to examine this report yourself, as well.

What are cytological tests?

Cytology is the study of body cells. Cytological tests involve examination of single cells under the microscope. These cells may be collected in various ways. The *Pap test* involves sucking up a small amount of liquid from that part of the vagina directly beneath the uterine cervix. This liquid contains old, sloughed-off cervical cells. The liquid is then spread on a glass slide, stained, and the cells examined for changes which would indicate the presence of cervical cancer.

Cells scraped directly from the uterine cervix may also be used for cytological examination.

Principle: Cervical cytology (Pap test) should be done once yearly, in every adult woman, as part of a complete physical exam.

Cytology may be done on sputum or on any body fluid which can be obtained in sufficient amounts. Needle aspiration of fluid from the abdomen is called a *paracentesis*. If the fluid is taken from the chest cavity, the procedure is called a *thoracentesis*. In either case, the fluid should be examined cytologically. It should also be cultured and tested chemically.

Amniocentesis is a relatively new procedure, in which a small amount of amniotic fluid is obtained from the sac which surrounds the fetus. This procedure must be done by a skilled operator, under x-ray guidance. Cytological examination of fetal cells in the fluid can enable the doctor to detect, before birth, a great many hereditary diseases.

Chromosome analysis (karyotyping) is a similar test. It involves taking a sterile blood sample, separating out the white blood cells, and examining their genetic material (chromosomes). The test is useful whenever genetic conditions involving chromosomal abnormalities are suspected (mongolism is the most common example). The test is costly, is generally done only in larger medical centers, and requires a skilled specialist to interpret.

What are radioisotope scans?

These are tests in which a small amount of a radioactive substance, the radioisotope, is injected into the body. Certain isotopes accumulate in certain body organs. Radioiodine, for instance, is taken up by the thyroid. A machine is then used to scan the organ and draw a picture of where the radioactivity is greatest.

Many body organs can now be scanned using this method. They include the brain, thyroid, lungs, liver, and kidneys. Main uses of scans are to detect tumors or areas of absent blood supply (infarction) in an organ.

Scans are done in special labs by doctors and technicians with training in the handling of radioisotopes. Many hospitals have *departments of nuclear medicine* to perform these tests, as well as to use radioactive materials for treatment purposes. Scans involve little risk or discomfort, making them valuable diagnostic aids.

What is meant by the term "screening tests"?

Only a relatively few tests qualify as screening tests. These are tests which can be used in large populations to pick out persons with a particular disease. Such tests must be specific for the disease, cheap, easy to do, and involve little or no risk.

Skin tests are an example of commonly used screening tests. These tests involve injection, under the skin, of a small amount of the test substance to see if the body will react by developing a rash at the test site.

Skin tests have two major uses. They are used to determine which persons in the population have been infected by a particular organism (see the TB skin test, below). They are also used to detect allergy (to ragweed, molds, x-ray dye, etc.).

The TB skin test is a good example of a screening test which should be more widely used. This test can be done by a doctor or nurse in seconds. The patient can "read" the results at home and call the doctor if the test is abnormal (redness or swelling at the test site). The TB skin test will be positive in virtually all people who have been infected with tubercle organisms.

Principle: The TB skin test should be a part of every diagnostic work-up, or checkup.

It makes sense to do this test routinely as a screening test for tuberculosis, since an infected person may show no physical signs of infection. (Even a chest x-ray may be normal.) And the TB test costs virtually pennies to perform.

What is "multiphasic screening"?

There are other tests which have proven valuable in screening for various conditions, particularly in apparently well ("asymptomatic") persons. Several years ago, the Kaiser Foundation Health Plan began offering a group of these screening tests to its subscribers. The test battery is administered (along with a history questionnaire) *before* the patient ever sees a doctor. The doctor, in turn, has the test results in front of him when the patient walks into his examining room.

This process is known as multiphasic screening.

Does multiphasic screening detect many health problems in persons who are outwardly "well"?

The evidence is that it does. Dr. Morris Collen, who developed the process, reports that of some 40,000 persons tested in a recent year at the Kaiser center, *nearly half* had one or more abnormalities requiring further diagnostic work-up. These included high blood pressure, diabetes, glaucoma, hearing loss, and others.

Principle: You should make an effort to have a multiphasic screening test battery not later than your fortieth birthday (and, ideally, each year or two thereafter).

Unfortunately, multiphasic testing centers are few and far between. Like Kaiser, some other large prepaid group practice plans offer this service. Some large corporations are also making efforts to test their employees.

If you do not have access to one of these sources, you may have to go to several different types of doctors (or hospitals outpatient clinics) to obtain the various tests.

Table 13 shows the multiphasic test battery in use at the Kaiser Plan. Many of the tests, you will note, can—and should—be done by any doctor (some merely involve drawing blood, collecting urine, etc.). Where you are likely to have to consult a particular kind of physician, I have so indicated.

TABLE 13   Multiphasic Screening Test Battery

TEST	ABNORMAL IN	OTHER TYPE OF PHYSICIAN/CLINIC FROM WHICH TO OBTAIN TEST
Audiometry	various hearing disorders	otolaryngologist (ear-nose-throat)
Blood type	general information	any M.D.
Chest x-ray	various cardio-pulmonary diseases	hospital OPD
Electrocardiogram	various cardio-pulmonary diseases	cardiologist, internist
Glucose tolerance test	diabetes, other disorders of carbohydrate metabolism	endocrinologist, internist
Hemoglobin	anemia (of any cause)	any M.D.

TABLE 13 Multiphasic Screening Test Battery

TEST	ABNORMAL IN	OTHER TYPE OF PHYSICIAN/CLINIC FROM WHICH TO OBTAIN TEST
Mammography[a]	breast cancer, other breast tumors	radiologist, some hospital OPDs, other clinics
Ocular tension and retinal photo	glaucoma, diabetes, hypertension, others	ophthalmologist
Pap smear (and gynecologic exam)	cervical cancer, other gynecologic disorders	gynecologist
Pulmonary function tests	emphysema, heart failure, other disorders	cardiologist
Pulse rate and blood pressure	various heart diseases, hypertension, others	any M.D.
Serum (blood) tests		
calcium	parathyroid, bone, kidney disease	any M.D.
cholesterol	atherosclerotic coronary heart disease	any M.D.
creatinine	decreased kidney function	any M.D.
rheumatoid factor	rheumatoid arthritis, other conditions	any M.D.
total protein and albumin	liver disease, others	any M.D.
transaminase	liver disease, others	any M.D.
uric acid	gout, certain anemias, other diseases	any M.D.
VDRL	syphilis	any M.D.
Sigmoidoscopy[b]	colon/rectal cancer, colitis	proctologist, surgeon, some internists
Urinalysis, urine culture, and colony count	urinary tract infection, kidney diseases, others	internist

TABLE 13   Multiphasic Screening Test Battery

TEST	ABNORMAL IN	OTHER TYPE OF PHYSICIAN/CLINIC FROM WHICH TO OBTAIN TEST
Visual acuity (eye chart)	various eye or neurologic diseases	ophthalmologist
Weight and skin thickness	obesity, various metabolic diseases, chronic infections, others	endocrinologist, internist
White blood cell count	infections (of any type)	any M.D.

NOTE: Tests are those used in the Kaiser Plan multiphasic testing program. In this program patients also answer a self-administered medical history before they see a physician.

ᵃ Mammography is done on women over age forty-five.

ᵇ Sigmoidoscopy is advised on all patients over age forty.

Despite their value, many of the tests in the multiphasic battery are used infrequently by office physicians. *Sigmoidoscopy* is an example. This test involves looking into the rectum and colon (lower bowel) with a sigmoidoscope—a stainless steel tube with a flashlight inside.‡ Using this instrument, the doctor can detect virtually all cases of colon/rectal cancer—more than 10 per cent of all cancer cases. Yet few physicians even own, much less use, a sigmoidoscope.

Which tests and procedures are most important?

The Kaiser multiphasic test battery constitutes a group of tests which have been found to have high "yields"—to detect many people with health problems. All of these tests are, clearly, important when it comes to preventing illness and detecting disease.

But there is another way of looking at the question of which tests are most important. This is by asking the question: Which tests are most useful in detecting the common causes of death and disability?

These tests are shown in Table 14.

‡ Laryngoscopy, gastroscopy, cystoscopy, etc., are similar procedures for examining other internal organs (larynx, stomach, bladder).

TABLE 14 Tests Useful in Detection of Common Causes of Death and
Disability (Outpatient Only)

CONDITION	TEST OR PROCEDURE
Causes of Death	
Cancer	
breast	x-ray mammography
cervix	Pap smear
colon/rectum	sigmoidoscopy
lung	chest x-ray
	sputum cytology
	bronchoscopy
pharynx and larynx	head mirror exam
	laryngoscopy
prostate	prostatic enzymes in blood
	cystoscopy
stomach and intestines	gastroscopy (stomach)
(above colon)	gastric cytology
	upper GI series (small
	intestine)
	barium enema (large intestine)
Diabetes	urine sugar, ketones
	glucose tolerance test
Emphysema	pulmonary function tests
	chest x-ray
Heart disease	"stress" EKG (coronary
	disease)
	EKG, heart enzymes (heart
	attack)
	venous pressure, circulation
	time, serum sodium, chest
	x-ray (heart failure)
Kidney disease (see also	urinalysis
Urinary tract infection)	24-hr. creatinine clearance
	24-hr. urine protein
	IVP (intravenous pyelogram)
Liver disease	liver function tests
	liver scan
	liver biopsy (closed)
Peptic ulcer	upper GI series

TABLE 14 Tests Useful in Detection of Common Causes of Death and
Disability (Outpatient Only)

CONDITION	TEST OR PROCEDURE
Causes of Death	
Pneumonia	chest x-ray sputum smear and culture
Stroke	lumbar puncture EEG (electroencephalogram) brain scan
Causes of Disability	
Allergy	skin tests pulmonary function tests (asthma)
Anemia	hemoglobin or hematocrit reticulocyte count microscopic exam of blood smear serum iron, B_{12}, folic acid bone marrow

Arthritis	x-ray of joint(s)
	microscopic exam and chemical
	    analysis of joint fluid, if any
	latex fixation (rheumatoid
	    arthritis)
	serum uric acid (gout)

Epilepsy	EEG
Gallstones	abdominal x-ray gallbladder series
Gastrointestinal infection	stool cultures microscopic exam of stool for ova and parasites
Hearing disorders	audiometry (hearing test)
Hypertension	blood pressure measurement
Mental retardation	psychological testing
Muscle disease	muscle enzymes EMG (electromyogram)
Tuberculosis	TB skin test chest x-ray (if skin test is "positive")

TABLE 14   Tests Useful in Detection of Common Causes of Death and
Disability (Outpatient Only)

Condition	Test or Procedure
Causes of Disability	
Urinary tract infection	"clean voided" urine for culture and colony count
Venereal disease	VDRL or other serology (syphilis) microscopic smear, culture
Visual disorders	eye chart direct ophthalmoscopy tonometry (glaucoma) gonioscopy (glaucoma) slit lamp exam (cataract, corneal disease)

NOTE: Causes of death from U.S. Vital Statistics.

Needless to say, these tests are not a complete diagnostic work-up for any of the conditions listed. A blood pressure measurement, for example, will only determine the presence or absence of hypertension (high blood pressure). To determine the type of hypertension, a dozen or more further tests and procedures are required.

The tests shown, however, are some of those which should probably be considered if you or your doctor seriously suspects one of the death-disability conditions. And, of course, many of the tests, as we have said, should be done yearly, regardless of your health or symptoms.

6

Drugs and doctors

Drugs are far and away the most common form of treatment, once a diagnosis has been made. In recent years, drugs have come to be commonly used for conditions, such as mental depression, for which no treatment was previously available. They have largely replaced surgery in the treatment of Parkinson's disease, certain types of cancer, and many cases of slipped intervertebral disks. New drugs which can dissolve gallstones and kidney stones—two common causes of surgery—are under investigation.

"I think all these things we're doing," predicts noted brain surgeon Irving Cooper, "will ultimately be treated by drugs."

Yet for all the benefits, drug treatment has its problems, too.

How dangerous are prescription drugs?

The evidence is that prescription drugs are a significant health danger. Adverse drugs reactions, it is estimated, kill 160,000 persons each year—more than breast cancer. They rank among the top ten causes of hospitalization.

The vast majority of these adverse drug reactions are to drugs prescribed by doctors. They are examples of what is called *iatrogenic* (physician-caused) illness.

Anyone who has worked in a hospital has seen this kind of illness. I can recall my first assignment as a medical student at Boston's Peter Bent Brigham Hospital. Each day I saw several patients, sent to the Brigham by physicians as "therapeutic problems." For these patients, and their physicians, the hospital was regarded as a last resort.

I came to recognize a common pattern, in these cases.

The patient—often a middle-aged woman—would arrive certain that she suffered from a grave and incurable illness. She would complain of increasing fatigue, loss of appetite, and other symptoms. Often she would present a note from her doctor detailing all the treatments he had tried without success.

The patient would open her purse and spill out her medications—a heap of hormones, diuretics, tranquilizers, vitamins, pills of every size and color—all prescribed by one or more physicians.

"None of these does any good," she would state.

On physical examination, many of these patients had strange rashes, enlarged livers, or other findings. Their lab tests were often quite abnormal. Sometimes these abnormalities were life-threatening.

"Tell me the truth, Doctor," one woman asked. "How sick am I?" This patient had an irregular heart rhythm, and a very low serum potassium. I was tempted to believe that she had some bizarre metabolic disease.

Fortunately, such was not the case. This woman, like so many others I saw, was a victim of iatrogenic disease. Her symptoms and abnormal metabolism were the result of the drugs she had been given. When the drugs were discontinued, her metabolism gradually returned to normal. Her appetite and energy returned. She was discharged with one mild drug, instead of the several potent ones she had been taking.

What is the most serious drug prescribing error?

My experience at the Brigham is, sadly, not unique. The prescribing by physicians of drugs which are not needed is the most common, and serious, drug error. George Baehr, a professor of medicine and former head of New York's huge Health Insurance Plan testified before a Senate committee on the problem.

"A few days ago," said Dr. Baehr, "I was consulted by a patient who took out of her bag eight different medications, *not one of which was indicated.*"

"Is this, in your experience," asked a senator, "a common occurrence?"

"Exceedingly common," replied Baehr.

Of the five billion dollars Americans spend for prescribed drugs each year, Dr. Baehr estimates that well over 50 per cent may be spent for drugs which are not "indicated."

What is an "indicated" drug?

An indicated drug is one which has been proven to help a particular diagnosis. In medical terms, a drug should be proven to be "effi-

cacious" for a given condition. If a drug does not help, it is said to be
non-indicated. If it actually causes harm, it is said to be *contra-indicated*.

Principle: You should assure yourself that any drug you take is indicated for your particular diagnosis.

Here are some instances:

Example 1: An antibiotic (penicillin) is indicated for pneumococcal
pneumonia. It is not indicated for influenza (a viral illness).

Example 2: Adrenal steroids (cortisone-like drugs) are indicated in
severe cases of rheumatoid arthritis. They are contra-
indicated in patients with tuberculosis.

Example 3: A diuretic (a urine-increasing drug) may be indicated
for the relief of fluid retention associated with heart failure. It is not indicated for weight loss.

Occasionally a patient may have two diseases, one which will be
helped by a drug; the other, harmed (a patient with severe arthritis
and tuberculosis, for instance). These situations make for tough
decisions on the part of the doctor. In most cases, however, this
kind of dilemma does not arise.

How can you determine if a drug is indicated?

One way is simply to ask your doctor, "Is this drug indicated for
my diagnosis?" Needless to say, this assumes that your doctor has
arrived at a final diagnosis, in your case. While there are instances
where treatment must precede making a positive diagnosis (certain
emergencies, for example), this is not usually true. In general, your
doctor should be sure of his diagnosis before embarking on a treatment regimen.

A second way to know whether or not a drug is indicated is to
consult the package insert. This is a slip of paper that comes inside
the carton of every prescription drug. Ask your doctor for one, or ask
him to instruct the druggist to give you one. The package insert lists
those conditions for which the drug is indicated. It also lists those
for which it is dangerous, or contra-indicated.

If you do not see your condition under those indicated, on the insert, it is a good idea to ask your doctor for an explanation.

What is meant by the term "drug of choice"?

Often there will be more than one indicated drug for your diagnosis. In this situation, the doctor's job is to select the *best* drug. If one drug is clearly superior to the others, it is termed the drug of choice.

Principle: Your doctor should be able to tell you why the drug he has chosen is the drug of choice for your condition.

Choosing the best drug can be a crucial decision. In infections, for instance, the infectious organism is often sensitive to several antibiotics. But it is usually more sensitive to some than to others. Choosing the best antibiotic can make a difference in how rapidly the infection is eradicated.

Sometimes two drugs will be equally effective but one may have many fewer *side effects,* making it the drug of choice.

You may have a condition which makes it inadvisable to use an effective drug. Persons with poor kidney function, for instance, should not have their infection treated with an antibiotic like streptomycin, which must be excreted by the kidney (or they should be treated using much smaller doses).

There are other things which can make one drug better than another. The *route of administration* may be important. A drug which can be administered orally is more desirable than one which must be given by injection. The drug's *cost* is obviously an important factor; all other things being equal, the cheapest drug should be the drug of choice.

How many drugs should your doctor use?

This will depend, of course, on your condition. In general, though, the best doctors will use the fewest drugs. They realize how dangerous drugs—any drugs—can be.

"Recognition of potential toxicity of drugs," writes Harvard professor and drug expert Dr. Richard Burack, "is why the best doctors write the smallest number of prescriptions."

Yet today it is not rare for patients to emerge from a doctor's office holding a half dozen prescriptions. Recently I visited the pharmacy of the Health Insurance Plan, one of the nation's largest prepaid health plans. The chief pharmacist told me that he had just filled eight prescriptions for a single patient who had just seen one of the plan's physicians.

On the other hand, more than one drug is often justified for treatment. Tuberculosis, for instance, is commonly treated by two antibiotics, which have been shown to be superior to either one alone. Occasionally a second drug is needed to combat the side effects of the first.

Generally, however, the principle still holds true: the best doctors will prescribe the fewest drugs for each patient they see. They will also use the fewest drugs in their practice, overall.

"From my own busy, private practice of internal medicine," says Harvard's Burack, "I know that 98 per cent of all patients can be adequately treated with *twenty-five or fewer drugs* and some of these need be used only rarely" (italics mine).

Yet one study showed that some doctors use as many as 500 different drugs in a single year!

Most experts agree that a doctor is doing well if he can know and keep up to date on the actions of one or two dozen drugs. (Some pharmacologists spend their whole lives studying the effects of one or two agents.) It's a safe bet, then, that those doctors who are members of the "500 Club"—those who dole out dozens of different drugs to their patients—can not possibly have a detailed knowledge of all these drugs.

This kind of physician you would do well to avoid.

What are drug "combinations"?

Drug combinations are two or more different drugs that have been combined in a single tablet or liquid. The drug industry soon discovered that drugs could be combined in a variety of enticing ways. There are combinations of two or more antibiotics. There are combinations of barbiturates and amphetamines. There are combinations of tranquilizers with pain-killers. And on and on.

These drug combinations go under a bewildering number of brand names, devised to sound catchy and to spur sales. Sometimes these names offer a clue to what is in the combination. Often they do not.

Principle: Drug combinations are rarely used by the best doctors.

The doctor who uses a combination is, in reality, prescribing several drugs. This automatically increases the likelihood of side effects. It also decreases the doctor's control over drug dosage: he cannot change the dose of one drug without giving more or less of whatever else is in the combination as well.

Finally, these brand-name combinations usually cost more; they often sell for two or three times as much as it would cost to buy their ingredients separately.

Let's look at an example:

Your doctor prescribes Dimetapp® for your "cold." He is really prescribing the following three drugs:

Brompheniramine Maleate	12 mg.
Phenylephrine Hydrochloride	15 mg.
Phenylpropanolamine Hydrochloride	15 mg.

Actually, the "business end" of this mixture is the phenylephrine—it's what relieves your stuffy nose. And you would be safer to take it as phenylephrine nose drops, rather than in tablet or liquid form (this doses your entire body—in some persons phenylephrine taken in this way has been shown to cause high blood pressure.)

Finally, you could buy phenylephrine nose drops at your drug store without a prescription—meaning you would save some money in the bargain. (Phenylephrine nose drops sell for about a dollar a bottle; you would pay about three dollars for a "Dimetapp" prescription.)

A doctor who uses this sort of a drug combination is practicing less than optimal medicine.

What is "shotgun" therapy?

"Shotgun" therapy is a more dangerous use of combinations of drugs. It is the use of such combinations to avoid making a complete and accurate diagnosis.

Example 1: Your doctor tells you that you are anemic, and writes a prescription for Trinsicon®. This is a drug combination which contains:

Vitamin B_{12}
Folic acid (another vitamin)
Iron
"intrinsic factor" (a substance needed in the stomach for the absorption of vitamin B_{12})

This is a good example of "shotgun" therapy. The doctor has not diagnosed your anemia completely. He has not determined whether it is iron-deficiency anemia due to a bleeding ulcer or cancer, or folic acid-deficiency anemia, or vitamin B_{12}-deficiency anemia, etc. He has merely prescribed a "shotgun" drug—in an effort to cover all these possibilities.

Example 2: Your doctor tells you that you have "a bowel infection" and he prescribes Tetrastatin®. This drug combination contains:

Tetracycline (an anti-bacterial)
Nystatin (an anti-fungal agent)
Glucosamine (an agent to increase intestinal absorption)

In this example, the doctor is prescribing a drug which is both anti-bacterial and anti-fungal. This may mean that he is unsure whether or not your infection is caused by a bacterium or by a fungus. A stool culture and a single drug—depending on the culture result—would be better medicine.*

Obviously, "shotgun" drug mixtures are a dangerous way to practice medicine. They encourage doctors to avoid making a definite and complete diagnosis. And they can "mask" the true nature of your anemia, infection, or other illness, making it harder to diagnose.

How can you tell if your doctor has prescribed a "combination"?

The best way is to ask him, as he writes your prescription, to tell you what is in the medication he is prescribing. If there are several drugs, ask him the purpose of each one. (There are some combinations whose use can be justified.)

Another way to find out what's in a prescribed medication is to consult the *package insert*. The insert must, by law, list all the ingredients, as well as their purposes. Ask your doctor to instruct the pharmacist to provide it for you.

What about doctors who use the newest drugs?

We all have been to such doctors. Often they will reach into their

* Some doctors—and drug companies—justify such a drug combination by saying that it is intended to prevent secondary fungal infection. In most patients, this is not a factor, however.

desk drawer and pull out a drug sample that the drug salesman has left with them that same morning.

"Here's something new," such a physician might say. "Let's see how it works."

Such new drugs may work fine. But they may also have side effects about which nothing is yet known. They may have contra-indications which have yet to be discovered.

Principle: In general, the oldest drugs are the safest ones.

These are the drugs about which most is known. Their side effects and adverse reactions have been best and longest studied. The best doctors will use these "established" drugs in preference to newer ones, whenever they can.

You can find out whether any drug has met the test of time, in terms of safety and usefulness, by consulting the two official drug compendia: the *U.S. Pharmacopeia* and the *National Formulary*. Or look for the letters *U.S.P.* or *N.F.* on the drug package and package insert.

What about doctors who give drugs by injection?

"Sure, I give my patients B_{12} shots," one doctor confessed to me in an off moment. "It's a nice red liquid. It looks good when you draw it up in the syringe."

Other doctors shoot their patients full of everything from steroids to amphetamines.

Principle: You should beware of any doctor who treats by injection.

This is particularly true if the doctor is unwilling to tell you what he is injecting, or if he says you need a "series of shots" to cure your illness.

There are very few adult conditions (with the exception of an acute asthma attack, heart attack, and other real emergencies) which require injections. Diabetics need injected insulin, but they can be taught to give it to themselves at home. Patients with "pernicious anemia" do need monthly B_{12} injections, but this is the only disease for which B_{12} is needed—and it is a very rare diagnosis indeed.

Mercurial diuretics are injected drugs which are useful in patients with heart failure and fluid retention. These drugs, too, can be self-injected, like insulin, after instruction. *They should not be used as "diet" drugs, however.*

With these and a few other exceptions (cancer chemotherapy, for example, and desensitization shots for various allergies) the use of injected drugs by a doctor in the long-term treatment of adults is cause for suspicion.

What about doctors who use "secret" remedies?

You should be equally suspicious of a doctor who uses any drug— whether by injection or otherwise—whose name and/or chemical structure he will not divulge. This is not all that uncommon. Doctors have been known to give their patients medications—often by injection—which they claim are their own, and which they will not describe.

Often these "unique" drugs are simply mixtures of several "feel-good" medicines, such as amphetamines and steroids. Sometimes they are potions the doctor himself has brewed.

Regardless of their source, the use of such secret drugs is good reason to look for another doctor. "The prescription or dispensing by a doctor of secret medicines . . ." says the New York County Medical Society, "is unethical."

How can you check to make sure your doctor is giving you a real drug?

There are several sources of information on bona fide drugs. I have already mentioned the two official drug compendia: the *U.S. Pharmacopeia* and the *National Formulary*. Most doctors rely on a volume called the *Physicians' Desk Reference*. (This volume has many faults, being essentially a drug industry list of brand-name drugs, but it is easy to understand and widely used.)

These and other drug references are listed in the Appendix. If you cannot find your doctor's "drug" in one of these sources, or if he does not have a package insert he can show you, you have adequate reason to suspect the drug is not legitimate.†

What should your doctor's prescription say?

You should, as an informed consumer, learn to read and understand your doctor's prescription. This is easier than most people

† An exception: experimental drugs. The doctor should have an FDA permit which authorizes use of any experimental drug for human use.

think. Nowadays doctors do not usually write their prescriptions in Latin, except for a few stock words. If you know what to look for, you can read any prescription.

Here is what your doctor's prescription should contain:

(1) the drug's name—either in generic or brand-name form (see below)
(2) the *form* in which the drug is to be taken (tablets, suppositories, drops, etc.)
(3) the *route of administration* (by mouth, by rectum, applied to the skin, etc.)
(4) the *strength* (milligrams per tablet, per cc., etc.)
(5) the *dosage* (one 10 mg. tablet three times a day, two drops of 1 per cent solution morning and night, etc.)
(6) *length of time* the drug is to be taken (one week, three weeks, as needed, etc.)
(7) other instructions (drug to be taken before meals, with milk, etc.)

Principle: You should examine your prescription to make sure it contains all relevant information. You should check the package insert to make sure your doctor's dosage, etc., are correct.

Here are some examples of how prescriptions may be written:

Example 1: A doctor wishes to treat a "strep" throat with a ten-day course of oral penicillin, one tablet three times a day. He writes:

Potassium penicillin G, U.S.P.
200,000 units/tab.
Sig. [take]: 1 tablet p.o. [by mouth] ½ hr. ac [before meals] t.i.d. [three times a day] × 10 days
Disp. [dispense]: 30 tabs.

Example 2: An elderly woman requires nitroglycerin tablets for the pain of coronary artery insufficiency ("angina"). The doctor wishes her to put one tablet under her tongue whenever she has pain in her chest. He writes:

Nitroglycerin [or Glyceryl Trinitrate], U.S.P.
1/25th gr./tab.
Sig.: tab. i. subl. [sublingual] prn [as needed for] pain
Disp.: 500 tabs.

Example 3: The doctor wishes to prescribe eye drops for his patient's glaucoma. He wants the patient to put two drops in each eye every six hours. He writes:

Pilocarpine HCl
1% solution
Sig.: Gtts.ii [two drops] o.u. [both eyes] q. 6h. [every six hours]
Disp.: 15cc. bottle

You should also make certain your doctor writes the word "Label" on your prescription. This instructs the pharmacist to label the drug vial (bottle, tube, etc.) with the drug's name. *This is your only guarantee of being able to know, at some later date, what the drug's name is.* It is also, of course, a great aid to any new doctor you might choose to consult (otherwise he has to contact the pharmacist or your old doctor, a laborious process).

Finally, your prescription should indicate whether or not it can be *refilled.* Your doctor may simply write, "Non-refillable." Or he may write, "Refill $\times$ 1 [$\times$ 2, $\times$ 3, etc.]."

For some drugs, such as narcotics, it is obviously undesirable to prescribe unlimited amounts. In New York State it is against the law to prescribe more than a thirty-day supply of certain drugs: barbiturates, non-barbiturate sedatives, amphetamines, and amphetamine-like substances. Doctors are not allowed to make prescriptions for such drugs refillable at all.

Regardless of the drug, if your doctor prescribes it for more than a few days' time, he should give you a *return appointment*. If, at that time, he wants you to continue taking the drug, he should also make plans to see you periodically (every month, three months, six months, etc.). The spacing of your return visits will depend on the drug. You may also require periodic lab tests (for example, the once-a-week blood clotting time test required of patients taking anticoagulants) to monitor the drug's effect.

What are generic and brand-name drugs?

A drug's generic name and its brand name are two different names for the same thing. The generic name is the drug's "official" name. The brand name is whatever catchy name the manufacturer thinks will sell best.

Drug manufacturers have long argued that their particular brand-name drugs are better than the same drug, manufactured by another company and sold under the generic name (at less cost, of course). There is, however, simply no difference. All the best hospitals buy generic-name drugs. So should you.

Principle: You should insist that your doctor prescribe drugs by their generic—not their brand—names.

It is to your advantage (usually) for your doctor to prescribe generically.‡ In other words, it is better for you if he writes for "Potassium penicillin G, U.S.P." rather than for "V-Cillin-K®" or for a variety of other brand names. The reason is simple. If he writes for a brand name, the pharmacist must—in most states—supply that brand name, regardless of its cost. If a generic name is on the prescription, the pharmacist is permitted to give you any manufacturer's product, provided it meets the official government drug standards. In general, the cost of generic-name drugs will be lower than if the same drugs are dispensed by their brand names.

There are several *specific* examples of incorrect drug use which you should know about and remember. Here are some:

(1) prescribing tetracycline (an antibiotic) for streptococcal sore throat (pharyngitis, tonsillitis). Penicillin G is the drug of choice.

(2) failing to treat streptococcal sore throat or skin infection for at least ten days—the period recommended by the American Heart Association as necessary for the prevention of rheumatic fever

(3) failing to treat urinary tract infections for at least a three-week period (some authorities suggest as long as six weeks in initial infections, longer for repeat ones); failing to obtain antibiotic "sensitivities" and to treat with the correct drug

(4) prescribing tranquilizers for mild, "self-limited" cases of depression

(5) prescribing antibiotics—either singly or in combination—for "colds," influenza, or other viral upper respiratory infections

(6) prescribing adrenal steroids (cortisone and its relatives) for depression or fatigue (these drugs, among their many effects, produce euphoria)

(7) prescribing anti-anemia combinations (they usually contain

‡ An exception: if a drug is a newer one it may still be protected by its patent: thus only one company may be making it. A common example is chlordiazeooxide, which also goes under the brand name of Librium®.

iron, folic acid, and vitamin B_{12}) without first determining the type and cause of the anemia

(8) prescribing thyroid hormone for fatigue—or for anything except proven thyroid hormone deficiency

(9) administering vitamin B_{12} by injection for anything but proven B_{12}-deficiency ("pernicious") anemia. A low or absent blood B_{12} level, along with a characteristic blood smear, is necessary evidence

(10) administering a mercurial diuretic by injection as a diet or weight-loss aid

(11) administering male hormones (testosterone and its relatives) to put on weight or build body mass

Finally, questions will always arise about drugs and their proper use. You should be aware of certain sources of information which you can use if you have a question about how your doctor is using drugs. Virtually all medical schools have a *department of pharmacology*. It is possible to contact this department and, often, to talk with one of the members, who can provide you with facts. You should, of course, know at least the type of drug you wish to discuss (antibiotic, barbiturate sedative, etc.).

Another source of information is a hospital's *department of clinical pharmacology*. These are rare and are usually found only in the largest, medical school-affiliated hospitals. (Often, you will have to contact the medical school itself.) A clinical pharmacologist is usually a physician or Ph.D. who specializes in the uses of drugs in human illness. Such a person—if you are fortunate to find one—may be invaluable in helping answer your drug questions.

You should also know the medical specialists who are most knowledgeable about the various types of drugs. In general, internists who specialize in *infectious disease* (usually found in hospitals) know most about antibiotics. Endocrinologists know most about hormones, including adrenal steroids, male and female hormones. Some psychiatrists (note: some) are quite knowledgeable about tranquilizers and stimulants (often called psychomotor stimulants or "mood elevators").

In the Appendix you will find a list of the basic sources of drug information used by physicians. Most can be understood by non-physicians, with the aid of a medical dictionary.

Finally, in review, here are the basic rules you should follow before you begin using any drug:

(1) Understand your diagnosis. Understand how it was arrived at and what parts of the history, physical exam, and other findings confirm it.

(2) Understand why the drug being prescribed is indicated for your diagnosis. Ask what kind of drug it is. Ask how it works in your body.

(3) Make sure your doctor tells you of the drug's possible side effects and adverse reactions. Make sure he asks you about any conditions you might have for which the drug is contra-indicated.

(4) Make sure you understand the prescription, particularly the dosage, route of administration, and how long the drug is to be taken. Ask your doctor to prescribe generically, and to write "Label" on the prescription.

(5) Make sure, if the drug is prescribed for more than a few days, your doctor gives you a return appointment. Try to obtain and read the drug's package insert as a check on what your doctor has told you about the drug.

7

Another opinion

"I just knew," says one woman, "my doctor didn't know what was wrong with me. I'd go to him with the same complaint and he'd give me the same prescription. I wasn't getting anywhere."

This patient switched doctors. In fact, she had to visit three doctors before finding one who could correctly diagnose her condition.

Seeking a second opinion used to be something people did with trepidation. They felt guilty at leaving one doctor for another.

Today things are different. People are growing more aggressive about their health care. They are less apt to stick with a doctor who cannot diagnose their problem. They are more sophisticated about other sources of care.

How often do doctors seek a second opinion?

Most everyone seems to accept the idea of a patient seeing more than one physician—except physicians themselves. The AMA still talks about the "doctor–patient relationship" as though most people still went to a single doctor for all their ills.

Doctors themselves tend to look askance at patients who seek other sources of care. They talk disparagingly of people who "shop around." I have seen physicians become openly hostile towards a patient who admits having tried another source of care.

"You'd better make up your mind," said one physician, "whether you're going to go to ——— hospital, or whether you're going to come here."

Doctors in private practice seldom refer their patients, regardless of their problem. In the United States, private GPs refer *only 2 per cent* of their patients to other physicians!

Where doctors are paid by salary, they are much more apt to refer. The interns and residents in a hospital clinic will refer or call consults on anywhere from 25 to 50 per cent of the patients they see.

This practice has been criticized as being inefficient (a patient with diabetes, for instance, might be sent to a foot clinic, an eye clinic, a kidney clinic, etc.), but it is far better than the doctor who holds on to his patient at all costs.

In prepaid group practice plans, where doctors are also on a fixed salary, they are less reluctant to refer a patient to another physician within the plan.

By and large, however, it is the patient who must decide when to switch doctors. It is the patient who must decide when to seek a second—or even a third and fourth—opinion.

This chapter will discuss how you can best make that decision.

The doctor who cannot make a correct diagnosis

This is the reason most people switch physicians, or seek another opinion. Sometimes they simply have a "feeling" that their doctor doesn't know what their diagnosis is. Other times there are more substantial clues:

—the doctor who persists in telling you that his diagnosis is "tentative," "presumptive," "preliminary," etc.
—the doctor who keeps ordering additional lab tests, the results of which are normal
—the doctor who seems to be putting you off, by waiting for test results or in other ways
—the doctor who diagnoses your condition incompletely ("anemia") or who substitutes a symptom for a diagnosis (see Chapter 3)

Principle: Failure to make a definitive diagnosis within a reasonable time (a few weeks, two or three visits in a non-acute situation) is a good reason to seek a second opinion.

If you have any doubt, you can put it to your doctor straight. You can ask: "Doctor, do you have a final diagnosis?" (If you want to sound more authoritative, you can ask for a "definitive" diagnosis.) Your doctor's response should be a pretty good guide to his certainty about your diagnosis.

Sometimes, of course, a doctor will make a diagnosis and start treatment. Yet there will be no improvement in your health status.

This, too, is a good reason to seek another opinion. There are, naturally, many conditions which do not get better, regardless of the treatment. Nevertheless, if your health status fails to improve with treatment, the only way you can be sure your doctor has made a correct diagnosis and is treating the right condition is to get another opinion.

The doctor who tells you your problem is emotional

This happens all the time. As we have seen (Table 5), psychoneurosis is the third most common diagnosis made by internists. Sometimes a doctor will tell you your problem is due to stress, "nerves," is "functional," or use other terms that indicate an emotional origin.

Principle: A diagnosis of emotionally caused disease is another reason to seek a second opinion.

I have already cited some examples of patients who were told they had an emotionally caused problem, only to find out their condition was not emotional at all (doctors use the word "organic"). There are many conditions which can masquerade as emotional ones. Porphyria —a rare metabolic disorder—is one example. Certain types of meningitis, or hydrocephaly (increased fluid inside the brain) are other examples.

Irving Cooper, the neurosurgeon, in his book *The Victim Is Always the Same,* writes about another rare disease: dystonia musculorum deformans. This is a genetic abnormality which begins in childhood and in which the limbs and body slowly become twisted into grotesque shapes. Many of these children and young adults are misdiagnosed as suffering from emotional illness.

One reason for this mistake, as Cooper says, is simply that most doctors have never seen a case of dystonia. When they do see a patient whose arms and legs are contorted into strange shapes, they often jump to the conclusion that the problem is an emotional one.

Of course there are also times when a doctor will fail to recognize a true emotional disease. (This is as serious an error as its opposite.) But more common, I suspect, is the mis-diagnosis of "organic" for emotional illness.

In any case, a diagnosis of emotional disease is a perfectly adequate reason to seek another doctor's opinion.

The doctor who diagnoses a disease with a bad "prognosis"

A condition's prognosis simply means its outcome. Doctors sometimes speak of a disease's "prognosis for survival" or "survival prognosis." They speak of the "prognosis for complete recovery," the "prognosis for recurrence," etc. Doctors may simply say that a disease has a "good prognosis"—an imprecise way of saying that the patient's chances for recovery are good.

Let's look at a common example: heart attacks.

The chances of surviving a first attack are about 60 per cent. Thus we might say that the prognosis for survival is "fair," "better than even," etc.

After a first attack, if one survives, the average life expectancy is about eight and a half years. Some 80 per cent of survivors will be able to return to work. Thus we might say that the prognosis among survivors for recovery is good.

Finally, about one fourth of survivors will have a second attack. We can say, then, that the prognosis for recurrence is significant.

Most people can sense when their doctor has made a diagnosis that carries with it a serious prognosis. Nevertheless, it is never inappropriate to ask about your prognosis. And you should ask (assuming that you really wish to know) in as precise a way as possible.

Here are some sample ways to ask about your prognosis:

"Doctor, what are my immediate chances for survival?"

"Doctor, can you tell me the average life expectancy (five-year survival rate, etc.) for my condition?"

"What are the chances that I will be able to return to work (care for myself, regain the use of my arm, etc.)?"

"What percent of people with my diagnosis suffer a recurrence (relapse, another attack, etc.)?"

"What is the likelihood that I will have another attack (seizure, flareup, etc.) within the next year?"

The prognosis in any condition often depends on several factors, other than the diagnosis itself. Your age, sex, the length of time the condition has been present—all may be important to your prognosis.

The best doctors will, of course, tell you your prognosis as precisely as they are able. In some instances they may have to go to the "litera-

ture" to look up the correct statistics. Occasionally, so little may be
known about a disease that a doctor may be reluctant even to guess as
to its prognosis. In most cases, though, he should be able to say
something that is based on actual reported experience.

**Principle: Any diagnosis which carries a serious prognosis is good
reason to seek a second opinion, for the purpose of confirming the
diagnosis.**

Other reasons for seeking a second opinion

There are a few other instances in which you might justifiably wish
to consult another doctor. Here are some of them:

(1) *When your doctor suggests surgery for either diagnosis or
treatment.* This is, most health experts agree, as good a reason as
any for seeking a second opinion. (Chapter 9 will discuss surgery in
more detail.)

(2) *When your doctor diagnoses a rare or unusual condition,*
regardless of its prognosis. Rare conditions are—in a word—rare.
When your doctor assigns you a rare diagnosis he is going "against
the odds." The likelihood is increased that he may be wrong. He may
be missing the real—and more common—cause of your complaints. Or he may be diagnosing a rare condition when nothing at
all is wrong.

In any case, a rare diagnosis is a logical reason for a second
opinion.

(3) *When your doctor diagnoses a condition which will require
long-term treatment.* Most doctors are understandably quite cautious
about making a diagnosis which implies long-term treatment. There
is, thus, less danger that a doctor will make such a diagnosis when
the condition is not present. You are, nevertheless, well justified in
seeking a second opinion when such a diagnosis has been made, or
suggested. Examples are: insulin-requiring diabetes; PKU (phenyl-
ketonuria) in children, which requires a special diet; hypothyroidism,
which requires thyroid hormone replacement, etc.

None of the above is meant to imply that you *must* seek another
opinion in these situations. You may be satisfied that your doctor's diagnosis is correct, even if the condition is one which carries a
serious prognosis. You may feel that it is too much trouble or expense
to corroborate his findings. You may be too ill to feel like doing anything.

Remember, however, it is your perfect right to demand an independent opinion. Even if you are hospitalized, you can still demand that your doctor find another physician—even a physician from another hospital—to render such an opinion.

Should you switch doctors if you think your doctor dislikes you?

It is a sad fact—but true—that many doctors dislike certain of their patients. Sometimes they resent a patient who has a problem that requires a lot of attention. Other times they feel hostility towards a patient for whom they are not sure what to do.

Howard Rusk, one of the pioneers of modern rehabilitation, once admitted to me that, as a young internist, he resented his patients who had suffered strokes. He had no idea what could be done for these patients, and tried to ignore them as much as possible.

"They'd begin a long tale of woe," Rusk recalls, "and I'd take their blood pressure . . . keep the stethoscope in my ears."

There can be thousands of reasons why your doctor might dislike you. He may dislike you because you are too rich. Or too poor. Or because you have a different "life-style." Often women fail to get along with male doctors (see Chapter 10).

For whatever the reason, if you feel that your doctor dislikes you, he probably does. And if he does, it can affect the quality of his medical care.

Therefore, a doctor who dislikes you is as good a reason as any for making a switch. It is a reason about which you should not feel guilty in the least.

A second opinion: Where should you go?

Many people are at a loss when it comes to seeking another opinion. They do not seem to know where they should turn. They ask whether or not they should go to a "specialist" and, if so, to what kind.

Principle: In seeking a second opinion you should, in general, seek another, different source of primary care.

If you, for instance, have been going to a private "solo" physician, you should consider the medical clinic of a medical school-affiliated hospital. Or one of the government's Neighborhood Health Centers. Or think of joining a prepaid group plan.

More and more, the hospital outpatient clinic has become an alternative source of primary care for many people. There is no doubt that care in the best hospital clinics is equal, if not superior, to that in most private "solo" doctors' offices.

What are the pros and cons of the hospital outpatient department?

"I go to my private doctor for most things," the mother of a small black boy told me, "but I come to the clinic to have his blood checked."

The boy had sickle-cell anemia. The mother knew that those of us who worked in the hospital's outpatient department cared for several children with this disease. She knew that we were highly attuned to its manifestations—as opposed to her private "solo" doctor, who rarely, if ever, saw a case.

This is one advantage of a busy hospital OPD: the doctors see large numbers of patients, many with unusual diseases. They are better prepared to recognize and treat these diseases.

The OPD of a top-notch hospital has a number of other advantages, too:

(1) The quality of care (delivered by interns and residents under supervision by senior staff physicians) is generally high.
(2) Lab and x-ray services are available on the spot.
(3) Doctors in virtually every medical and surgical specialty are available for consultation.
(4) The doctors are all salaried; they have no economic reason not to refer you, if necessary, or to see you more often than needed.
(5) The price of a visit is generally on a par with what you would pay to visit a private specialist; prices are usually adjusted according to your ability to pay.

There are also some drawbacks to the hospital OPD:

(1) If you have to make a return visit, you may not get the same doctor who saw you the first time.
(2) You may (though not necessarily) have a longer wait than you would in a private doctor's office.
(3) The care you receive may be more "impersonal"; your doctor may have little time for "small talk."
(4) You may, if the clinic is crowded, receive an overly rapid history and physical exam (this is also a risk in a private doctor's office).

Are there "tricks" to using the hospital OPD?

There are a number of ways to minimize the drawbacks of the OPD and to use it more effectively.

The first thing to remember is to *telephone* before you visit the clinic (even, if possible, in an emergency). Talk to the nurse in charge or, if possible, to a doctor. Tell your problem *briefly* over the phone.

This can save you a lot of trouble. If the clinic is jammed with people when you call, the nurse or doctor may suggest that you come later in the day. Sometimes they may give you advice over the phone that can save a visit entirely.

Talking to a clinic physician is a good idea because later, when you visit the clinic, you can tell the nurse at the desk that you have already spoken to Dr. So-and-so. Sometimes (especially if the problem is an urgent one) this can expedite your seeing a doctor.

Make an appointment over the phone if your problem is not an emergency. More and more hospitals are trying to discourage "walkins" and encourage appointments. If the clinic accepts appointments, the hospital staff will appreciate your calling ahead to make one.

Make sure you know the clinic's *name and location.* The nurse or other person on the phone may tell you to come to the general medical clinic. Or they may give you an appointment to a specialty clinic (cardiac, orthopedic, renal, etc.). In any case, make sure you get it straight.

Find out if you should bring any *biologic specimens.* A nurse or doctor can usually advise you if you should bring a urine or stool specimen, as well as how to collect the specimen. You may be told to stop at the clinic desk, pick up a lab or x-ray requisition, and have the necessary test done *before* seeing a doctor. Often this can save you a lot of time.

Are there ways to "pull rank" in the clinic?

Generally, the clinic takes patients in the order in which they arrive, or have made appointments. I have seen people push their way to the desk, waving a letter from a private doctor and demanding to be seen immediately.

Such "rank pulling" should—and generally does—have little

effect. If you go to a clinic, you should not expect any "special treatment" over the other patients, who may be just as ill as you.

If, on the other hand, you think your case (your child's, your father's, etc.) is a genuine emergency, you should so inform the person at the desk. If you (your child's, etc.) condition *deteriorates* while you are waiting, you should inform the staff.

No nurse or doctor is callous enough to fail to give priority to a true emergency (a heart attack, for example). But many times (especially at peak hours) the desk nurse may "eyeball" a patient and, if he does not look sick enough to be an emergency, may make him wait his turn.

What are the Neighborhood Health Centers and how good are they?

These centers are funded by the federal government (the Department of Health, Education and Welfare). There are now more than 100 in various parts of the nation. Though originally set up for low-income families, most will now accept members of the general public. The care offered is fairly comprehensive and prices are on a par with those in the community or even lower.

Principle: The quality of primary care in Neighborhood Health Centers is as good as that in the best hospital OPDs.

These centers have been extensively evaluated. It seems safe to say that they deliver care which is as good (if not slightly better than) that in the best hospital clinics (Table 3). This means that, where they exist, you may be able to consider these centers as another alternative source of primary care, if you decide to seek a second opinion.

Should you refer yourself to a specialist?

In general, it is best not to refer yourself to a specialist (other than an internist or pediatrician who delivers primary care). This problem is solved if you go to a hospital OPD (or a Neighborhood Health Center). If you need more specialized care, the doctor who sees you first will refer you.

The risk in picking a specialist yourself is that you may pick the "wrong" type of specialist. Let's take an example:

Case 7–1: A twenty-five-year-old medical student wakes up one morning with severe pain in his right lower jaw, in the region of his wisdom tooth. He suspects an infection in the tooth and calls his dentist for an appointment. The dentist examines the student, finds some redness of the gums, and prescribes a mouthwash and aspirin. The pain seems better for a day but then becomes much worse. This time the student goes to a primary care physician (internist), who makes a tentative diagnosis of sinusitis, and refers him to an ENT specialist. The ENT specialist conducts an exam, and orders sinus x-rays. The diagnosis is confirmed, treatment instituted, and the patient recovers uneventfully.

This case shows how easy it is to pick the wrong specialist. In this case the medical student suspected a tooth infection, from the location of his pain, and referred himself to a dentist. But, as it turned out, he did not have a dental problem at all. The pain in his lower jaw was actually due to an infection in his sinuses—an unusual, but not unheard-of phenomenon.

Many people refer themselves to specialists. People who think they need eyeglasses go to an ophthalmologist. Women often go directly to a gynecologist. Dentists, who can be considered the equivalent of medical specialists, are almost always consulted directly.

It is not necessarily bad for you to go directly to a specialist.

You should, however, be aware of the pitfalls. You should be aware that you run the risk of choosing the wrong specialist—one who might overlook things of consequence.

On the other hand, visiting a specialist has its pluses. An orthopedist stands a better chance of diagnosing your torn knee cartilage than an internist. A neurologist might spot that slight tremor in your fingers that another observer might miss.

Table 15 lists the various specialists (non-primary-care) and the sorts of problems they are best suited to handle. Excluded are surgical specialists (see Chapter 9), child health, and obstetrics-gynecology (see Chapter 10). Also excluded are anesthesiologists, radiologists and pathologists, all of whom you are not likely to consult unless referred by another doctor.

TABLE 15   Non-Primary-Care Specialists and Their Areas of Expertise
(Adult Non-surgical Specialties Only)

Specialty	*Areas of expertise*
Allergy and Immunology	conditions of excessive sensitivity to ingestion of, or contact with, foreign substances (pollens, molds, dust, etc.)

TABLE 15   Non-Primary-Care Specialists and Their Areas of Expertise
(Adult Non-surgical Specialties Only)

Specialty	Areas of expertise
Cardiovascular disease	congenital (present or developing at birth) heart disease, rheumatic heart disease, degenerative heart disease, disorders of heart rhythm
aDermatology	conditions of the skin and scalp: rashes, abnormal pigmentation, growths, infections, etc.
Endocrinology and Metabolism	conditions involving hormones and the glands that secrete them (thyroid, parathyroids, adrenals, gonads [testes or ovaries], and pituitary); conditions involving growth and development
Gastroenterology	conditions involving the esophagus, stomach, small and large intestines; also related organs such as the liver and gallbladder; common problems: ulcers, intestinal malabsorption, regional enteritis, ulcerative colitis
Hematology	conditions of the blood and blood-forming system; common problems: anemias, polycythemias (abnormal thickening of the blood), leukemia and other blood cancers, hemophilia and other disorders of blood clotting
Infectious Disease	conditions involving infectious agents (bacteria, viruses, parasites) and use of anti-microbial agents
Nephrology	conditions involving the kidneys; common problems: nephritis, nephrosis, renal failure, hypertension
Neurology	conditions of the central nervous system (brain and spinal cord), and of the peripheral nerves and muscles; common problems: dementias (loss of mental capacity and degenerative brain disease), learning disorders, cerebral palsy, epilepsy (seizure disorders), mental retardation
Oncology	conditions involving tumors—either benign or malignant (cancerous)—and their treatment
aOphthalmology	conditions of the eye and surrounding structures; common problems: near- and far-sightedness, cataracts, infections, injuries and foreign bodies, retinal detachment, glaucoma
aOtolaryngology (ENT)	conditions of the ears, nose, throat, and larynx; common problems: sinus infection, hearing loss, hoarseness and laryngitis

TABLE 15   Non-Primary-Care Specialists and Their Areas of Expertise
(Adult Non-surgical Specialties Only)

Specialty	Areas of expertise
Pulmonary Disease	conditions of the lungs; common problems: asthma, emphysema, "black lung" and other occupational lung diseases
Physiatry (Physical Medicine and Rehabilitation)	conditions which involve disability; common problems: paralysis, aphasia
Psychiatry	conditions of the mind and emotions; common problems: depression, schizophrenia and other psychoses, marital and sexual problems
Rheumatology	conditions of the joints and so-called rheumatoid-group diseases; common conditions: rheumatoid arthritis, rheumatic fever, arthritis and other manifestations of systemic lupus erythematosus and other diseases
[a]Urology	conditions of the urine and urinary tract, and reproductive organs (males); common problems: urinary tract infections, kidney and bladder stones, congenital abnormalities, prostate enlargement

[a] Designates specialties which involve surgery, to a varying degree. For primarily surgical specialties, see Chapter 9, Table 26.

Other places to go for a second opinion

There are many other sources, often overlooked, where you can get a second opinion (or a first one, for that matter). Most large cities operate *public health clinics*. In New York City, where I live, the health department runs clinics for the diagnosis and treatment of venereal disease, tuberculosis, tropical diseases, heart and orthopedic conditions, and others. Your city may have similar public health clinics.

Another resource are the various *disease-oriented private* organizations. These include the American Cancer Society, the Arthritis Foundation, United Cerebral Palsy Associations, etc. Many of these groups operate clinics. Others provide information on diagnosis and treatment. The best way to find these agencies in your local area is to consult the Yellow Pages under "Associations," "Social Service Organizations," etc.

8

Hospitals and post-hospital care

There is an old—and probably apocryphal—story doctors at the prestigious Massachusetts General Hospital used to tell. It seems a little old man walked into the MGH outpatient clinic one day to get a new pair of eyeglasses. By mistake someone directed him to the gastrointestinal clinic. Once there he got into the wrong line. Before he knew it, he found himself on his hands and knees on an examining table, having a sigmoidoscopic exam. During the procedure the instrument accidentally perforated his bowel. The unlucky fellow was admitted to the hospital, where he underwent surgery to repair his torn bowel, developed peritonitis, and died.

And all for a new pair of eyeglasses!

This incident probably never happened. But its black humor does make a point. A hospital—any hospital—can be a hazardous place. Once you pass through its portals, things can have a way of going awry.

How good are U.S. hospitals?

Each year one in ten Americans is admitted to a hospital. Some receive excellent care. But many do not. In the Columbia studies of hospital care, roughly one third of all patients received substandard care.

Duncan Neuhauser, a hospital expert now at Harvard, studied thirty Chicago hospitals. He found that some had death rates three times as great as others. Neuhauser estimated that overall, hospital death rates could be lowered by 50 per cent!

The National Commission on Medical Malpractice found that nearly 8 per cent of hospital patients were the victims of medical errors which made their condition worse. A larger number, presumably, were victims of errors which—fortunately—did not worsen their health status.

Is it possible to identify "good" and "bad" hospitals?

"If I were sick and had to go to the hospital," said John Knowles, former chief of the Massachusetts General, "there are only a few places in the country I'd trust myself to. You could almost count them on the fingers of both hands."

A few years back, the *Ladies' Home Journal* asked Knowles, and several other health experts, to pick what they thought were the nation's "best" hospitals—those they would choose for themselves or their families. There are more than 7,000 U.S. hospitals. Considering this large number, one might expect that one expert's list of the "best" hospitals would hardly resemble another's.

On the contrary. There was surprising agreement: the hospitals on one expert's "best" list were, by and large, those on every list! The hospitals picked by the *Ladies' Home Journal* jury are listed in Table 16.

Harvard's Neuhauser did the same thing in a slightly more scientific way: he asked several Chicago doctors to rate a group of hospitals in that city. Their ratings showed amazing agreement with one another—and with the hospitals' death rates!

The *Ladies' Home Journal* survey of "best" hospitals was vehemently attacked by an unsigned editorial in the *Journal of the American Hospital Association*. The editorial criticized the survey for "creating unsettling doubts" in the minds of Americans over what it said "is universally acknowledged to be the best hospital and medical care in the world."

Yet in the next breath, the AHA journal made a startling admission:

"It's easy," stated the editorial, "to single out the best in any group."

Precisely so. It *is* easy—if you know what to look for. And when it comes to hospitals, most doctors and other health professionals know what to look for. Even "the nurse who lives on the block," says Professor Neuhauser, has a pretty good idea which hospitals in town are of high caliber, and which are not.

What should you look for in choosing a hospital?

There is a "pecking order" among hospitals. And this order is more than just a matter of prestige. It is a matter of quality. What's

TABLE 16   Outstanding U.S. Hospitals as Chosen by Experts

Barnes, St. Louis, Mo.
Baylor University Medical Center, Dallas, Tex.
Beth Israel Hospital, Boston, Mass.
Cedars-Sinai, Los Angeles, Calif.
Cleveland Clinic Hospital, Cleveland, Ohio
Columbia-Presbyterian, New York, N.Y.
Duke Hospital, Durham, N.C.
Hartford Hospital, Hartford, Conn.
Henry Ford, Detroit, Mich.
Hospital of the University of Pennsylvania, Philadelphia, Pa.
Johns Hopkins, Baltimore, Md.
Massachusetts General, Boston, Mass.
Methodist Hospital, Houston, Tex.
Michael Reese, Chicago, Ill.
Montefiore Hospital, New York, N.Y.
Mount Sinai, New York, N.Y.
New York Hospital, New York, N.Y.
New York University Medical Center, New York, N.Y.
Palo Alto-Stanford, Palo Alto, Calif.
Peter Bent Brigham, Boston, Mass.
Presbyterian-St. Luke's, Chicago, Ill.
Rochester Methodist Hospital, Rochester, Minn.
St. Mary's, Rochester, Minn.
Strong Memorial Hospital of the University of Rochester,
   Rochester, N.Y.
University Hospital, Ann Arbor, Mich.
University Hospital, Seattle, Wash.
University Hospitals, Cleveland, Ohio
University Hospitals, Madison, Wis.
University Hospital and Hillman Clinic, Birmingham, Ala.
University of California Medical Center, San Francisco, Calif.
University of Chicago, Chicago, Ill.
University of Minnesota Hospital, Minneapolis, Minn.
Vanderbilt University Hospital, Nashville, Tenn.
Yale-New Haven, New Haven, Conn.

SOURCE: *Ladies' Home Journal*, © February 1967, Downe Publishing Inc.
Reprinted with the permission of *Ladies' Home Journal*.

more, it is generally agreed upon by those in the best position to
know—doctors, hospital administrators, and other health professionals.

"I wouldn't go to a hospital," says a New York administrator, "that
wasn't affiliated with a medical school."

Most other health workers agree. The best hospitals are those which have internship and residency training programs and are medical school-affiliated. Next best are those with interns and/or residents but without medical school ties. Still lower in the order are hospitals without interns or residents, but which are adequate enough to be "accredited" by the Joint Commission on Accreditation of Hospitals. And worst are those hospitals—about one fourth of the total—which are not even accredited.

Principle: You should choose a hospital which trains interns and residents and, if possible, one which is also affiliated with a medical school.

In the *Ladies' Home Journal* list of "best" hospitals, all were "teaching hospitals" (interns and residents), and all except a couple were medical school-affiliated.

Overwhelmingly, doctors themselves choose such hospitals for their own or their families' care. And with good reason. In the Columbia hospital studies, chances of getting substandard care were *more than three times as high* in hospitals without medical school ties. Chances of getting substandard care go up as you go down the hospital "pecking order" (Table 17).

TABLE 17 Quality of Care in Different Types of Hospitals

TYPE OF HOSPITAL	PERCENTAGE OF PATIENTS RECEIVING ADEQUATE CARE	
	Columbia study #1	Columbia study #2
Medical school-affiliated	79	86
Approved for internship and/or residency, but not medical school-affiliated	61	55
Accredited only	29	47
Not accredited	34	a

a By the time this study was done, nearly all New York hospitals studied were accredited.

SOURCES:
  Study #1: "The Quantity, Quality and Costs of Medical and Hospital Care Secured by a Sample of Teamster Families in the New York Area," Columbia University School of Public Health and Administrative Medicine, 1962.
  Study #2: "A Study of the Quality of Hospital Care Secured by a Sample of Teamster Family Members in New York City," Columbia University School of Public Health and Administrative Medicine, 1964.

Needless to say, even in a medical school-affiliated hospital there is still plenty of opportunity to receive sub-optimal care (in the Columbia studies chances were about one in five!). But, clearly, these hospitals should be your first choice, wherever possible.

How can you find a medical school-affiliated hospital?

This may not be an easy task. Less than 10 per cent of all hospitals —about 450 in all—have medical school ties. Another 15 per cent (1,300 hospitals) train interns and/or residents. The rest—or some three quarters of all hospitals—neither have training programs nor are medical school-linked. And of these, roughly 1,600 institutions are unaccredited.

TABLE 18   U.S. Hospitals—Per Cent with Medical School Affiliation or Some Teaching Program

	NUMBER	PER CENT
All hospitals[a]	6,236	100
Medical school affiliation	448	7
Teaching program		
Residency	1,019	16
Internship	787	13

[a] Excludes psychiatric, tuberculosis, and long-term care hospitals. Includes all other federal, state, and local government, and for-profit hospitals.

SOURCE: Piore, N., et al., *A Statistical Profile of Hospital Outpatient Services in the United States,* Association for the Aid of Crippled Children (New York), 1971.

It is fairly easy to find out which hospitals in your area are medical school-affiliated or have training programs. One way is to ask a doctor or nurse. Another way is to call the office of the hospital's administrator and inquire. Still another method, probably the best, is to consult the *Directory of Approved Internships and Residencies.* This is a soft-cover volume published by the AMA to aid medical students in selecting hospitals for their future training. The *Directory* may be found in many libraries, and in all medical libraries (usually bound with volumes of the AMA *Journal*).

If you wish to check the accreditation status of any hospital, you may consult *Accredited Hospitals.* This volume is published by the Joint Commission on Accreditation of Hospitals. The JCAH is a non-profit body which conducts periodic surveys of hospital records and procedures (see Chapter 11).

TABLE 19   U.S. Hospitals—Medical School Affiliation,
Residency, and Internship

HOSPITAL TYPE	NUMBER	MED. SCH. AFFILIATION		RESIDENCY		INTERNSHIP	
		No.	Per Cent	No.	Per Cent	No.	Per Cent
Federal (VA, Public Health Service, etc.)	416	84	19	134	13	57	7
Non-federal[a]	5,820	364	81	885	87	730	93
Non-profit	5,051	362	81	879	86	729	93
less than 100 beds	3,317	10	2	28	3	1	b
100–299 beds	1,798	99	22	306	30	212	26
300–499 beds	504	138	31	362	35	331	42
over 500 beds	201	117	26	189	19	186	24
Profit	769	2	b	6	1	1	b
TOTAL	6,236	448	100	1,019	100	787	100

a Excludes psychiatric, tuberculosis, and long-term care hospitals.
b Less than 1%—totals may add to more than 100% due to rounding.

SOURCE: Piore, N., et al., *A Statistical Profile of Hospital Outpatient Services in the United States,* Association for the Aid of Crippled Children (New York), 1971.

What are "proprietary" hospitals?

Proprietary hospitals are ones which are owned and operated as profit-making institutions. Proprietaries comprise only about 10 per cent of all hospitals (the majority of hospitals are so-called "voluntary" or non-profit ones).

Principle: In general, you should avoid proprietary hospitals.

In the Columbia studies, proprietary hospitals delivered the worst caliber of care. These hospitals are usually small. They are (with one or two exceptions) not affiliated with medical schools. Often such hospitals specialize in a certain type of lucrative service—psychiatric care or simple surgical procedures. Not infrequently, proprietaries are poorly equipped or have serious physical deficiencies.

"We don't even have a functioning OR [operating room]," the assistant administrator of one proprietary admitted to me. Despite this lack, the administrator told me, the hospital still does biopsies (a lucrative item)—some under general anesthesia!

According to Roger Rapoport, writing in *Harper's Magazine,* for-profit hospitals, in their efforts to keep costs low and profits healthy, often eliminate services which fail to make money. According to Rapoport, when Hospital Corporation of America—a big for-profit chain—took over a hospital in Selma, Alabama, they closed the hospital's obstetrics floor and replaced it with a coronary care unit. Obstetrics, it seems, was not profitable while coronary care was.

The head of a large for-profit chain boasted that his patients had hospital stays of only five to six days, instead of the more typical seven to eight days found in most non-profit hospitals.

"We do this," he told the reporter, "because most of the patient profit is generated during his first three days in the hospital. . . . After that the patient is merely recuperating and we are lucky to break even . . ."

One only wonders how many of those patients who are "merely recuperating" have been discharged from proprietary hospitals only to have a relapse at home and wind up in the emergency room of another institution.

Needless to say, this is the kind of hospital "efficiency" most of us could do without.

Are large hospitals better than smaller ones?

This is a question health experts have debated for years. One thing upon which all agree: large hospitals generally have a wider array of services. A large hospital can afford to have a cystic fibrosis clinic, or a surgeon who does only retinal surgery, or hyperbaric chamber. A large hospital has enough patients to keep such specialized services occupied—and, more important, *to do them well.*

Open-heart surgery is a good example. This is a service needed by very few people. Experts agree that a hospital's open-heart unit needs to do some 200–300 cases each year to keep its quality up to par. Only the very largest hospitals can keep up such a volume (in one survey of sixty-three large hospitals with open-heart facilities, more than 40 per cent averaged less than a single case each week—a frightening fact.)

Principle: You should, if possible, choose a larger hospital (more than 500 beds). You should avoid hospitals which have less than 100 beds.

The less-than-100-bed hospitals are dangerous places. Almost none (there are more than 3,000 in the country!) are medical school-affiliated. These tiny hospitals have death rates that are *40 per cent higher* than other hospitals, when the severity of their cases is taken into account.

In the *Ladies' Home Journal* list of top hospitals, all but three are larger than 500 beds. And only one has less than 300 beds.

There are some very good small hospitals (the Hunterdon Medical Center in Flemington, New Jersey and Thayer Hospital in Waterville, Maine, are two that are excellent). But, in general, the smaller hospital simply cannot compete with the largest when it comes to providing services.

You can find out the size of any hospital by consulting the *Hospital Guide Issue* of the American Hospital Association's journal. If this journal is not available in your local library, you can request a copy from the AHA, 840 North Lake Shore Drive, Chicago, Ill. 60611.

What services should a hospital provide?

More important than size, as we have said, is the services offered by the hospital. You would not wish to have surgery in a hospital which had no blood bank (29 per cent of all private hospitals). Or a recovery room for postoperative patients (20 per cent). Or a pathology lab (50 per cent).

Table 20 lists the various services which hospitals can provide. You can find out if your local hospitals provide these services by consulting the AHA *Guide Issue*.

Some of these services deserve special mention:

Intensive care units (ICUs)

An ICU is just what it sounds like: a room or area where seriously ill patients receive closer-than-normal scrutiny. An ICU should have specially trained nurses—roughly one for every one or two patients. It should have equipment for continuously monitoring the patients' electrocardiograms. It should have respirators and trained inhalation therapists to assist the patients' breathing, if needed.

ICUs have proven most valuable in the care of persons who have had heart attacks (acute myocardial infarctions). In one study, your chances of dying from a heart attack were *25 per cent less* if you were treated in an ICU!

130 TALK BACK TO YOUR DOCTOR

TABLE 20 Hospital Services Listed in AHA *Guide Issue*

Postoperative recovery room
ICU—cardiac
ICU
Open-heart surgery
Pharmacy
X-ray therapy
Cobalt therapy
Radium therapy
Diagnostic radioisotopes (brain scans, liver scans, etc.)
Therapeutic radioisotopes (usually for treatment of malignancy)
Histopathology lab
Organ bank (corneas, kidneys, etc.)
Blood bank
EEG (electroencephalogram, or "brain wave")
Inhalation therapy (respirators, etc.)
Premature nursery
Self-care unit
Extended care unit
Renal (kidney) dialysis (both in- and out-patient)
Burn unit
Physical therapy
Occupational therapy
Rehabilitation
Psychiatry
Psychology
Outpatient department/emergency ward
Social service
Family planning
Genetic counseling
Abortion (in- and out-patient)
Home care
Dentistry
Podiatry
Speech therapy

Yet many heart attack victims—perhaps half—are treated in hospitals which have no ICU.

"I really pity the patients who get stuck in our hospital in that situation," says the administrator of a large proprietary hospital which has no ICU and yet which treats heart attack victims.

An ICU is of value, of course, for any seriously ill patient. (See Chapter 10 for the use of intensive care for newborn infants.) The problem is that *any* hospitalized patient may, at any time, take a "turn for the worse" and become seriously ill. This is why it is best, if you have to go to the hospital, to pick one with an ICU.

For heart attack victims, I believe that anything less than ICU-level care in the first forty-eight to seventy-two hours (the period when most deaths occur) is simply not acceptable medicine in this day and age. If you are at high risk for a heart attack (obese, diabetic, high cholesterol, sedentary job, angina, etc.), it would seem prudent to make sure that your doctor uses an ICU hospital. If you have had a heart attack already, it would seem doubly prudent.

Physical therapy (PT)

Physical therapy is one aspect of rehabilitation. It can be most useful in helping you recover from strokes, fractures, and other disorders which involve muscular power and co-ordination. Pulmonary PT is used after surgery to help patients expand their lungs and thus prevent lung infections. (See also Chapter 9 for a discussion of rehabilitation.)

Dietary counseling

This is an item absent from the AHA list. But it can be of vital importance to you. A trained dietician knows a good deal that many doctors do not. She (most are women) can help you plan your diet both in and outside the hospital. She can be invaluable if you have insulin-requiring diabetes, for example. Or if you have heart failure and need a low-salt diet. Or if you have kidney failure and require a low-potassium diet. Or for a variety of other conditions.

Psychological testing

This is a service most often used in children. It is of special value where a child is thought not to be developing normally (see Chapter 10) or where a child is not learning up to par in school. A trained psychologist can often assist the doctor in determining whether such problems are due to mental retardation, or to another cause.

Social service

Trained social workers can help with many problems vital to your health. If your child has lead poisoning, all the medical care in the world will be valueless if he returns to an apartment which has not been de-leaded. A social worker may be of value in such an instance. Housing, financial aid, post-hospital care, homemaker services—all are areas where a social worker can make a big difference.

Genetic counseling

A geneticist (usually a doctor or a Ph.D.) can help in such matters as predicting the chance of a genetic disease occurring in your offspring, and in other matters where hereditary problems are involved. If a member of your family has a cleft palate, for instance, the counselor can tell you the chances of this defect reoccurring in subsequent offspring.

Should you choose a hospital for its "efficiency"?

There is nothing wrong with efficiency—as long as it does not happen at the expense of high-quality care. Hospitals with shorter lengths of stay and higher occupancy rates are—assuming they adhere to a high level of care—operating more efficiently. So are hospitals which have lower daily costs (room rates, for example).

Principle: Once you have assured yourself about quality, you may wish to consider a hospital's efficiency: its length of stay, occupancy rate, and daily cost.

If you have a choice, let's say, between two hospitals—both medical school-affiliated—you might wish to take these "efficiency factors" into account. You might wish to choose the hospital with the lower daily rate, or length of stay. Or the higher occupancy rate (which means that more of the hospital's beds are filled on any given day).*

Beware, though: use these criteria only *after* you have considered the hospital's quality. (Remember, proprietary hospitals pride themselves on their efficiency, and have lengths of stay which are only five to six days.)

In Pennsylvania, former Insurance Commissioner Herbert Denenberg believed consumers should know more about hospital efficiency. Commissioner Denenberg published "A Shopper's Guide to

* Occupancy rates are, I believe, a good measure of a hospital's efficiency. The best hospitals will keep all their beds working all the time, and will have occupancy rates of 90–100%.

Hospitals." The guide contains data on length of stay, occupancy rates, and daily costs for various hospitals.

You may have trouble obtaining this kind of data on your local hospitals. One possible source is your state insurance department or health department. Your local hospital league and hospital planning agency are other sources. Local Blue Cross plans also collect such data, though they may be reluctant to share it with consumers.

Should you—or your doctor—choose your hospital?

The choice of hospital is not always made by the patient. Usually, in fact, it is the doctor who decides where *he* prefers that you be hospitalized.

"I didn't want to go to Hospital X," I have heard people complain, "but my doctor sent me there."

Your doctor cannot hospitalize you anywhere. He can only send you to a hospital where he has *admitting privileges*. (This is why, in selecting a doctor, his hospital affiliations are of paramount importance—see Chapter 2.) Most doctors, however, have admitting privileges at *more than one hospital* (some can admit to as many as five or six hospitals).† You may have, therefore—even with the same doctor—a wide choice of hospitals.

Principle: You should ask your doctor the names of all hospitals at which he has admitting privileges; you should discuss with him the pros and cons of each.

I recall the wife of a friend, whose doctor advised her to enter the hospital. The doctor had admitting privileges at two hospitals—a large, medical school-affiliated one and a smaller, non-affiliated hospital. The better hospital, however, had a wait for beds. The doctor advised his patient—even though her condition was not urgent—to enter the second hospital and "get things over with." She was admitted and stayed in the hospital nearly two weeks, at a cost of more than a thousand dollars. Many of her diagnostic tests were of questionable value, due to the hospital's outmoded equipment. At the time of her discharge, no final diagnosis had been made. She

---

† It is, of course, one of the great scandals of American health care that a sizable number of doctors have no hospital ties, a situation which undoubtedly undermines the quality of their care.

subsequently went to a second physician, at a top-notch hospital, where she had to undergo the entire diagnostic work-up again.

The story's point is clear: a lot of your time, energy, and money can be wasted if you let your doctor "send" you to a less-than-adequate hospital. If you are not satisfied with your doctor's plans for your hospital admission, you should seriously consider finding a doctor at the hospital of your choice, or simply going there as a "ward" or "clinic" patient (see below).

How can you avoid unnecessary hospitalization?

Thousands of Americans are hospitalized each year who need no hospital care whatsoever. At least *10 per cent* of hospital admissions, studies show, are *not medically indicated.*

Why do these admissions occur?

Often they are matters of convenience—for the doctor. Doctors frequently admit patients for diagnostic work-ups which could readily be done on an outpatient basis. These doctors find it easier, however, to "work up" their patients in the hospital—particularly if it is a hospital where interns and residents do most of the work.

Needless to say, such convenience admissions are hardly a good practice. Hospitalization—as the story at the start of this chapter illustrates—has its hazards. Simply being in a hospital bed carries a small, but real risk. I have seen many patients given other patients' medications, by mistake. I have seen the wrong patients sent to the hospital x-ray department, by mistake. Worst of all, I have seen patients who entered the hospital perfectly well, acquire infections with hospital germs—a particularly hard kind of infection to cure. (I have never—in answer to the inevitable question—seen the wrong patient go to surgery, but I have no doubt it could occur.)

Principle: You should avoid, in general, hospitalization for a diagnostic "work-up" and should—if at all possible—have such a work-up on an outpatient basis.

A frequent reason heard for hospitalization is insurance. "The patient's insurance won't cover it if we do the tests as an outpatient," I have heard doctors say.

Insurance coverage for outpatient diagnostic tests, it is true, leaves a lot to be desired. Many companies, however, have broadened their benefits. Many now cover "pre-surgical testing"—tests which must be done prior to an operation. Other policies will cover certain outpatient tests.

Principle: Make sure what outpatient benefits your insurance policy has, before accepting hospitalization for purely economic reasons.

Finally, you should ask your doctor: "Is this hospital admission really necessary?" Make sure he can satisfy you that there are cogent reasons for your admission. Make sure you are satisfied that these reasons outweigh the risks.

Will joining a prepaid health plan keep you out of the hospital?

Enrolling in a prepaid plan is an excellent way to avoid hospitalization. People who join such plans are hospitalized 20–50 per cent fewer times than people who obtain their care in the traditional manner. (And plan members' health status is, if anything, *better*.)

Principle: In the long run, enrolling in a prepaid plan is probably your best way to avoid hospitalization.

Why is this so? Possibly because prepaid plans emphasize regular checkups and other preventive care (see Chapter 5). Possibly because these plans stress continuing education for their doctors, and because they monitor the caliber of their care.

Whatever the reason, the facts are clear enough. A national commission found that patients in California's Kaiser Plan use 30 per cent fewer hospital days each year. Studies of New York's Health Insurance Plan showed that its enrollees use fewer hospital days than a comparable New York population outside the plan.

Paul Ellwood, a physician and former head of the American Rehabilitation Foundation, culled data from prepaid plans all over the nation. He found the same results: people in these plans had almost *one third fewer hospitalizations* than people in the same locales who obtained care in the usual catch-as-catch-can way and whose bills were paid by Blue Cross (Table 21).

Prepaid plans, then, can be recommended not only because they provide high-caliber out-of-hospital care (see Chapter 2, Table 3) —but because they keep you out of the hospital!

TABLE 21   Yearly Hospital Care Needed—Persons Enrolled
in Prepaid Health Plans and in Blue Cross

	PREPAID PLANS	BLUE CROSS	DIFFERENCE
Hospital admissions per 100 enrollees	8.3	12.3	4.0
Length of stay (days/hospital admission)	6.6	7.0	0.4
Total hospital days per 100 enrollees/yr.	56.2	86.4	30.2

SOURCE: Ellwood, P., and Herbert, M., *Harvard Business Review*, July–August 1973.

How can you minimize your hospital stay?

Once committed to entering the hospital, you should bend your energies to staying *no longer than medically necessary.* This statement may surprise you. But the plain facts are that large numbers of people—once in the hospital—stay longer than they need to. In a recent study by the New York City Health Services Administration, some 30 per cent of patients hospitalized more than twenty-one days had *no medical reason* for being in the hospital. This study was done in New York's municipal hospitals. But essentially the same situation exists in private ones. As many as 15 per cent of all hospital days may be unneeded, from a medical point of view.

What causes unnecessarily long hospital stays?

Weekends and holidays play a role. Everyone who has worked in hospitals knows that, on weekends and holidays, they operate on a "skeleton" basis. Only vital services are maintained. Staffs are cut to the bone.

Sometimes this shutdown results in dangerously poor care. Consider this case history, from one of the Columbia hospital studies:

A middle-aged man had a history of a hernia which he had been able to reduce [force back in] manually in the past. He was admitted to the hospital after two days in which reduction of the hernia had been impossible. . . . and *two days later* it was necessary to operate. [Italics mine.]

"He should have been operated on at once," said the surgical expert who rated the case as having received "poor" care. *"The two day delay,"* the expert went on, *"may have had something to do with the fact that the patient entered the hospital on the fourth of July."*

The unfortunate man with a hernia, obviously, could not choose the day on which he entered the hospital. But many times it is possible to make such a choice, since most hospital admissions are "elective," and not emergency, ones.

Principle: If you can, avoid entering the hospital before weekends or holidays.

One hospital administrator I know suggests that Tuesday (or Monday night) is probably the best time to enter the hospital. This, he explains, is the time when the hospital, and its staff, has recovered from the weekend and is probably most productive.

A hospital stay is not a vacation. The best doctors plan to keep their patients busy during each moment of their hospitalization. These doctors schedule everything in advance, so that your day will not be idle for a moment—a "must" at today's hospital prices of $100 or more per day.

Principle: You should ask your doctor—before you enter the hospital—to estimate your discharge date.

This little mental exercise will make him think about just how long you are likely to be in the hospital. It will make him plan your hospital stay.

Hospital stays will vary depending on your age, your illness, whether you require surgery, etc. Some average stays are shown (Tables 22 and 23).

TABLE 22   Average Length of Hospital Stay According to Age

Age	Length of Stay (Days)
0–1 years	7.0
1–4	4.6
5–14	4.5
15–24	5.5
25–34	6.5
35–44	7.9
45–64	10.0
65 and over	14.0

SOURCE: *Statistical Abstract of the United States,* 1971.

You may be able to obtain more detailed data on hospital stays for specific diagnoses, in your locale, from your Blue Cross plan or other hospital insurer. When your doctor's estimated discharge date (or your actual hospital stay) is out of line with the average, you should ask him why. If he cannot explain the difference, you may wish to obtain another length-of-stay estimate from another doctor.

TABLE 23　Average Hospital Stays for Various Illnesses[a]

Type of Illness	Average Stay (days)
Allergic, Endocrine, Metabolic disease	10.5
Diabetes	12.6
Other conditions (asthma, thyroid disease)	8.9
Anemias and other blood disease	10.4
Bone and joint disease	9.9
Arthritis	13.1
Bursitis, synovitis, etc.	4.8
Fractured femur (hip, upper leg)	13.8
Other fractures	43.0
Sprains, dislocations, etc.	16.7
Circulatory disease	12.9
Arteries and veins (hemorrhoids, varicose veins, phlebitis, etc.)	11.1
Coronary heart disease (heart attack)	14.8
Other heart disease	12.7
Hypertension	11.0
Gastrointestinal disease	8.0
Appendicitis	7.8
Gall bladder	11.6
Gastritis, gastroenteritis, etc.	5.4
Peptic ulcer	12.3
Genitourinary disease	6.5
Breast disease	3.1
Menstrual disorders	3.0
Prostatic hyperplasia (enlargement)	13.7
Urinary calculi (stones)	6.8
Urinary tract infections	6.3
Infectious and parasitic disease	7.9
Neoplasms (tumors)	11.9
Benign	6.6
Malignant	15.5
Nervous system disease	10.3
Cerebrovascular accident (stroke)	17.4
Head injury with brain damage (concussion, etc.)	16.2
Other nervous system	7.3
Pregnancy (uncomplicated)	4.5
Respiratory disease	6.0

TABLE 23   Average Hospital Stays for Various Illnesses

Type of Illness	Average Stay (days)
Acute upper respiratory infection	4.4
Pulmonary infection (pneumonias, bronchitis, etc.)	8.5
Skin disease	8.8

a Data are from a sample of 11,356 patients, surgical and non-surgical, in 66 acute short-term New England hospitals, 1970. For data on hospital stays for surgical procedures see Table 28, p. 174.

SOURCE: Peterson, O. L., et al., "The impact of Medicare on hospital utilization and financing," Grant no. 10-P-56003/1-02, Social Security Administration, Department of Health, Education and Welfare, Washington, D.C.

How important is a hospital's nursing care?

Nursing care is a vital part of your hospital stay. I have seen the efforts of the best physicians nullified by poor nursing care. (I have also seen poor doctors "saved" by alert and competent nurses!)

It is not uncommon, for instance, for nurses to fail to notice that the liquid in an intravenous bottle is nearly finished. I have seen patients over whom a doctor has labored for an hour, to find a vein and start an intravenous solution—and all his labor (not to mention the patient's discomfort) has to be repeated because a nurse has not noticed an IV bottle run dry.

Some nursing errors are more serious. Consider this one, told me by a nurse herself:

My father was in the hospital for heart failure . . . he was in an oxygen tent . . . We came in one night to find that his oxygen had run out . . . He was just in a big plastic bag.

"We got him a private-duty nurse that night," she adds.

In this case, poor nursing care could have proven disastrous. The patient, his circulation already seriously impaired, could easily have died from suffocation.

Lack of skilled nurses is not uncommon, even in the largest hospitals. "There are wards at this hospital," says the chief of medicine at a large municipal institution, "that are uncovered by an R.N. for entire shifts."

Other hospitals have, even during the daytime hours, only one R.N. for a dozen or more patients—an unsatisfactory ratio.

Other hospitals, however, are better run. They make sure there are one or more R.N.s on every floor (ward) for each of the three daily shifts (days, evenings, nights). During the day, when most of the hospital's business takes place, they make sure that each R.N. has no more than five to six patients to care for.

Principle: You should beware of hospitals where (1) there is not at least one R.N. per floor at all times, or where (2) one R.N. has responsibility for more than eight to ten patients.

If you find yourself (or a relative) in one of these situations, you may wish to consider *private-duty nursing*. This means, essentially, hiring your own private nurse. Most hospitals or communities have nurse registries, with rosters of R.N.s or L.P.N.s who are available for private-duty nursing care. Such care is expensive, however. And it is usually not covered by health insurance, including Medicare.

Private-duty nursing, then, is hardly a good solution. It means that you are paying for something the hospital should provide, as part of their care. It is far better—and cheaper—to choose a hospital with good nursing coverage *beforehand,* if at all possible. (And remember: in any hospital, nursing coverage may well vary depending on the floor or ward.)

What is a medication error?

A medication error is when you receive (a) the wrong medicine, or (b) the correct medicine in an incorrect dose or form, or by the wrong route of administration. A medication error can also mean not getting a drug which you are supposed to receive.

How often do these errors happen?

In most hospitals this is a closely guarded secret. But anyone who has worked in a hospital knows that medication errors are certainly not rare. Milton Silverman and Dr. Philip R. Lee, in their book *Pills, Profits, and Politics,* assert that "from two to eight per cent of all drug doses given in hospitals are in error—wrong drug, wrong dose, wrong route of administration, wrong patient, or failure to give the prescribed drug."

Medication errors happen for many reasons. The doctor makes an error when writing in the "order book." A nurse makes an error when copying the doctor's order from the book into her card file.

Or—as often happens—the nurse doling out cups of medicines simply gives you someone else's cup.

Principle: You should know what medications your doctor has prescribed for you, and what they look like. If a nurse gives you a new medication, you should make sure your doctor's orders have changed (ask her to check the order book).

"I think," says one experienced R.N., "the patient should always question a new pill." This nurse readily admits that she herself has been saved from making a medication error by a patient who said, "That's not the kind of pill I usually get," or, "I've never been given that kind of medicine before."

This is the sort of alertness, on your part, that can prevent you from being the victim of a medication error.

If you do take the wrong medication, your doctor should be notified as soon as the error is noticed. Many drugs, in a single dose, are not harmful. Others can be neutralized in various ways. The key thing is to make sure that your hospital physician knows that an error has occurred, and that he knows *promptly*.

Should you go to a public hospital for your hospital stay?

I recall, during my internship at the Boston City Hospital, an interesting case. A middle-aged advertising executive was seriously injured in an automobile accident on Boston's Southeast Expressway. Since the expressway runs right by the City Hospital, the police rushed him there. He was seen in the emergency room and admitted immediately. He was given blood, and x-rays of every part of his body were taken. A urinary catheter was inserted to monitor his urine output and to check for blood in his urine.

The next day the man was better. His condition had stabilized and he was alert. His arms and legs were in casts for multiple fractures but there was no reason why he could not have been transported to another hospital.

His family, in fact, desired such a transfer.

"You don't want to stay here, Robert," his wife said as he lay in bed in the middle of a ward with only a few flimsy curtains to separate him from the other patients.

The man, however, refused to be transferred. He knew quite well that the care he had received was good care. He had been impressed by the no-nonsense doctors in the BCH emergency room. Perhaps he sensed, correctly, that the City Hospital saw more cases like his than any private hospital in the area.

In any case, the man refused transfer. He stayed on the ward, despite his wife's pleadings that he should be "someplace nicer." He improved rapidly and in a few days was able to sit up and to eat. He seemed even to enjoy his surroundings. He talked to his fellow patients. He compared experiences with them. When the time finally came for him to go home, he seemed a bit reluctant to leave.

"I never knew," he said, "that being in a hospital could be such a pleasant experience."

The ad exec, like many people who experience municipal hospital care for the first time, was pleasantly surprised. The horror stories he had heard about public hospitals did not turn out to be true. He found the quality of care to be excellent.

Public hospitals (most are run by cities, hence the name "municipals") are not easy to generalize about. Many suffer from serious shortages of staff and equipment. Many operate under the handicap of old, dilapidated buildings. In some, the length of stay is far longer than it is in private hospitals, due partly to these problems.

The best public hospitals, however, do manage to deliver high-caliber care.

Principle: The quality of care in the best public hospitals (those with medical school affiliation and full-time department heads and staffs) is probably as good as that in the best private hospitals.

The main reasons why this is so is that the best public hospitals attract top-grade students from the best medical schools, to be interns and then residents. They choose these hospitals to finish their training because they know they will see the toughest cases and will have more responsibility than in a private hospital.

Public hospitals are a good learning environment for interns and residents. And this makes them a good care environment for patients. (I have already noted that at least one study has shown that interns and residents provide better care than other physicians.)

Should you be a "ward" or "teaching service" patient?

Even private hospitals have their "ward" or "teaching service" patients. Most of the people I know recoil in horror, however, when asked if they would enter the hospital as a ward or teaching case.

"I want a private room," one woman told me. "That's what I'm paying for—privacy."

I recently visited a friend, a woman financial analyst, in the hospital. She had gotten pneumonia and had developed an unusual —and serious—complication: pulmonary emboli. A pulmonary embolus is a blood clot that comes from one of the veins in the body, passes through the heart, and lodges in one of the arteries that carry blood to the lungs. A pulmonary embolus can be as sudden and grave as a heart attack. The patient may die in a few moments, unless help is available.

My friend had already "thrown" a few small emboli. Her doctors were treating her with anti-coagulant drugs and hoping that she would not have any more.

When I saw her, she was ensconced in an elegant private room. She was surrounded by flowers and get-well cards. Suspended from the ceiling opposite her bed was a color television set that she could operate by remote control.

"This," she informed me, "is the best room in the place."

I looked around. The heavy door to the hall was closed. Outside, the nearest nursing station was a good fifty yards away. My friend's only contact with the outside world was the call button, hung well above the head of her bed.

Could this woman, I wondered, summon aid if she were suddenly stricken? She would have, it occurred to me, a better chance of turning on her television set, since the control button was nearer to her hand.

We Americans have a penchant for privacy. But sometimes I think we might carry it a bit too far. If I myself were gravely ill, or even ill enough to be hospitalized, I would think twice before allowing myself to be shut away in a private room. I would probably want to be on an open ward, where, if I were to take a turn for the worse, someone—even a fellow patient—might notice and summon help.

On the ward or teaching service of a top-notch hospital your care will be the responsibility of one doctor (usually a resident) but many other persons will also visit you. You will be seen by medical students and their physician preceptors. (Remember, it's often a medical student who picks up a key sign or symptom that everyone else has missed.) You will be seen on regular daily "rounds" by your doctor and other interns and residents, several times each day. Once or twice a week your doctor's chief resident and his "attending" physician will look in on you.

All this means just one thing: as a ward patient you will receive *several times the medical attention* you would as a private or semi-private patient. The least change in your condition is more than likely to be noticed by someone.

TABLE 24

A TYPICAL TEACHING HOSPITAL HIERARCHY AND LINES OF RESPONSIBILITY FOR CARE OF "WARD" PATIENTS

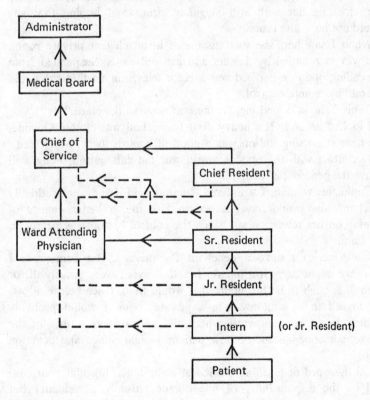

Key:

solid lines (————): usual lines of responsibility

dotted lines (— — — —): other lines of responsibility

How is a hospital teaching service organized?

A hospital teaching service is a hierarchy. Here's how it usually works:

An intern or resident is assigned to your case. He is "your doctor." He, in turn, is responsible to a senior resident, or sometimes directly to the chief resident. The chief resident is responsible to the chief of the service (who should be a full-time Board-certified physician— an expert in his field).

In addition, the intern or resident in charge of your case also reports to his "attending"—another Board-certified specialist—who also follows the progress of the other patients on your ward or floor. (The "attending" jobs are usually rotated several times each year among the several physicians on the department chief's staff.)

Table 24 shows a typical teaching hospital hierarchy.

Principle: If you are not satisfied with your ward care, you should not hesitate to ask to see your doctor's superior. (If necessary, ask to see his chief resident, "attending," or the chief of the service.)

This is another advantage of being a ward or teaching service patient: you have someone—indeed, a lot of people—to whom you can complain if you are not satisfied with your care. As a private patient, by contrast, you are stuck with only your private physician —for better or for worse.

Also, of course, the hierarchy tends to encourage good-quality care. It does this because each doctor—from the intern on up— knows that someone else is looking over his shoulder.

"In a teaching hospital," as John Knowles puts it, "the setup tends to keep everybody honest."

How can the hospital hierarchy get you in trouble?

While there are obvious advantages to having several doctors caring for you, there may be disadvantages as well. Sometimes important things get overlooked. They fall between the cracks. Sometimes important bits of information on your condition fail to get communicated from one doctor to another, with disastrous results. Here is an example of such a disaster, taken from an actual legal case:

Case 8–1: A male construction worker was injured when a nail pierced his right leg and fractured his fibula. On being taken to a hospital, he informed the medical student who took his history that he was allergic to penicillin. This information was passed along to the nurse anesthetist. There was, however, a question as to whether the information concerning his allergy was given to the resident who performed the surgery, and who wrote the postoperative orders. The information was not given to the staff surgeon who was in charge of the resident's activities. The construction worker was given large doses of penicillin postoperatively. He suffered a cerebrovascular accident (stroke) followed by severe physical and personality changes . . .

This case shows how, on occasion, crucial facts can get "lost in the shuffle" among the hospital hierarchy. You should be aware that this can happen. You should *never assume* that what you tell one doctor will be communicated to all your doctors. You may feel funny, repeating the same story three or four times, but rest assured that it is necessary.

If you are a diabetic who needs daily insulin, for instance, make sure you tell this to each physician you see. Tell the floor nurse. Make sure whichever doctor writes your "orders" does not neglect to note it in the order book. (The above catastrophe could have been averted if one of the patient's doctors had marked his order book sheet with the words "Allergic to penicillin.")

What are your rights as a hospital patient?

Hospitals can be intimidating places. Many people are unsure, once in a hospital, what their rights are. Many surrender their rights unnecessarily.

Here are some common questions I have heard patients ask, in one form or another:

"Do I have the right to see my hospital record?" (Yes.)

"Do I have the right to refuse to be examined by a medical student?" (Yes, though you will probably benefit more by consenting to the exam.)

"Do I have the right to refuse a diagnostic test, or procedure?" (Yes.)

"Do I have the right to refuse treatment?" (Yes, except in unusual instances where your illness poses a threat to others, or where the hospital first obtains a court order.)

"Do I have the right to demand that my records be kept secret?" (Definitely.)

"Can I leave the hospital at any time?" (Yes, though you may be required to sign a form which states that the hospital is no longer responsible for your care.)

Recently, the American Hospital Association set forth a "Bill of Rights" for hospital patients. This "Bill of Rights" may be found in the Appendix. If you have any question regarding your rights as a hospital patient, you may wish to write or call the AHA, 840 North Lake Shore Drive, Chicago, Ill. 60611 (312 645-9400).

What is meant by "informed consent"?

Informed consent is one of your most important rights as a patient. This means that, before any procedure or treatment, your doctor must inform you of its risks and consequences (see Chapter 5 on the risks of diagnostic procedures). He must, after this explanation, have you sign a *consent form*.

Principle: You should not feel obliged to sign a consent form until you are satisfied that you have been fully informed concerning the procedure or treatment in question.

What kinds of things require consent forms?

In general, almost any procedure which entails any element of risk. A lumbar puncture (spinal tap) is an example. Anything which involves anesthesia. Any surgery.

You should make sure that the consent form states the specific procedure for which you are being asked to give consent. The form should *not,* for example, merely say "surgery." It should state the surgical procedure to be done ("skin graft, left thigh," "mitral valvuloplasty," "closed reduction of fracture of ulna," etc.).

Do not sign a blank consent form. Do not let the doctor convince you to sign a blank form, saying, "I'll fill in the procedure later." Or, "We're not sure exactly what the surgery will be at this time." Such excuses are not given by competent doctors, or in competent hospitals. Nor do such hospitals try to get their patients to sign consent forms for "any medical or surgical procedure" or other such all-inclusive terms.

Should you take part in a research project?

There is an aspect of some hospitals—particularly those allied with medical schools—that bothers many people: research. I have had many people tell me they fear that they will be used as "guinea pigs" at a medical center, without their knowledge or consent.

Are such fears justified?

Most research does take place at medical school-affiliated hospitals. Research is one of the functions of such hospitals. In all medical school hospitals, however, any research on humans is subject to certain controls. Each research project must be approved by a hospital research committee. More important, every patient who takes part in the project must first give informed consent.

Principle: You should be sure you understand the benefits and risks of any research project before you give consent to participate.

You may be asked to take part in a project where there might be direct benefit to you (as, for example, testing a new drug treatment for your disease). Or you may be asked to take part in a project which can only benefit future patients. Both projects might be worthwhile. You should, nevertheless, make sure you understand which is which.

In many research projects there is a "control group." This is a group of patients, assigned at random, who may receive no treatment, or the "old" treatment (in contrast to the "experimental group," who get the treatment being tested). Many people feel they would rather get some treatment, regardless of what it is. If you feel this way, you might not wish to participate in a research project where there is a chance you will be randomly assigned to the control group.

Finally, you should of course ask about the risks of the project. You should satisfy yourself that these risks are justified in your condition. You might even ask the researcher for his previous *published papers* on the subject under investigation. While you may not understand them completely, you may find it useful to read them before giving your consent. You may wish to ask other doctors (an intern or resident not involved in the project, for instance) for their opinions of the research's worth.

Most of the research I have seen has been done responsibly and ethically. But there are abuses. The best way to protect yourself against such abuses is to make sure you understand the purposes of any research project *before* you give your consent to take part.

Should you have a health advocate?

A health advocate is someone who can represent your interests in dealing with doctors and other health personnel. The job of a health advocate is to make sure you, the patient, are getting proper care and attention.

Some people might scoff at the idea of health advocacy. Why, they might ask, do I need such help? I am an educated person. I am able to look after my own interests.

Unfortunately, as we have seen, the patient may not always be so lucky. He may be too incapacitated to look out for his own best interests. He may be powerless to deal with the "system" from his hospital bed.

Principle: Anyone who enters a hospital, or other health care institution, ought to consider having a health advocate.

Consider the following example of how an advocate can be useful:

Case 8–2: A woman graduate student was admitted to the university infirmary because of seizures. She was treated with anti-epileptic drugs, and informed that she would be transferred to a large hospital for a full diagnostic work-up as soon as a bed was available. She waited several days for the transfer, but it did not take place. Her seizures, at first partly controlled, began to recur and to become more frequent. She began to have personality changes. During lucid moments she pleaded with her doctors to transfer her to the larger hospital, without success. Finally, her boyfriend—a third-year law student—took matters into his own hands. He demanded that the patient be transferred at once. He threatened to notify the university authorities. He enlisted the aid of friends to "pressure" the woman's physician. The next day, the patient was informed that a bed was available in the hospital. She was transferred for her diagnostic work-up.

In this case, advocacy was clearly essential. The patient, partially disabled, was not able to get her physician to act. She needed an advocate to get action.

This kind of situation is not uncommon. I have seen patients languish in a hospital bed for days, waiting for a diagnostic test or other procedure. Often their doctor will tell them there are scheduling difficulties, or offer some other excuse for inaction. These patients need a health advocate. They need someone who can demand action on their behalf.

In the above case, the advocate happened to be a law student. (Perhaps the patient's doctor acted quickly out of fear of a malpractice suit.) But a health advocate can be anyone. An advocate need not have any knowledge of law or of medicine. The advocate's sole function is to represent your interests—regardless of what they may be—when you are not totally able to do so yourself.

What about your post-hospital care?

The time to start thinking about your post-hospital needs is when you enter the hospital. Talk to your doctor about post-hospital care early in your hospital stay. Do not assume he will think of it on his own!

Principle: Poor discharge planning is a major cause of prolonged hospital stays.

I have seen doctors suddenly realize—on the day of discharge—that their patient needed to be taught a special diet. Or special exercises. Or how to inject insulin. I have seen discharge delayed for several days because the doctor did not think to tell a social worker in advance that his patient would need nursing home or other institutional care following discharge.

In these instances, the doctor simply failed to "think ahead." You can avoid this problem by asking him, long before your discharge, about post-hospital care.

What is "home care"?

One kind of post-hospital care you should know about is *home care*. Home care can not only get you out of the hospital earlier, it may also save you—or someone in your family—from having to go to a nursing home.

Many hospitals have home care programs. These programs are usually run by a nurse. The idea of home care is to provide skilled nursing and other services at home—and thus to enable the patient, and his family, to manage by themselves.

Here is an example:

Case 8–3: A 26-year-old woman had pneumonia. During her illness she suffered a pulmonary embolus (a blood clot in the pulmonary circulation). She was hospitalized and placed on an anti-coagulant (a drug to decrease the clotting of the blood). When she was out of danger, her doctor told her she could go home. She had to have daily injections of the anti-coagulant, however, as well as twice-weekly blood samples drawn to measure clotting time. As a result, her discharge was delayed for several weeks.

This patient is an example of someone who could have benefited from home care. In a home care program, a nurse would be sent to her home to administer her injections. A lab technician would be sent to draw blood for the clotting test. Without home care, this patient would have to remain in the hospital even though she was completely well.

Another example might be a patient who needs daily dressing changes. A home care nurse visit will allow him to leave the hospital.

Home care also includes physical therapy services—done at home by a registered physical therapist. Home care can, in some instances, even include observation alone (as long as it is by a nurse), and equipment such as "walkers" or wheelchairs.

These kinds of services are all included in home care. They will all be paid for by Medicare if you are over sixty-five and a Social Security beneficiary. They *may* also be paid for by your Blue Cross plan.

Home care can be, in other words, a way for you to leave the hospital without it costing you money for private nurses or other services. Even home health aides (nurse's aides) may be included in many instances.

Principle: You should consider home care, whenever skilled nursing or other rehabilitation services are needed after a hospital stay.

Do not assume that your doctor knows about home care. The twenty-six-year-old woman cited above was in a hospital with a home care program. Yet her physician did not know about it.

"Nine out of ten doctors," says one home care nurse who did a survey, "knew very little about home care." And this, too, in a hospital with a home care program.

Most hospitals with home care programs will take referrals from hospitals which do not have such programs. This is important to remember if you are in one of the latter hospitals.

Your local *Visiting Nurse Association* is another source of home

care. The VNA may be contacted by your doctor, the hospital
social worker, or even by you. In general, though they will charge
you for home nurse visits, they will adjust their charges according
to your ability to pay.

Finally, your *local health department* may employ nurses who will
make home visits, for certain purposes.

How successful is rehabilitation?

Rehabilitation is the "forgotten science" of modern medicine.
Most doctors and other health workers have little idea of its benefits. Often they fail to recognize when a patient can be helped by
rehabilitation services.

Consider this case, told me by a hospital nurse, a member of a
team who evaluate patients' rehabilitation potential:

We were asked to see an elderly woman . . . who had had a stroke.
She was on Valium, Benadryl, Elavil—half a dozen different drugs.
She was totally disoriented, tied to a stretcher, screaming constantly.
We told her family "We see no rehabilitation potential." Yet, after
a few weeks at home, I got a call from her daughter, who asked us to
come out to see her. When we got there she was sitting up in a chair,
knitting. She greeted us by name!

Stroke, according to rehab expert Dr. Howard Rusk, is a disease
where patients are often mislabeled "hopeless"—when they actually
have a good deal of rehabilitation potential. Stroke patients, Rusk
notes, are usually evaluated too early to appreciate their potential
for improvement.

"One third," he told me, "were able to get back to some kind of
gainful work . . . 90 per cent we were able to teach to meet the
needs of daily living."

**Principle: Every disabled patient deserves a rehabilitation evaluation
before hospital discharge, and again after several weeks.**

Ideally, this evaluation should be done by a *physiatrist*—a doctor
who is Board-certified in physical medicine and rehabilitation. Sadly,
there are very few such specialists: about 1,700 for the entire country. As a second best choice, the evaluation might be done by
a *physical therapist,* or by a nurse who has had special training in rehabilitation.

You may also wish to have an evaluation done at one of several rehabilitation centers—places which do nothing but skilled rehabilitation (see below).

In which conditions is rehabilitation particularly appropriate? Here are a few of the more common:

strokes—especially with muscle paralysis or weakness, loss of speech, loss of memory and other higher mental functions

accidents—especially where paraplegia (waist-down paralysis) or quadriplegia (neck-down paralysis) are present

amputations—loss of part or all of arms or legs, or even lower part of trunk

burns—to prevent muscle contractures

blindness and/or deafness

cerebral palsy—to prevent muscle contractures, to improve gait, coordination

heart attacks—gradually to build up physical strength and restore mental confidence

post-surgery—example: arm and shoulder exercises following breast cancer surgery

post-fractures—to restore muscle strength after cast removal

This list is hardly complete. But it does provide an idea of the myriad of situations in which complete or partial rehabilitation should be possible—situations involving everything from the highest mental processes to the function of individual muscles, or groups of muscles.

Additional information on rehabilitation

Here are some ways you can obtain more information on rehabilitation evaluation and care:

(1) Contact the National Rehabilitation Association or one of the many other private health and social welfare agencies (American Cancer Society, American Heart Association, The Arthritis Foundation, National Kidney Foundation, etc.). Some supply services. Others will give you the names of centers where you may obtain services. See the Yellow Pages under "Associations," "Social Service Organizations," etc.

(2) Contact a general rehabilitation center. Examples of general centers are: Woodrow Wilson Center, Fishersville, Va.; the Hot Springs Rehabilitation Center, Hot Springs, Ark.; the Georgia Rehabilitation Center, Warm Springs, Ga.; the Institute for the

Crippled and Disabled, New York, N.Y.; the Institute of Rehabilitation Medicine, New York, N.Y.; the Kessler Institute of Rehabilitation, West Orange, N.J.; and the Rehabilitation Institute of Chicago, Chicago, Ill.

(3) Consult the May 1969 issue of *American Annals of the Deaf,* which lists 405 *speech and hearing clinics* in the United States and Canada.

(4) Contact your state or local health department. Every state has a crippled children's program. Most have other rehabilitation services as well.

(5) Contact a rehabilitation center for the *blind.* Examples include: Industrial Home for the Blind, Brooklyn, N.Y.; North Carolina Rehabilitation Center for the Blind, Butner, N.C.; South West Rehabilitation Center, Little Rock, Ark.; Kansas Rehabilitation Center for Adult Blind, Topeka, Kans.; St. Paul's Rehabilitation Center for the Blind, Newton, Mass.; Minneapolis Society for the Blind, Minneapolis, Minn.; Adjustment Training Center, Florida Council for the Blind, Holly Hill, Daytona Beach, Fla.

(6) Contact the Rehabilitation Services Administration, Social and Rehabilitation Service, U. S. Department of Health, Education and Welfare, Washington, D.C. 20201, or your regional HEW office.

(7) Contact your state vocational rehabilitation agency (a federal-state program in all states and territories).

What about nursing homes?

Something must be said about nursing homes, since so many patients—no doubt too many—are discharged from the hospital to one of these institutions.

A nursing home, in my opinion, should be virtually a "last resort." It should be used only after the patient has had a trial at some form of rehabilitation, either in a rehab center or at home.

Consider the elderly woman with a stroke mentioned above. She was able to recover fairly well at home, even without any formal rehabilitation. What would have happened to this woman had she gone directly from a hospital to a nursing home? She would have been placed in unfamiliar surroundings. She would undoubtedly have been given one or more drugs, possibly a tranquilizer (a serious cause of disorientation in old people).

In a nursing home, it's safe to say the old woman would probably have deteriorated. She probably would have gotten worse, not better. Nursing homes are dangerous places. Too often, sending someone to a nursing home is the same as signing their death certificate.

A study done at the Johns Hopkins School of Public Health found that over 10 per cent of people sent to nursing homes were dead or back in the hospital *within four weeks.* Of these, three quarters were dead!

In another study, more than two thirds of all nursing home patients had not had an adequate physical exam within a year—despite the fact that most were taking one to four drugs!

These studies point out the poor level of care in most nursing homes. Few even think of rehabilitating their patients. Most give merely custodial care.

If you must consider using a nursing home, you should look for the following things:

(1) skilled nursing care—one registered nurse (R.N.) and one licensed practical nurse (L.P.N.) on duty at all times for every thirty patients. There should also be an aide for each five patients

(2) rehabilitation—patients gotten out of bed, encouraged to use walkers, etc. A physical therapist in attendance to give exercises, prevent stiffening of the limbs ("contractures") in bedridden patients

(3) physician care—a doctor's visit, including a complete history and physical exam, once each month

(5) lab tests—a complete blood count (CBC), urinalysis, chest film, Pap smear (females), fasting blood sugar, and stool exam for blood—all at least once every few months.

(6) records—daily nurses' notes on each patient, kept in his own record

(7) vital signs—pulse, blood pressure, temperature, respiratory rate, and weight—all checked by a nurse at least once a week and, ideally, once each day

(8) dietary care—the services of a full-time dietician

(9) other services—speech therapy, occupational therapy, dental care, recreational and spiritual activities, etc.

You should visit several prospective nursing homes with these things in mind. In general, as with hospitals, *non-profit nursing homes provide the best care.* (Unlike hospitals, however, most nursing homes are for-profit operations.)

When you visit the nursing home, make sure you see all parts of it. Look in the kitchen, the baths and showers, the physical and occupational therapy sections.

Ask the administrator questions: "What is your R.N.-to-patient ratio?" "Your L.P.N.-to-patient ratio?" "Your nurse's aide-to-patient ratio?"

Use your own eyes and ears. Look to see how many patients are up and around, as opposed to lying in bed. Listen to the noise level —too quiet homes may be a sign that all the patients are drugged into a stupor. Use your nose: the smell of urine or feces can mean only one thing: somewhere a patient is lying in them.

These are the hard, unpleasant things you must look for if you are to make a sensible nursing home choice. You will have very little to guide you but your own wits and inquisitiveness. Nursing home administrators may not always be eager to answer your questions, or to make a thorough inspection of their premises.

One administrator, writes Susan Jacoby in a New York *Times* special article on nursing homes, "told me not to ask questions from a 'so-called consumer checklist.'" Nursing home personnel, Ms. Jacoby notes, often avoided her questions or claimed not to know the answers.

There are two sources of "objective" information about nursing homes, of which you should be aware. These are:

(1) State health departments—Many rank homes by quality; Connecticut, for instance, has an A-to-E ranking system, with those homes which offer the most services (though not necessarily the best care) getting an A rating.

(2) Federal government—By law, nursing home inspection reports for Medicare and Medicaid must be available to the public. These reports may be found at the regional offices of HEW's Social Security Administration (for Medicare) or the Social and Rehabilitation Service (for Medicaid). (If a home is not good enough to meet Medicare criteria, it should not even be considered, since these quality criteria are minimal, indeed.)

Finally, the Department of Health, Education and Welfare publishes a consumer checklist for nursing homes. The stock number is 1761–00032. It is available from the Superintendent of Documents, U. S. Government Printing Office, Washington, D.C. 20402 ($.40).

9

Surgeons and surgery

One of my classmates in medical school had always wanted to be a surgeon. Even while still in college, he had haunted the experimental labs, eager for a chance to assist in an operation on one of the animals. In medical school he was already more skilled in surgical procedure than any of us.

Once he actually got onto the surgical wards, his bias was clearly evident. He was constantly urging surgery. He would criticize other doctors for failing to realize that their patients' salvation obviously lay in the hands of the surgeons.

"This guy with ulcers," he'd say. "They've had him up there on the medical service three days now. They've given him more than six pints of blood and he's still bleeding. When are they gonna realize he needs an operation?"

An exasperated look would come into his eyes, a look of incomprehension.

"Why," I once asked my classmate, "did you choose surgery?"

He looked at me as though the question were a ridiculous one.

"Because," he replied, "I like to cut."

American doctors, like my friend, seem to be enamored of surgery as a form of treatment. Operation rates in this country are double those in England and Wales. If you are hospitalized, the chances you will wind up on the operating table are fifty-fifty—nearly twice as high as in Sweden.

There is something about surgery that seems to appeal to us—both doctors and patients alike. Maybe it's the notion that the surgeon, with a stroke of the scalpel, can wipe away disease and save our life. Indeed, many doctors look upon surgeons as the only members of their profession who can actually "cure" their patients. More surgery, they feel, means less disease and fewer deaths.

It is only recently that a few physicians have started to question this assumption.

"More surgery," bluntly asserts Dr. John Bunker, "means *more* deaths."

Bunker is a Harvard professor and has spent more time studying surgery and surgeons than probably anyone else. Those locales, he points out, where operation rates are highest, also have higher death rates. Indeed, Bunker points out that death rates in the United States are much higher—under age sixty-five—than in most other developed nations. He raises the possibility that these excess deaths may be due to our national love for surgery.

How dangerous is surgery?

All surgery carries some element of risk. A routine D and C can result in a postoperative uterine infection. The surgeon doing a tonsillectomy may accidentally perforate the internal carotid artery and be faced with a rapidly exsanguinating patient.

These complications, though rare, do happen.

In one study of several thousand operations in thirty-four different hospitals, the death rate from surgery was about 2 per cent. The operations ran the gamut from tonsillectomies and hernia repairs to open-heart procedures. Emergency surgery as well as scheduled or "elective" surgery was included. Only operations which required *general anesthesia* (where the patient is "put to sleep") were included.*

From this careful study, then, it seems clear that the risk of death from surgery is not inconsequential. Even elective operations (95 per cent of all surgery) carry with them, in John Bunker's words, a "discrete and measurable risk of death."

Here are the most common causes of death during and after surgery:

—uncontrolled hermorrhage (bleeding)
—infection
—metabolic disorders (abnormal blood sodium, potassium, sugar, etc.)
—body temperature disorders
—embolism

These complications are often related as much to the anesthesia as to the surgery itself. A long operation under general anesthesia

---

* This is sometimes called "major" surgery. Major surgery has also been defined as surgery in which a "major body cavity" is opened.

increases your risk of developing post-op pneumonia. General anesthesia for long periods in a chilly operating room can lower body temperature, which can result in death. (There is also a rare and dangerous disease in which patients react to anesthesia with "hyperthermia" or very high body temperatures.)

These anesthesia risks are part and parcel of the risks of surgery (see below for more on anesthesia).

Which operations are most often done—and overdone?

Recently, a young public health worker and former surgeon, Edward Hughes, decided to examine the habits of his surgical colleagues. Hughes looked at the operations most often done by two different groups of surgeons—those working in a large medical school-affiliated hospital, and a second group in a smaller, unaffiliated suburban one.

He found some striking differences (Table 25).

TABLE 25   Most Common Surgical Procedures in Two Hospitals

MEDICAL SCHOOL-AFFILIATED HOSPITAL	SUBURBAN (NON-AFFILIATED) HOSPITAL
(1) Hernia repair	Hernia repair
(2) Appendectomy	Removal of skin lesion
(3) Gallbladder removal (cholecystectomy)	Appendectomy
(4) Breast biopsy	Gallbladder removal
(5) Removal of stomach, partial (partial gastrectomy)	Breast biopsy
(6) Removal of large intestine, partial	Hemorrhoidectomy
(7) Removal of skin lesion	Tonsillectomy
(8) Open reduction of bone fracture	D and C of uterus
(9) Interruption of vagus nerve (vagotomy)	Excision of varicose veins
(10) Abdominal exploration	Suture of skin
(11) Amputation of leg	Hernia repair, abdominal wall
(12) Incision of peripheral blood vessel	Incision of skin and subcutaneous tissues
(13) Incision of skin and subcutaneous tissues	Removal of uterus (hysterectomy)
(14) Colostomy	Removal of thyroid, partial (thyroidectomy, partial)
(15) Skin graft	Closed reduction of fracture
(16) Excision of varicose veins	Removal of veins

TABLE 25   Most Common Surgical Procedures in Two Hospitals

MEDICAL SCHOOL-AFFILIATED HOSPITAL	SUBURBAN (NON-AFFILIATED) HOSPITAL
(17) Biopsy of lymph node	Removal of breast (radical mastectomy)
(18) Hernia repair, abdominal wall	Removal of stomach, partial (partial gastrectomy)
(19) Repair of diaphragmatic hernia	Removal of large intestine, partial
(20) Closure of colostomy or other artificial stoma	Excision of lesion of muscle, tendon, etc.

SOURCE: Adapted from Hughes, E. F. X., et al. "Operative Workloads in One Hospital's General Surgical Residency Program," *New Engl. J. of Med.*, vol. 289, 1973.

The suburban surgeons did many more operations. And they seemed to have certain "favorites"—operations that were done much more often than at the larger medical center.

These "overdone" operations are:

Hemorrhoid repair (hemorrhoidectomy)
Tonsillectomy (with or without adenoidectomy)
D and C (dilation and curettage of uterus)
Hysterectomy (removal of uterus and, usually, ovaries)
Thyroidectomy
Varicose vein removal
Radical mastectomy (removal of breast and surrounding tissue)

Interestingly enough, these procedures are not only more often done in suburbia than at the major medical center, they are more often done in the United States, as a whole, than in either England or Wales, along with two other operations—hernia repairs and gallbladder removals.

Are these operations done "too much"?

There can be little doubt that they are. In one of the Columbia hospital studies, half of all hysterectomies were done for questionable indications. It is hard to believe that there are enough persons who need part or all of their thyroid gland excised to make this one of the most popular procedures on the surgical hit parade!

How can you avoid unneeded surgery?

Any operation—even the "favorites" listed above—can have its valid indications. There are several things you can do to make sure that you undergo surgery only when it is needed.

Principle: You should not go to a general surgeon (or a surgical specialist) for your primary medical care.

This might seem like an obvious rule. Yet I know a surprising number of people who disregard it. I know people who use surgeons as their family doctors. Or women whose gynecologist is their sole source of health advice.

This is a dangerous practice. Surgeons tend to have a way of finding things which require surgery. (It is probably no accident that doctors in general, who have the most contact with surgeons, also undergo the most surgery!) On the other hand, "medical men" (internists, family practice specialists, pediatricians, etc.) tend to try to avoid surgery, if possible.

If your primary care physician—usually an internist—refers you for surgery, you can be fairly sure he is doing it as a "last resort."

Principle: You should obtain the opinions of at least two surgeons before having surgery.

This is another way—perhaps the best—to protect yourself against unneeded surgery. The United Mine Workers found, a few years ago, that their members were having too much surgery. So the union instituted this rule—that all operations be endorsed by a preoperative surgical specialist's consultation. The results: 75 per cent less hysterectomies, 60 per cent less appendectomies, 35 per cent fewer hemorrhoidectomies.

You can get a second surgical opinion by simply going to the outpatient department of any medical school-affiliated hospital, or any teaching hospital. Or you can ask your primary care physician (*not* the surgeon) to refer you to another surgeon.

Principle: You should make sure that all surgeons you consult are Board-certified in the appropriate specialty. Each should also, ideally, be a Fellow of the American College of Surgeons (F.A.C.S.).

Half of all the operations in the United States are done by GPs or other physicians who are not Board-certified surgeons. Any doctor can call himself a "surgeon." This term may mean only that, on occasion, he performs surgery. Needless to say, this is not the kind of "surgeon" you would want taking out your gallbladder.

In the Columbia hospital studies, the chances of receiving satis-

162 TALK BACK TO YOUR DOCTOR

factory care were *one and one half times greater* if the surgeon was
Board-certified! (For a discussion of surgery by interns and residents, see below.) Table 26 lists the various surgical specialties in
which physicians can be Board-certified.

TABLE 26 Surgical Specialties and Their Major Functions

SPECIALTY	FUNCTIONS
General surgery	surgery of all parts of the body, particularly the abdomen; most common operations being for conditions of the intestines, including hernias
Neurosurgery	surgery of the brain, spine, and peripheral nerves
Obstetrics and Gynecology	surgery of the female reproductive organs (vagina, uterus, tubes and ovaries); surgery connected with childbirth (Cesarean section)
Ophthalmology	surgery of the eye and surrounding structures
Orthopedic surgery	surgery of the bones, tendons, muscles, joints, etc.
Otolaryngology	surgery of the ear, nose, throat, and larynx
Plastic surgery	surgery for repair and improvement of deformities, particularly of the skin and subcutaneous tissues
Proctology	surgery of the colon and rectum
Thoracic surgery	surgery of the lungs, esophagus and related organs in the chest including surgery of the heart and blood vessels
Urology	surgery of the urinary tract (kidneys, ureters, bladder, urethra) and of the male genitals

You can find out if any surgeon is Board-certified by looking in
the *Directory of Medical Specialists*. Or you may call your local
county medical society. Or you may ask the surgeon directly. (To
find out if any surgeon is a Fellow of the American College of Surgeons, write the college at 55 E. Erie St., Chicago, Ill. 60611. The
Directory also has this information.)

**Principle: You should insist that your surgeon(s) allow you to make
an informed choice regarding surgery.**

No surgeon should "sell" you the idea of surgery. He should present the facts you need to make an informed decision for yourself.

If he does not—or can not—do this, you should consult another surgeon.

If I were advised to have surgery, I would want to know several things in order to make an informed decision. I would want to know, first, the likelihood that my condition would be cured, remedied, or made better by the procedure. I would want to know the risk of death or serious disability from the operation, or from its complications. Finally, I would want to know the likelihood of benefit and the risks of *not* having surgery, or of having some other treatment.

Let's take a specific and common example. Suppose I had an abdominal hernia. I know, as a physician, that for a young man with a hernia surgery is considered the treatment of choice (the only other treatment is wearing a truss). To allow the hernia to go untreated is dangerous because it can "strangulate"—become swollen and unable to be pushed back into the abdomen. If this happens, surgery carries a much higher death rate—some 10–25 per cent.

Since my chances of surviving surgery, as a young, healthy person would be quite good—virtually 100 per cent—and the risks of not having surgery would be considerable, an operation would seem justified.

Here are some other specific examples:

Case 9–1: A forty-seven-year-old woman is found by Pap smear to have early (non-invasive) cervical cancer. If untreated, her cancer will progress to invasive disease and, eventually, to death in a few years. With surgery, her chance of a five-year cure is nearly 100 per cent. No other form of treatment (drugs, radiation) has this high a five-year survival rate for this type of cancer. The surgical mortality is low (about 0.5 per cent). The total dollar costs are about $1,000 and the hospital stay, about ten days. If the ovaries are also removed, the patient may need hormone replacement treatment, at an added cost.

Comment: In this case, surgery is clearly indicated. Not having surgery will almost surely result in death within perhaps three to six years. Surgery can virtually guarantee a permanent cure.

Best decision: Surgery.

Case 9–2: A forty-seven-year-old woman is found on x-ray to have stones in her gallbladder. She has had no symptoms that can be ascribed to the stones. Without surgery there is a small, but definite chance that her gallstones could cause trouble (an acute inflammation of the gallbladder and surrounding structures). The chances of this might be 1–2 per cent over the next ten years. Surgery to remedy such an acute "flare-up" would entail a much higher mortality (perhaps 10 per cent) than "elective" surgery (again, about 0.5 per cent). The costs of surgery are about $1,000 and the hospital stay is ten days.

Comment: In this case the decision is less straightforward. Like the hernia example, surgery here is for preventive reasons—to eliminate the small, but serious, chance of a flare-up. On the other hand, if the surgeon is unskilled the operation can cause complications which require more surgery.

Best decision: Probably surgery.

Case 9–3: A sixty-eight-year-old man is discovered to have an abdominal hernia. The chances of the hernia strangulating are about 1–4 per cent over the rest of his lifetime. Were this to occur, emergency surgery would be needed and would carry a mortality rate of 10–25 per cent. The mortality rate for "elective" surgery in a man this age is 1.3 per cent. The chances of the hernia "coming back" are, with a good surgeon, about 2 per cent, and this would require another operation.† The only other effective form of treatment is wearing a truss (corset).

Comment: This case (for which I am indebted to Professor Duncan Neuhauser of the Harvard School of Public Health) presents a new dilemma. The chances of the elderly patient dying from the operation and a possible repeat operation (assuming a good surgeon) are:

$$.013 + (.02)(.013) = 1.33\%$$

The chances of the patient dying from *not* having surgery are, at the most:

$$(.04)(.25) = 1\%$$

Thus it seems that even with the best surgeon, the patient would still be better off not having surgery and wearing a truss.

Best decision: Probably no surgery.

Sometimes, as this last case shows, balancing the risks of surgery versus no surgery can be important, and hard. There may be key facts which are not precisely available. There may be a new surgical technique, or a new medical treatment, which alters the balance.

In any event, your primary care physician and surgeon bear the responsibility of presenting you with the best, most up-to-date information on hand. They have the responsibility of allowing you, and only you, to make an informed choice.

† This "repeat rate" may be as high as 20 per cent with a poor surgeon!

Will joining a prepaid health plan save you from surgery?

Again, as with hospital care in general, the answer is a resounding "yes!" Wherever they have been studied, prepaid plans have saved their enrollees thousands of surgical admissions.

Why is this so?

Some have suggested it is because prepaid plans employ salaried doctors who have no dollar incentive to operate on their patients. Others have pointed out that prepaid plans emphasize preventive care which might prevent certain types of surgery.

Whatever the reason, joining a prepaid plan can diminish the chances that you will require surgery—perhaps by as much as half!

Your chances of having surgery will also be less if you obtain your primary care from a Neighborhood Health Center (see Chapter 2). At one such center, run by Tufts University Medical School in Boston, surgical admissions fell by more than 75 per cent after the center opened. These primary care centers (where doctors are also, by the way, on salary) seem to be doing a good job of keeping their patients out of the operating room.

What should you know about your surgical anesthesia?

Anesthesia (literally, absence of feeling) is a prerequisite for surgery. And, in many instances, this means general anesthesia in which the patient is "asleep" during the operation. In other cases, "local" or "regional" anesthesia can be used.

Principle: In general, the risk of surgery is less if general anesthesia can be avoided.

I remember an eighty-year-old man, frail-looking, who showed up on the surgical service one day with a hernia. He wanted the hernia repaired, but the surgeons were none too anxious to operate. They feared that, given general anesthesia, he would not survive the procedure. They were afraid he would develop pneumonia, or other lung complications from inhaling the anesthetic gases.

But the old man was adamant. He wanted his hernia fixed. He asked the surgeons why they had to put him to sleep. He asked the same question of his anesthetist.

The anesthetist agreed. General anesthesia was not needed. Local anesthesia with Novocaine could, he thought, probably be used, though he warned the patient that—if trouble developed—it might be necessary to resort to general anesthesia.

The operation took place. The patient was wheeled into the OR, washed, and draped. Then the local anesthetic was injected around the nerves in his groin, numbing the entire area of the hernia. The surgeon made sure the whole region was numb. Then, carefully, he made his incision. The whole procedure went without a hitch. The old man was awake all the time, but he felt nothing except the pressure of the surgeon's fingers.

"It felt," he said later, "like they were playing the piano on my stomach."

This case illustrates an important point. Many surgical procedures usually done under general anesthesia can be done under another type, if necessary. If you are aged, or if you have a history of lung problems such as asthma or emphysema, you should seriously investigate these other types of anesthesia, in order to lessen the risk of surgery.

Principle: You should make certain that your anesthesia will be done by a Board-certified anesthesiologist.

An anesthesiologist is a doctor who is a specialist in anesthesia. It is his job (usually with the surgeon) to select the most appropriate type of anesthesia to be used. During surgery he is also responsible for maintaining all the body's vital functions.

In the United States *less than half* of all anesthesia is administered by a physician anesthesiologist!‡

Someone who is not an anesthesiologist—but who administers anesthesia—is called an "anesthetist." In smaller hospitals, it is common to use a *nurse anesthetist* to administer anesthesia. Some hospitals even use registered nurses *with no special training* to administer anesthesia.

I believe if it is important enough to put someone to sleep for surgery, it is important enough to use an anesthesiologist. Virtually all doctors, I am sure, would demand one for their own operation. Consumers should do the same.

You should be familiar with the different types of anesthesia in common use. *Inhalation anesthesia* is the most common form. Ether,

‡ This includes teaching hospital cases where anesthesia is given by an anesthesia resident, with a Board-certified anesthesiologist inside, or in close proximity to, the OR during the surgery.

nitrous oxide ("laughing gas"), halothane—all are anesthetic gases which are given to the patient (usually in combination with oxygen) to inhale. The gases pass from the lungs into the bloodstream, and are carried to the brain, where they induce anesthesia.

Intravenous anesthesia is where a drug—usually sodium pentothal —is injected directly into the bloodstream via a vein. This method will put the patient to sleep almost at once. It is commonly used for quick procedures, such as abortions. It is also often used before inhalation anesthesia, since it is much more pleasant to be put to sleep with pentothal than with a gas such as ether.

Spinal anesthesia is a form in which a needle is introduced into the fluid surrounding the spinal cord (as in a spinal tap) and a drug is injected. The drug is actually a local anesthetic. It "blocks" pain impulses in the spinal cord and causes anesthesia in the legs and pelvis. This form of anesthesia has proven most useful in childbirth.

Epidural anesthesia is similar to spinal in that a local anesthetic is injected through a needle. But the drug is injected into an area (the epidural sac) which is outside of the spinal fluid. Epidural anesthesia has advantages over spinal, especially in childbirth. Its disadvantage is that it requires a skilled operator to administer.

Local anesthetic drugs can also be administered around a peripheral nerve, a *nerve block*. For example, anesthesia can be caused in the hand by injecting a local anesthetic such Novocaine or Xylocaine around a nerve in the elbow. (This is the kind of anesthesia our aged hernia patient had.) Finally, such drugs may, of course, be injected into the skin and other tissues for minor surgery, such as excision of a skin cyst.

Everyone has heard of patients who have a bad reaction to anesthesia. This can be a truly tragic occurrence. People can have adverse reactions to anesthetic drugs, as with any other kind of drug. These reactions can be so serious as to involve cardiac and/or breathing arrest—a life-threatening state.

It is your doctor's job—either the surgeon or anesthesiologist—to ask you about any prior drug allergies you might have experienced. He should also ask about any prior anesthesia you have had—and how it was tolerated. Many anesthetic drugs such as Novocaine (Xylocaine, Pontocaine, etc.) can be tested for an allergic reaction by placing a drop in the patient's eye, or under the skin. Though not foolproof, your doctor can employ this test to determine the safety of these local anesthetic agents.

Your doctor should also ask you about any past history of liver or kidney disease, before anesthesia. Certain anesthetic agents are eliminated from the body by these organs. Pre-existing impairment could affect the doctor's choice of the anesthetic drug.

Finally, your doctor should ask about any other drugs you might be taking. Anesthetics can cause dangerous reactions with a number of other drugs, particularly tranquilizers, anti-depressants, sedatives, and drugs to lower blood pressure.

Should you choose a surgeon who works "part time"?

More than one hundred years ago, Sir James Simpson, a Scottish physician and discoverer of the anesthetic property of chloroform, made another important discovery. He found that those surgeons who did the most amputations had the lowest mortality rates following this procedure. Doctors who did few amputations, had high rates.

James Simpson's observation still holds true today. A recent study showed that one surgeon who did a great deal of open-heart surgery had a death rate of below 5 per cent, while twelve others who "were technically qualified but lacked practice" had a 30 per cent death rate. One of these twelve lost every patient!

Principle: You should select a surgeon who operates at least ten hours each week.

Edward Hughes, himself a former surgeon, queried a number of other surgeons, in a medical school-affiliated hospital. All agreed that surgery is no place for a "part-timer." According to these expert surgeons, any doctor who does surgery ought to operate about ten hours each week to keep his skills up to par.

The American Board of Surgery requires that, in their last year of training, surgical residents should do at least 150 major operations during the year. This number comes out to roughly ten hours of OR time per week.

Many surgeons, however, spend far less time in the OR. Hughes found that his suburban general surgeons spent, on average, about *five hours* at the operating table. Some 10,000 GPs do "part-time" surgery.

Clearly, it is to your advantage to avoid surgeons who do only a few operations per week. You would do well to ascertain that your prospective surgeon operates every day, for a minimum of two hours.

Which operations carry the most risk?

Some operations are more dangerous than others. They require more surgical dexterity and experience. They require more decisions "at the table" and are less able to be performed "by the book."

Some operations require the set-up and use of complex equipment, such as a heart-lung machine used in open-heart surgery. Or they require more meticulous attention to postoperative details.

Principle: Your surgeon should be able to tell you the risk of death or disability involved in your operation. He should also be able to tell you the operation's success rate.

In general, the longer time an operation requires, the greater its complexity—and thus its risk. I have listed several surgical procedures, and have grouped them according to their complexity and the amount of OR time they involve (Table 27).

TABLE 27   Common Surgical Procedures and Their Degree of Difficulty

Group I: Least Difficult (OR time usually less than 1 hour)
Tonsillectomy
D and C
Breast biopsy
Circumcision
Hemorrhoidectomy
Incision and drainage of superficial abscess
Skin graft (except face)
Biopsy of superficial lymph nodes
Repair of vagina and/or rectum

Group II: Somewhat Difficult (OR time usually 1–2 hours)
Appendectomy
Hernia repair
Varicose vein excision
Colostomy
Leg amputation
Gallbladder removal (cholecystectomy)
Spleen removal (splenectomy)
Thyroid removal, partial (thyroidectomy, partial)
Removal of uterus and/or ovaries (hysterectomy and/or ovariectomy)
Repair of bladder

Group III: Fairly Difficult (OR time usually 2–3 hours)
Total breast removal (radical mastectomy)
Removal of part of intestines or stomach (colectomy, gastrectomy, etc.)
Hip repair and insertion of artificial hip (arthroplasty)

TABLE 27 Common Surgical Procedures and Their Degree of Difficulty

Group III: Fairly Difficult (OR time usually 2–3 hours)
  Repair of muscles or ligaments
  Removal of lung, partial (lobectomy)

Group IV: Most Difficult (OR time usually over 3 hours)
  Repair of kidney and/or ureters
  Repair of aorta or peripheral arteries
  Repair of peripheral nerves
  Radical neck dissection (cancer removal procedure)
  Repair of heart valve(s) with insertion of artificial valve(s) (valvuloplasty)
  Repair of congenital heart lesions (closure of atrial or ventricular septal
    defect)

What tests should your surgeon do before surgery?

Surgery presents your body with a severe stress. Anything which renders you less capable of meeting this stress will increase your risk. Advanced age, concurrent illness or infection, poor nutrition— all these can increase the risk from surgery. (Available data suggest that the risk of death from surgery in persons over 65 is 2–4 times that in younger adults.)

The best surgeons will look you over quite carefully before surgery. They will think of you, coldly, as a "good" or a "not-so-good" risk. Sometimes they will delay surgery for the purpose of getting you in better shape (losing weight, clearing up an infection, etc.).

Needless to say, it is to your best interest to avoid being a "poor" risk. *It is up to you to help your surgeon make this assessment.* You should make sure he knows about all your medical (non-surgical) conditions, no matter how trivial they may seem. Make sure he knows if you are below your normal weight or otherwise debilitated. Tell him if you have had a recent respiratory infection or other acute illness.

Your surgeon, in turn, ought to make sure you have had the following prior to any major surgery:

(1) a chest x-ray
(2) an electrocardiogram
(3) a complete blood count (CBC)
(4) a urinalysis
(5) a skin test for tuberculosis
(6) pulmonary function studies, for surgery inside the chest
(7) a blood sugar (fasting) and a test of kidney function (creatinine, blood urea nitrogen)

In addition, you should have a "medical consult" in the hospital if you have any concurrent non-surgical illness (diabetes, for instance). Finally, you should be visited by the anesthesiologist or anesthesia resident prior to your operation, as well as by a pulmonary physiotherapist, who will instruct you in postoperative breathing exercises (to minimize the likelihood of lung infection).

These preoperative precautions are all part of good surgery. The surgeon who ignores them does so at his—and at your—peril. Yet all too many surgeons do. In one survey, done by the Commission on Professional and Hospital Activities, nearly half of all patients over age forty had no electrocardiogram prior to surgery. Nearly one-third had no chest x-ray. You should make certain you are not the recipient of this kind of careless preparation.

Is it safe to be operated on by an intern or resident?

Many persons who would readily consent to being a "ward" patient—and to being cared for by interns and residents—for a medical ailment, balk at doing the same for a surgical one. Surgery, they argue, is one area where experience is paramount. It is an area where one mistake can result in death on the operating table.

"I wouldn't want an intern doing his first appendectomy on me," one friend told me, with conviction.

The same person quickly acknowledged that surgeons must come from somewhere—in other words, that every surgeon must, at some time, perform his first appendectomy, his first gallbladder removal, his first open-heart operation, etc.

"But not on me," he repeated.

Is an intern, or a resident, a "worse" surgeon than someone who is fully trained? This is not as easy a question to answer as one might think.

An intern doing his first hernia repair (a traditional "beginning" procedure for surgeons-in-training) might, it's true, be a little shaky. On the other hand, a hernia is not a very risky operation (I'm speaking of an "elective" hernia, of course). The fledgling surgeon will have "prepared" for his debut by assisting another surgeon. When he makes his first incision, he will do so under the direct supervision of a more senior surgeon.

Such a "teaching" hernia case will, doubtless, take a bit longer

than one done by an experienced surgeon. But this added time should
not be long enough to entail added risk.

In a top-notch teaching hospital, then, there should be virtually
no difference between the results of an intern's first hernia, and a
senior staff man's. For you, the patient, the quality of care should be
exactly the same.

But what about "harder," more dangerous procedures?

Here too, it is difficult to say who does the better job. There have
been few studies of this issue—and their results are far from definitive. In one, patients operated upon by residents for gallbladder
disease had death rates twice as high as those operated upon by
fully trained Board-certified surgeons. On the other hand, it is well
known that teaching hospitals attract sicker patients, and this may
have explained the difference in mortality.

In the Columbia hospital studies, interns and residents handled
nearly all their cases in an "optimal" manner—a higher percentage
than that of fully trained surgeons.

From my own personal experience, I think I would actually prefer
being a "ward" surgical patient—including being operated upon by
an intern or resident—for most surgical conditions (assuming, of
course, that the "ward" was one in a medical school hospital). By
and large, I'd rather take my chances with the "ward" system than
with most general surgeons. A resident on a busy "ward" service will
operate often. He will operate under the supervision of expert surgeons. And—perhaps most important—he is not likely to "bite off
more than he can chew": to operate "over his head."

I would, I think, prefer to have a fully trained surgeon (still in a
medical school hospital) for certain very complex procedures—
open-heart surgery is one example. These are situations where, I
believe, experience and teamwork count for a great deal. Even in
such situations, however, I would be the first to admit that there is
no objective evidence that a surgical resident, working under
proper supervision, will do any worse a job of open-heart surgery
than will the fully trained surgeon.

I would stress, again, that I am talking about surgical residents in
medical school-affiliated hospitals. These hospitals would be my first
choice—and that of most doctors—for all but the most minor surgery.
Modern surgery demands many people—surgeons, anesthesiologists,
scrub nurses, technicians—who operate together many times each
week. The large teaching hospital best meets this condition.

How long should you stay in the hospital for surgery?

Surgery need not entail a long hospital stay. In fact, surgical patients generally stay in the hospital less time than non-surgical cases. But it is also true that *surgical patients often stay in the hospital longer than is medically necessary.*

One common reason is *delay of surgery.* Operating room space is scarce. Use of the OR must be scheduled in advance. Elective surgery may have to be canceled if an emergency case comes along.

Often, however, the only reason for delay of surgery is hospital or physician inefficiency. Sometimes your doctor may neglect to schedule your OR time. Or he may tell his secretary, who forgets. Or the OR supervisor may get the request but, for whatever reason, it may get lost in the shuffle.

In any case, it is to your interest to make sure—before you enter the hospital—that OR space is reserved for your surgery. If there are diagnostic tests (x-rays, endoscopy, etc.), these should, of course, be scheduled as well. (As mentioned before, it is best to have as many diagnostic procedures as possible done as an outpatient, before entering the hospital.)

You can influence your hospital stay by timing your day of admission. As mentioned earlier, do not enter the hospital before a weekend or holiday. The best time to enter the hospital is at the start of a full work week.

Also, it is best if your surgery is done during the week, rather than just before a weekend, when nursing and other staffs are likely to be at less than full strength.

One disadvantage to being a "ward" patient is that you will stay in the hospital longer. Ward stays may be as much as two to four days longer than those for non-ward (private and semiprivate) patients.

Why do ward patients stay longer?

Often their longer stay is due to the inexperience of the intern or resident "working up" the case. In July and August, interns and residents are likely to be new at their hospitals. They do not know the routine. They have to get used to new ways of scheduling procedures and surgery. This often results in needless delays. If you do enter the hospital as a "ward" patient, you should try to avoid the months of July and August.

Ward patients also stay longer for another reason: often priority for OR space and other procedures is given to patients of private physicians. This is, unfortunately, a fact, though it may be denied by hospitals and doctors. A private surgeon may do his own case first and then, time permitting, he may do a ward case, supervising the intern or resident (acting as the attending physician).

This practice of giving priority to private or semiprivate patients is not only unfortunate, it is indefensible. Yet I have seen it happen in the best hospitals. (Not, of course, where an "emergency" is involved.) It is something you should be aware of, though it is not necessarily a reason for you not to be a ward patient.

Table 28 shows hospital stays for various surgical procedures. You can use it as a guide to how long your surgical stay should be.

TABLE 28 Length of Stay for Common Surgical Procedures

	DAYS
Tonsillectomy	1–2
D and C	1–3
Breast biopsy	3–4
Varicose vein excision	5–6
Hemorrhoidectomy	5–6
Thyroidectomy	5–7
Lens (cataract) extraction	5–7
Appendectomy	5–7
Mastectomy	8–10
Hysterectomy	8–10
Cholecystectomy (gall-bladder removal)	13–15
Prostatectomy	14–16
Vagotomy and pyloroplasty (ulcer operation)	13–15
Gastrectomy (stomach removal)	25–26
Colectomy (removal part or all of large bowel)	26–27
Splenectomy (removal of spleen)	24–26
Lobectomy (removal one lobe of lung)	26–27
Surgery on arteries of legs, arms, etc.	28–30
Open-heart surgery	more than 1 month

How crucial is postoperative care?

Postoperative care is as important in keeping down your stay and in getting you out of the hospital healthy as what happens in the operating room. Pulmonary physiotherapy (post-op breathing exercises) has been mentioned. Ordinary physiotherapy may also be useful, particularly when surgery has involved joints or muscles.

Principle: You should not consent to surgery in a hospital without adequate facilities for postoperative care.

Many hospitals lack such facilities. Amazing as it may seem, some one fifth of all private hospitals have no *recovery room* for their post-op patients.

What is a recovery room?

A recovery room is, essentially, an intensive care unit for post-surgical cases. It should have equipment for continuous monitoring of heart action and respirators for assisting breathing, if necessary. It should have a machine for administering external cardiac shock in cases of heart stoppage. It should have materials for giving intravenous fluids and blood.

Most important, the recovery room should have its own staff. It should be run by a physician anesthesiologist. It should have registered nurses—about one per one to two patients—who have been trained to deal with post-op problems. It should be visited by respiratory therapists, who will help you cough and inflate your lungs as soon as you awaken from anesthesia.

All these things, and more, make an adequate recovery room.

You can determine if your hospital *says* it has a recovery room by consulting the American Hospital Association's *Guide Issue* (see Chapter 8). In addition, you should also ask your own doctor about the adequacy of the hospital's post-op care. If you have doubts, ask a hospital nurse. Or make a visit yourself, if possible.

10

Women and children last

When it comes to health care, women and children are definitely the "forgotten" health consumers. These two groups are forgotten in many regards. They do not have the benefit—as do most males—of job-related health exams. They often lack decent health insurance coverage. The care they do receive is frequently cursory and below par.

Do women receive poorer health care than men?

This is a question which, to my knowledge, has never been rigorously studied. Women live longer than men. But this may have little to do with the kind of medical care they get. Women may, in other words, live longer *despite*—and not because of—their medical care.

The most frequent complaint I hear from women is that their doctor does not give their case the attention which it deserves—or as much attention as he would give a man with the same problem. Doctors, they say, do not take as careful a history. They rush through the physical exam. They fail to do enough diagnostic tests.

"This guy never touched me," says one woman. "He just sat there behind his desk, and wrote out a prescription."

Principle: The failure to do an adequate diagnostic work-up is something women should be aware of.

Here are some examples, taken from hospital records:

Case 10–1: Forty-two-year-old female . . . Admitted for cough, back pain. Discharge diagnosis: acute pyelonephritis [kidney infection], bronchopneumonia. No clinical or x-ray evidence of pneumonia. No urine culture. No urinary tract studies.

Case 10–2: Twenty-four-year-old . . . Headache, nausea, vomiting. Discharge diagnosis: migraine. No neurological examination. Therapy bizarre: steroids, antibiotics, vitamin B_{12}, etc.

Case 10–3: Thirty-four-year-old . . . Admitted for fever, nausea, abdominal pain . . . treated as pyelitis [kidney infection] . . . Gynecological examination inadequate. No smear or culture. Urine culture negative, hence antibiotics (3) not indicated . . .

Case 10–4: Forty-three-year-old . . . Bronchial pneumonia. History of three prior respiratory illnesses and father dying of tuberculosis. No investigation of tuberculosis made . . .

Case 10–5: Fifty-eight-year-old . . . Diabetic with five-month history of loss of vision. No central nervous system evaluation. No fundoscopic [eye exam with ophthalmoscope]. Albuminuria [albumin in urine] not investigated . . .

All these cases represent a common phenomenon: the failure of physicians to do an adequate diagnostic work-up on their patients, all of whom were women. Needless to say, any of these patients could have as easily been a male. But, from my own personal experience, I believe that women are more likely to be the victims of this kind of "short-shrift" diagnosis than men.

Are women intimidated by doctors?

Many women tend to be awed by their (male) physicians. As a result, they fail to be as demanding in regard to their care as they ought to be. They fail to demand an adequate explanation from him of his diagnosis and treatment.

"Why," I once asked a woman friend who had called me for advice, "didn't you ask your doctor about that during your visit?"

"I don't know," she replied. "I was so nervous. All I wanted to do was get out of there."

As someone who has been a patient myself, I can understand this reaction. There is a tremendous temptation, when visiting the doctor, to grab your prescription and run—without any discussion or questions. The attitude of many doctors toward women patients only encourages this sort of behavior.

You should fight this impulse. You should, as I have said earlier, make certain that you fully understand your diagnosis and how it was arrived at. You should understand the rationale for your treatment.

You should not feel guilty about "wasting the doctor's time with questions." As mentioned earlier, your doctor ought to spend at least one half hour with you. I have spoken to many women who—despite the fact that they were in their doctor's office considerably less time—still felt guilty at prolonging their visit by questions!

Your questions are a useful way to "slow up" any doctor who is trying to rush you out of his office. Asking one question will also give you time, if you are flustered, to think of others. While I do not advocate "questions for questions' sake," this can be a useful technique for you to overcome your anxiety at a doctor's brusqueness.

I have already suggested many questions you might wish to ask, in earlier chapters. Here are a few of the most useful:

"Doctor, what is my final diagnosis?"

"How common is my condition?"

"What is the prognosis for complete recovery in my condition?"

"What body organ systems are involved?"

"What evidence substantiates my diagnosis?"

"Are there any other effective means of treatment?"

"What is the natural history of this disease?" (i.e., what will happen without any treatment?)

Are doctors too quick to diagnose "emotional" disease in women?

There is little doubt that this is a common phenomenon. Many doctors are quick to ascribe a woman's symptoms to "nerves" or to label them psychosomatic. All too often, as in the case of the woman swimmer cited earlier, the cause turns out to be distinctly physical —and not emotional at all.

How can you combat this tendency?

The best way is by making sure that your doctor does not label your symptoms as emotional *before* he has ruled out all possible "organic" or non-emotional causes. This means, at the least, that he should do a complete history and physical exam, as well as the basic blood and urine tests. Generally, x-rays and blood chemistries will be in order also.

As I have mentioned, a diagnosis of emotional illness is *a perfectly good reason* to seek another medical opinion. If your symptoms are severe or incapacitating ones, and your primary care doctor diagnoses them as emotional, you might also want to see a psychiatrist, in order to confirm the diagnosis and help decide upon treatment.

Sometimes merely asking your doctor if you should visit a psychiatrist will make him "reconsider" his diagnosis. It may make him think of other "organic" diseases he ought to rule out, before he sends the psychiatrist your medical record. This can be a useful technique in dealing with a physician who has too hastily made a diagnosis of emotional illness.

Are doctors too quick to treat women with drugs?

Many doctors, I believe, are quicker to reach for the prescription pad for a woman patient than for a man. Look closely at the people waiting in the pharmacy line at any large hospital. The vast majority will be women.

Since emotional disease tends to be overdiagnosed in women, many of the most abused drugs are the so-called mind-altering or psychotropic ones. In a recent article on the abuses of anti-depressant drugs, five of the six cases cited were women! Here are two cases from this article:

Case 10–6: A twenty-four-year-old single female graduate student failed an important examination and developed depression, insomnia, and agitation, together with an inability to perform her work. She was started on desipramine . . . within two or three days . . . she complained of being "so tired I could hardly struggle to my feet." . . . Because of her persistent lassitude, she eventually requested termination of the medication: "I would rather feel a little depressed than so totally worn out" . . .

Case 10–7: Following the end of a turbulent love affair, a twenty-six-year-old teacher . . . experienced severe despondency, insomnia, and an inability to work. She was given desipramine . . . but within an hour after the first dose suffered an acute confusional episode . . . weakness, somnolence, blurring of vision, dryness of the mouth, and mild disorientation. . . . She wished no more anti-depressant medication. . . . She had a past history of idiosyncratic reactions to many different types of drugs . . .

In a third case, a sixty-year-old woman became so dizzy from another psychotropic drug that she almost plunged from a subway platform during rush hour.

One can only wonder whether, if the patient were a male, these doctors (two male psychiatrists) would have prescribed such potent drugs for reasons such as a failed examination or a terminated love affair.

In any event, if you are female, you should be wary of physicians who seem overly anxious to prescribe psychotropics (tranquilizers, anti-depressants, barbiturates, etc.) for experiences which are a part of everyday living.

Do doctors withhold needed drugs from women?

One young woman, in a small town, went to her doctor for severe menstrual cramps. The physician would not, however, prescribe any analgesic (pain-killer). According to the patient, he tried instead to convince her the problem was "all in my head."

There is a common belief that women are able to withstand pain more readily than men. (As far as I know, there is no physiological reason why this should be so.) This belief may occasionally be used as an excuse for withholding analgesics when such drugs are indicated.

Another example of inadequate use of drugs in women is in the treatment of urinary tract infections. Urinary tract infections (cystitis, pyelitis, pyelonephritis) are common. Every woman, as part of her complete physical exam, should have a urinalysis *and* a "clean voided" urine (see p. 72) obtained for a culture and colony count. A colony count of over 100,000 bacteria per cc. of urine indicates a urinary tract infection.

Most authorities suggest at least three weeks of antibiotic treatment for a first infection, longer for a repeat one. Yet these infections are often treated for an inadequate period of time. The average prescription for Gantrisin, the most widely used urinary antibiotic, is written for only forty-seven tablets—enough for only six days of treatment.

Other common errors in the treatment of this common women's infection include:

(1) starting antibiotics before obtaining a "clean voided" urine for culture and colony count
(2) failure to obtain antibiotic "sensitivities"
(3) failure to obtain a colony count two to three days after treatment is begun (to make sure the infection is being cleared up)

and three to four weeks after treatment has ended (to make sure the infection remains cleared up)

(4) failure to do tests of kidney function (IVP, creatinine clearance, etc.) to see if the infection has caused kidney damage

Do doctors perform too much surgery on women?

Women undergo more surgery than do men—about 20 per cent more, according to one source. U.S. women, moreover, have a disturbingly higher rate of surgery than women in at least two other countries—England and Sweden—where health levels are better.

Certain operations are performed much more often on U.S. women than on their English sisters (Table 29). Hysterectomies*

TABLE 29   Surgery on Women, U.S. and England

OPERATION	U.S.[a]	ENGLAND[a]
Appendectomy	180.0	223.5
Breast surgery (all types)	278.0	171.7
partial mastectomy	196.0	100.6
complete (simple) mastectomy	15.0	27.2
radical mastectomy	51.0	25.1
other	16.0	18.8
Cholecystectomy	273.0	89.9
Hemorrhoidectomy	137.0	31.4
Herniorrhaphy	51.1	29.2
Hysterectomy	516.0	213.2
Thyroidectomy	68.5	42.3
Tonsillectomy	641.0	321.9
Average (all 8 operations)	268.0	140.2

[a] Operations are expressed at the rate of each procedure per 100,000 female population.

SOURCE: Bunker, J. F., *New Engl. J. of Med.,* vol. 282, 1970. Reprinted by permission.

are an example of an operation that is often done without proper indications. In the first Columbia hospital study, *one third* of all hysterectomies were done for questionable reasons. Half of all hyster-

* The term hysterectomy, though commonly used, is really inaccurate. The correct term should be hystero-salpingo-oophorectomy, since the procedure usually involves removal of the Fallopian tubes and ovaries, as well as the uterus.

ectomies done in proprietary hospitals were open to question as to
their necessity.

Here is what the study said about these questionable hysterectomies:

> All cases showed minimal or non-existent uterine pathology; only two
> had a prior dilatation or curettage. . . . All but four of the cases . . .
> had normal hemoglobin [indicating that blood loss had not been ex-
> cessive]. Even in the four cases which showed some evidence of blood
> loss, the surveyor felt that a dilatation and curettage and transfusions
> were indicated as an initial step.

One unfortunate woman had a D and C which revealed no abnormality. Nevertheless, according to the study's expert surveyor,
"the surgeon had the gall to go ahead and perform a total hysterectomy anyway."

The following are some other sample cases of women who were
subjected to unneeded or overly quick surgery:

> **Case 10–8:** Fifty-two-year-old . . . Cholecystectomy performed. His-
> tory, physical, and diagnostic studies did not indicate presence of gall-
> bladder disease . . .

> **Case 10–9:** Forty-two-year-old . . . twelve hospital admissions since
> 1950 included five surgical procedures for gynecological conditions,
> cholecystectomy . . . normal findings on all . . .

> **Case 10–10:** Forty-seven-year-old . . . two week-history of rectal
> bleeding. Hemorrhoidectomy. No barium enema. No sigmoidos-
> copy . . .

> **Case 10–11:** Forty-seven-year-old . . . Hysterectomy. Complete his-
> tory: "bleeds twice monthly during past six months" . . . size of uterus
> not stated in physical or in operative note. No pathological findings re-
> ported by pathologist . . .

Needless to say, if you are female and are urged to have one of
the "big four" operations—hysterectomy, cholecystectomy, breast
surgery, or thyroidectomy—you would probably do well to consult
another Board-certified surgeon, preferably one on the staff of a
medical school-affiliated hospital. The extra trouble may save you
an operation.

If you must have surgery, make sure you have an adequate preoperative checkup by an internist (see Chapter 9). Many doctors simply fail to do such a check on their female patients.†

Should a woman use a woman doctor?

This is, obviously, a choice each woman must make for herself. I can only say, from my own experience, that many women prefer women doctors. They feel that such doctors understand them better than a male physician might.

One friend of mine went to a male gynecologist. The experience was definitely not a mutually enjoyable one.

"He asked me a lot of questions," she said, "I thought were none of his business."

The male physician, my friend thought, was too "judgmental" when it came to matters of sexual behavior and life-style—matters she considered her own prerogative. She switched to a woman gynecologist and has never regretted the change.

Male doctors often treat women patients with an attitude of condescension that makes them seek women physicians. One woman had surgery for a uterine fibroid. Her surgeon did not visit her before the operation, or afterwards. The morning she was to be discharged she asked to see her doctor. When he arrived, she asked him to tell her about the operation.

"I took it out," he replied, "so what more do you need to know?"

These kinds of incidents are convincing more and more women to seek physicians of their own sex.

What are the odds of your finding a woman doctor?

The odds—while not good—are getting better. A few years ago, fewer than 3 per cent of all doctors were women. Now the figure is about 10 per cent. Another encouraging note: the number of women in medical schools is rising rapidly. More than 15 per cent of all medical students are female. This means that, in a few years, fairly large numbers of women physicians will be interns and residents and, eventually, fully trained doctors.

† One of the Columbia hospital studies, for example, notes that "of the 17 women 45 years of age or older that were subjected to major surgery, only one received an electrocardiogram preoperatively."

Your chances of finding a woman doctor will also depend on what specialty you require. Certain specialties have a higher percentage of women than others. Pediatrics, psychiatry, and anesthesiology are examples. Surgery is a specialty which, traditionally, has not had many women. When I was in medical school, there was a chief surgeon at one hospital who swore that, as long as he remained chief, his hospital would never have a female surgical intern. (Soon after, fortunately, this physician retired.)

Obstetrics-gynecology is another specialty with few women—an unfortunate circumstance in that it is the medical specialty which deals with illnesses of women.

In the final analysis, you should choose a doctor for his/her competence, ability to communicate, and compassion—and not gender. (We have all met women doctors who had little sympathy for women or ability to relate to them.) If you do have a sex preference in your choice of a physician, make sure you do not sacrifice these other important qualities.

Where are women doctors most likely to be found?

In our still unliberated society, women doctors—like other women —usually bear the major responsibility for raising their families. This means that they seek medical positions which have regular hours, as opposed to the twenty-four-hour day of the "solo" practitioner.

A woman physician is more likely to seek a salaried position on the staff of a teaching hospital, for instance. Or in a Neighborhood Health Center. Or in a prepaid group practice. These are the kinds of places you are most likely to find female doctors. Incidentally, they are also the kinds of places you are more likely to receive high-caliber care!

Should a woman practice "self-examination"?

A number of women, and women's groups, have become interested in self-examination of their own bodies. Self-examination clinics have been set up to teach women, for instance, to use a flashlight and a speculum to examine their own vagina and uterine cervix. Some clinics advocate self-treatment of conditions such as vaginal infections, as well.

Is self-examination conducive to good-quality care?

Self-examination can have immense benefits. For years now, health experts have urged women to conduct monthly self-examination of their breasts for breast cancer. There is no doubt that such self-exams could save many lives. Yet it was only recently that the technique for self-examination of the breasts was demonstrated on television—a terrible commentary on how our society fails to deal forthrightly with health problems.

Principle: You should perform self-examination of your breasts once each month. (For films and literature, write the American Cancer Society, 219 E. 42nd St., New York, N.Y. 10017 [212 867-3700].)

Self-examination of the vagina and uterine cervix can also be beneficial—if you know what to look for, and if you have adequate tools to do the proper job. There is, of course, nothing "magical" about learning to insert a speculum or to manipulate a light source. There are even kits available which a woman can use to screen herself for cervical cancer (in much the same manner as when your doctor takes a Pap smear).

But self-examination has its perils, too. A woman who relies only on looking at her own cervix with a mirror, as a means of ruling out cervical cancer, is practicing the same brand of substandard medicine this book seeks to warn against. Similarly, the woman who treats her own vaginal infection with yogurt, without a microscopic smear or a culture, is in effect practicing sub-optimal medicine.

This kind of self-exam and/or self-treatment is really cutting off one's nose to spite one's face. I personally believe that women who are incensed and frustrated by the shortcomings of doctors should—rather than falling back on self-examination and self-treatment—take steps to bring the caliber of physician care up to their own expectations (see Chapter 11). In so doing, they will benefit not only themselves, but their husbands and other men as well.

Family planning and abortion

Prevention of pregnancy is another area about which women have a justifiable concern. Yet, though it is now possible to prevent unwanted pregnancies, many thousands of women still do not have access to family planning services.

Not a few doctors, too, show a lack of knowledge about methods of pregnancy prevention.

One woman told me that she consulted a New York gynecologist, a man with a fashionable clientele, for birth control advice. This physician assured her that contraceptive foam was as effective in preventing pregnancy as other methods, such as "the pill" or a diaphragm. A few months later, the woman was pregnant and had to undergo an abortion.

In this case, the doctor—knowingly or unknowingly—gave his patient incorrect advice. And *this is not an isolated incident.* I have heard of other instances. Similar stories have been presented in testimony before congressional committees.

Sometimes a doctor will deny contraceptive advice because a woman is unmarried or a teen-ager, and he does not approve of her sexual activities. Other times the physician simply lacks the knowledge to prescribe contraception.

Principle: As a woman, you have the right to complete information and use of any method of pregnancy prevention. Any physician who denies you this right is practicing substandard medicine.

There are several methods of pregnancy prevention. Each has its pros and cons. These several methods are listed in Table 30.

The pros and cons of the various pregnancy prevention methods do not make for an easy decision. Some informed doctors believe, for instance, that "the pill" entails too much risk. Harvard's Richard Burack, in his *Handbook of Prescription Drugs,* has this opinion:

> The *Handbook* refuses to advise the use of any oral contraceptive drug solely for its contraceptive effect. There are sobering reports of death from thromboembolism [blood clotting] which seems to be due to them. Therefore it is not sensible to dose a healthy person . . . to do what for practical purposes can be accomplished as well with mechanical devices . . .

Burack's argument, in my opinion, has much merit. It is, however, often ignored by other physicians.

As Table 30 indicates, a diaphragm—if properly fitted and used— is nearly as effective as "the pill." Furthermore, even if pregnancy does result, the risk of an early abortion is still considerably less than the risk of "the pill."

On the other hand, many women will no doubt accept the risk of an oral contraceptive, in return for its virtual assurance that they will not become pregnant and have to suffer the trauma of an abortion.

In any event, the choice should be the patient's. Her doctor's

WOMEN AND CHILDREN LAST

TABLE 30 Pros and Cons of Various Pregnancy Prevention Methods

METHOD	% EFFECTIVE-NESS	RISK OF DEATH[a]			SIDE EFFECTS
		(1)	(2)	(3)	
"The pill"	virtually 100	1–3	13–34	14–37	blood clotting (4–7 X normal), water retention, vomiting, etc.
Intrauterine device (IUD)	96–98	7–17	unkn'n	—	uterine infection (about 5% above normal), pain
Diaphragm	90–98	14–35	0	14–35	occasional allergy to rubber
Condom	85–95	23–58	0	23–58	none
Foam, jellies	80	46–116	0	46–116	occasional vaginal irritation
Rhythm method	75	57–145	0	57–145	none
Abortion	—	3.7/100,000 abortions[b]			uterine infection, bleeding
Natural pregnancy	—	228–576	—	228–576	—

[a] Risk of death in 1,000,000 users/year
  (1) due to pregnancy while on method
  (2) due to method itself
  (3) Total of (1) plus (2)
The first number is for women aged 20–34 years, the second for women aged 35–44 years. Data are from the Birth Control Handbook, McGill University Student Society (Montreal), 1971, and the author's own estimates.
[b] New York City abortion program data.

TABLE 31 Abortion Methods in Use

METHOD	RISK[a] —[b]	TIME OF PREGNANCY	ANESTHESIA	HOSPITALIZATION
Menstrual extraction		first 2 weeks after missed period	none	no
Vacuum aspiration	1.1	up to 16 weeks	local	no (if done before 12 weeks)
D and C	2.4	up to 16 weeks	local or general	overnight
Saline injection	18.8	after 16 weeks	local	no or overnight
Hysterotomy	208.3	after 20 weeks	general	yes

[a] Risk expressed as deaths per 100,000 procedures. SOURCE: Tietze, C., et al., *Journal of the A.M.A.*, July 1973.

[b] Menstrual extraction is still experimental and done in only a few places. Since the procedure uses no anesthesia and is done very early, the risk of death may be expected to be negligible.

role should be solely to provide her with the best and most up-to-date information (even the data in Table 30 may no longer be current when this book is published) to make her choice.

What are the risks of abortion?

The risks of a *legal* abortion, performed in a hospital or clinic, are quite low. In New York City, after nearly a half million legal abortions of all types, the death rate was only five per 100,000 procedures. Newer data indicate that it is even lower.

The risk of abortion is lower if the abortion is done early in pregnancy. In New York, if the abortion was done during the first twelve weeks, there was less than one death in every 50,000 procedures. Abortion after twelve weeks carried nine times the risk!

Principle: If you elect an abortion, you should have it as early as possible.

The safest abortion method is vacuum aspiration. This method depends on suction to remove the fetus from the uterus. Local anesthesia can be used, the procedure takes about five minutes, and hospitalization is not necessary if the aspiration is done within the first twelve weeks.

Table 31 shows the various types of abortion procedures, their risk, the anesthesia and hospitalization required, and the pregnancy period during which they can be used.

Is it dangerous to have an abortion in a non-hospital clinic?

This controversy arose in New York City when abortion first became legal. Non-hospital or "free-standing" clinics were doing dozens of abortions a day—with, they claimed, a safety record comparable to that of hospitals.

The question boils down to this: does the clinic have the staff and equipment to cope with the risks of abortion? The most important of these risks are (1) an acute adverse reaction to an anesthetic drug, and (2) excessive bleeding.

Any clinic that does abortions should be prepared to handle these emergencies. This means that it should have doctors trained in resuscitation, a defibrillator and other equipment for the same purpose, and blood or blood substitutes on hand.

New York now licenses all such clinics. You should check before your abortion to see if your clinic is state-licensed or otherwise approved. You should ask about the availability of staff and equipment for emergency use.

What can you do if you are denied an abortion?

Abortion on demand—at least through the first trimester of pregnancy (three months)—is the law of the land, according to the Supreme Court. This has not stopped some states, however, from trying to restrict the ability of women to obtain abortions. It has not stopped some doctors and hospitals from placing barriers in the path of women who wish an abortion.

Principle: You should not let anyone deny you an abortion, in any state, during the first three months of pregnancy.

After three months, the Supreme Court has ruled, the various states may decide for themselves how liberal they wish to be regarding abortions. Even during this period, of course, there is nothing to prevent you from traveling to New York or another state where abortion is legal.

If, for any reason, you are denied an abortion by the caprice of a local doctor or hospital, you can also seek legal help. The American Civil Liberties Union (ACLU) has helped many women who were the victims of local barriers to legal abortion. So have legal aid offices and many private lawyers.

For further information on your right to abortion, you can call or write: ACLU, 22 E. 40th St., New York, N.Y. 10016 (212 725-1222); or National Abortion Rights Action League, 250 W. 57th St., New York, N.Y. 10019 (212 541-8887). Planned Parenthood, in your area, is another source of abortion facts, as well as information on family planning.

What is sterilization?

Sterilization is a permanent form of birth control, for persons who do not desire any further children. There are essentially two types of sterilization: *tubal ligation* (in the woman) and *vasectomy* (in the male).

Again, many doctors give their patients poor advice concerning sterilization. One couple visited their physician because they wanted information on sterilization. The doctor advised the woman to have a tubal ligation—and did not mention the option of vasectomy at all!

Vasectomy, as this doctor should have known, is a simpler procedure. It can be done in the surgeon's office under local anesthesia. Tubal ligation, by contrast, is traditionally done under general anesthesia, and is major surgery (the abdomen is opened and the Fallopian tubes are tied off).

It should be mentioned that there is now a technique for doing tubal ligation in a simpler way. This involves inserting an instrument called a laparoscope into the abdomen. In some medical centers this technique is being performed on an outpatient or overnight-stay basis.

If you are a woman, your sterilization should be performed by a Board-certified gynecologist. The same principles should apply as for other types of surgery. If you are a man, you should consult a Board-certified *urologist,* who is usually best qualified to deal with surgery of the male reproductive organs.

What is prenatal care?

Prenatal care is the care a pregnant woman receives during the nine months of pregnancy. It is one of the most important—and most under-used—kinds of health care.

In New York City, records are kept of how many women avail themselves of prenatal care. The results are startling. About one third of all pregnant women use no prenatal care or make only one or two visits, late in pregnancy.

Principle: You should start prenatal care during the first trimester (first three months) of pregnancy.

Health experts all agree that numerous health problems—of mothers and infants both—can be averted by early and continued prenatal care. I myself have seen many women who just "walk in" to the hospital to have their babies—without any prenatal care at all. Often these women have gained too much weight during pregnancy. Sometimes they have high blood pressure. Not seldom their babies are born with problems that could have been detected earlier.

The American College of Obstetrics and Gynecology (ACOG)

has established standards for adequate prenatal care. The college's standards are as follows:

> 0–28 weeks: 1 visit every 4 weeks
> 28–36 weeks: 1 visit every 2 weeks
> 36+ weeks: 1 visit every week

In addition, the college recommends one *postpartum* visit, six to eight weeks after delivery.

There are certain specific things your doctor—preferably a Board-certified obstetrician—should do at each prenatal visit. Most of these things are part of a complete history and physical exam. They deserve special mention, however, due to their importance in pregnant woman. Your doctor, for instance, should measure your weight at every prenatal visit. He should take your blood pressure. He should obtain a hemoglobin (or hematocrit) at least once during the first and third trimesters.

Table 32 lists the most important prenatal care items. If the care

TABLE 32   Recommended Prenatal Care Examination Items

History, including history of prior pregnancies
  (birth weights, Apgar scores, length of pregnancies,
  complications)

Physical exam, including
  height
  aweight
  ablood pressure
  pelvic measurements

Laboratory
  hemoglobin or hematocrit (1, 3)
  aurinalysis (including urine for sugar and albumin)
  Rh factor and blood type
  serological test for syphilis (1, 3)
  Pap smear
  vaginal smear
  sickle-cell prep (non-whites only)
  skin test for tuberculosis

Other
  nutritional counseling
  dental care

a Each prenatal visit.
(1, 3) First and third trimester.

SOURCE: Morehead, M., et al., Am. J. Publ. H., July 1971.

you receive does not include these basic items, it cannot be considered high-caliber prenatal care.

You can obtain prenatal care from a private "solo" obstetrician, or one who works in a group practice plan. Most large hospitals also run prenatal care clinics, as do the federal government's Neighborhood Health Centers. Finally, the government funds some sixty Maternal and Infant Care (MIC) centers, in various locales, which offer high-caliber prenatal, post-natal, and family planning services.

What is a "high-risk" pregnancy?

Contrary to popular opinion, many pregnancies—some 40 per cent, in fact—are abnormal. This means that problems are present which can increase the risk of death or disability for mother or infant. These pregnancies are called "high-risk" ones.

Principle: Your doctor should make an effort to identify any "high-risk" pregnancy—and to tell you if yours falls in this group.

Sadly, many doctors make no such effort. Or, if they do, they neglect to tell their patients that they are "high-risk."

"Half the time," says newborn expert Dr. Stanley James of women with pregnancy problems, "they don't even know they're high-risk."

Table 33 lists the most common conditions which increase the risk of pregnancy. *Most of these conditions,* you will note, *can be identified by prenatal care.*

TABLE 33 Conditions Which Increase the Risk of Pregnancy to Mother and/or Infant

CONDITION	CONDITION CAN BE IDENTIFIED		
	At 1st Prenatal Visit	During Pregnancy	During Labor
Mother under age 18 or over 40	X		
First pregnancy over age 32	X		
Previous abortion or lost baby	X		
Previous delivery within 1 year	X		
6 or more children	X		
Toxemia[a]		X	
Uterine abnormalities (double uterus, fibroids, etc.)	X	X	
Bleeding during pregnancy		X	
Rh-sensitized	X	X	
Cephalo-pelvic disproportion	X	X	

TABLE 33 Conditions Which Increase the Risk of Pregnancy to
Mother and/or Infant

CONDITION	At 1st Prenatal Visit	During Pregnancy	During Labor
	CONDITION CAN BE IDENTIFIED		
(mother's pelvis too small for infant's head)			
Medical illness (diabetes, asthma, heart disease, TB, syphilis, urinary tract infection, German measles, etc.)	X	X	
Previous Cesarean section (means subsequent babies must be delivered by section)	X		
Breech (or other) abnormal position of baby		X	X
Prolonged labor (over 24 hrs.)			X
Premature rupture of membranes (more than 24 hrs. before birth)			X
Bleeding during labor			X
Fetal distress (abnormal fetal heart rate or fetal acidosis)			X

ᵃ Toxemia is defined as one or more of the following after the 24th week: (1) blood pressure more than 140 systolic or 90 diastolic (normal 120/80); (2) 1+ or more urine protein; and (3) swelling of hands or face.

Who should deliver your baby?

I remember quite clearly the first baby I delivered as a third-year medical student. The mother was in her early thirties. She had already had a couple of previous children. Her pregnancy had been uncomplicated. Her baby was being born at "term" (forty weeks) and it was estimated, by physical exam, to be full-sized.

The pregnancy was, in other words, not a "high-risk" one.

As expected, everything went well. The baby—a seven-pound boy—virtually "delivered himself." He bawled lustily as soon as he was delivered. All I had to do was cut his umbilical cord and place him in a bassinet for the happy mother to see.

Delivering a baby, as I found, is easy so long as everything goes the way it should. Also, of course, I had the benefit of a more experienced senior obstetrics resident at my elbow, just in case. The resident had, in fact, selected my first delivery. He had made as sure as he could that it would be a normal one.

Even so, he was standing there, ready to step in should any trouble occur. There was a Board-certified anesthesiologist in attendance, ready to help too. And a pediatric resident, waiting to take the baby from me.

Not all deliveries get so much attention.

In one southern community, according to Senator Walter Mondale, some 60 per cent of all women have no professional care at the time of delivery!

Who delivers babies in the United States?

The answer: almost everybody! A study in Iowa, a few years ago, showed no less than *five different types of doctors*—including osteopathic physicians—doing deliveries in that state.

Principle: You should have your baby delivered by a Board-certified obstetrician (or obstetrical resident) who performs at least 100 deliveries a year.

As with surgery, there are two things that are important in any doctor who delivers babies: his training, and the number of babies he delivers.

In the Iowa study, most of the doctors doing deliveries were *not* Board-certified. Most were GPs who delivered *less than 50 babies each year!* (The average GP delivered only 32 babies a year. Even the Board-certified doctors were not "overworked": they delivered an average of 157 babies a year—or about 3 per week.)

Many states license *nurse midwives* to do deliveries. These are nurses who have completed a training course (usually two years) in obstetrics. The nurse midwife usually works under the supervision of a physician, generally in a hospital. Nurse midwives have shown that they are capable of delivering high-caliber care, in uncomplicated (non-high-risk) deliveries.

Should you have your baby in a hospital?

Nearly all U.S. babies are born in hospitals. In other parts of the world, this is not the case. In Amsterdam, a recent visitor found that most births were done at home, if they were not "high-risk." Deliveries were performed by nurse midwives, who were very competent. And infant mortality was far lower than in the United States.

Clearly, a hospital is not necessary for having a baby.

Nevertheless, you are taking a chance, in this country, if you elect to "buck the system" and have your baby at home. First, as I have said, many doctors are not adept at singling out "high-risk" pregnancies. This means that you could be "high-risk" and not know

it. Secondly, you will have trouble finding qualified medical help
for a home delivery. Most doctors will not deliver babies at home.
And there are too few licensed nurse midwives.

I find it easy to understand, given the impersonal care at many
hospitals, why some women would prefer to have their baby at home.
Given the way the health system is set up, however, I do not believe this is a wise choice, generally. Unless you are sure that the
person(s) in charge of your home delivery are prepared for any
eventuality—for instance, resuscitation of the newborn infant (see
below)—I would not advise having your baby at home.

**Principle: You should choose a hospital maternity service which
delivers at least 1,500–2,000 babies each year (500 in rural areas).
This means a maternity service with at least 30–40 beds (20 in rural
areas).**

Hospitals (like doctors) which do the fewest deliveries, have the
poorest quality of care. In the Iowa study, of hospitals which delivered less than 100 babies per year, *more than half* had maternity
services which were rated "poor." Of hospitals with less than 250
births, one third were rated "poor."

In these less-than-250-birth hospitals, virtually none of the anesthesia was done by a Board-certified anesthesiologist. Anesthesia was
usually done, instead, by a registered nurse with *no special training*
in anesthesia.

What is "perinatal" care?

When the Kienast quintuplets were born at New York's Columbia-
Presbyterian Medical Center a few years ago, many experts expected
one or more of the infants to die. They reasoned that the quints'
small size—plus the sheer logistics of delivering five babies in a few
minutes—would create serious hazards.

In fact, all five babies came through with flying colors. They were
practically "routine" newborns.

What was not routine was the care they received during the
perinatal period—the period surrounding birth.‡

Mrs. Kienast had had a history of previous "lost" babies (spontane-
ous abortions). As a result, she was hospitalized and placed on bed

‡ Technically, the term "perinatal" refers to the period from twenty-eight weeks
of pregnancy to the time the infant is seven days old. The term "neonatal"
refers to the period from birth to age twenty-eight days.

rest during the last several weeks of her pregnancy. Her infants' heart rates were monitored electronically.

Since it was expected that the babies would be of smaller-than-normal size, the pediatric staff was alerted. Several were on hand just waiting to take the infants and to bring them to the newborn intensive care unit (see below).

The perinatal period is the most dangerous time of pregnancy for both mother and child. It is the time when most deaths occur—as well as most physician errors. Experts estimate that optimal perinatal care for everyone could reduce infant deaths by anywhere from 25–50 per cent. Needless to say, it is in the consumer's interest to know what is "optimal" care.

Should you have "fetal monitoring"?

Fetal monitoring is a way of checking on the status of your infant during (and, as mentioned, sometimes before) labor. Fetal monitoring is really two techniques. The unborn baby's heart is monitored by electrodes pasted to the mother's belly (really a continuous electrocardiogram). Second, the baby's blood oxygen and pH (acidity) levels are monitored by blood samples taken from the infant's scalp, when the head has been pushed low enough during labor.

Principle: If you are a "high-risk" pregnancy, you should try to have your baby at a hospital where fetal monitoring is done.

"Our highest-risk patients," says Columbia-Presbyterian electronics expert Henry Rey, "do better than *all* our patients ten years ago." Since the hospital began fetal monitoring of high-risk pregnancies, there has been a 50 per cent decline in infant deaths and in infants born severely "depressed" due to oxygen lack.

Sadly, it is usually only the large medical school hospitals that offer fetal monitoring. It is a technique which—while not overly complicated—does require special equipment and physicians and technicians who can use it.

"There are plenty of hospitals," says Columbia's Rey, "where monitoring is unknown."

How can you find a hospital with fetal monitoring?

The best way is to contact the hospitals in your locale and speak with the chief of obstetrics (or the chief residents). They should be able to tell you if the hospital uses fetal monitoring (make sure you ask both about the fetal heart rate *and* fetal "blood gas" or "scalp sample" measurements). You might also want to ask what proportion of all pregnant women are monitored.

Should the same doctor who gives you prenatal care deliver your baby?

There are, of course, advantages to having the doctor who has followed you through pregnancy deliver your infant. But this is far from a necessity. Your prenatal care physician may discover that you are "high-risk." Yet he may not have admitting privileges at a hospital best suited to care for your pregnancy—preferably a medical school-affiliated one.

This is one of the most serious weaknesses of American health care. In most other nations, a "high-risk" woman would automatically be sent to the hospital she needs. In the United States she must, in effect, refer herself.

Principle: You should consider—if your pregnancy is "high-risk"— switching your obstetrician or, if need be, going to a medical school hospital as a "ward" patient.

You should not, needless to say, wait until you go into labor to make this change. Let's say that you develop toxemia, with high blood pressure, during your third trimester. What was a normal pregnancy has now become a "high-risk" one. You should, in this instance, seriously consider going to a medical school hospital (or at least a large teaching hospital) for your delivery. If your prenatal care physician does not have admitting privileges at such a hospital, you should seriously consider (1) switching to an obstetrician who does, or (2) making an appointment in the hospital's prenatal care clinic as soon as possible.

What about drugs during labor and delivery?

The most important protection against the hazards of drugs (including anesthesia) during birth is the person who is administering them. A well-trained doctor or anesthesiologist is, naturally, less likely to make errors in the use of drugs.

The best doctors will be aware that virtually all drugs used to ease pain can affect the infant, by crossing the placenta. In particular, the small or premature infant will be most affected. Babies whose mothers have been given general anesthesia or pain-killing drugs during labor, will be less responsive at birth than those whose mothers have had "local" anesthesia or no drugs at all. Every doctor, myself included, has seen infants born so badly drugged that they had to be resuscitated (see below). This usually occurs when pain-killers are given too close to the time of delivery (four hours is sometimes cited as the "safe" period; when drugs, such as Demerol, are given closer than four hours before the baby is delivered, the infant's system does not have a chance to get rid of the drug and he is born with high levels still in his circulation).

Principle: You should discuss with your obstetrician his policy on the use of drugs, early in your pregnancy.

With anesthesia, too, your best guarantee against mishap is the person administering the anesthesia. First choice is a Board-certified anesthesiologist (or anesthesia resident, under the supervision of an anesthesiologist). Second would be a trained nurse anesthetist. Last, and a poor choice, would be a registered nurse without any anesthesia training. (In the Iowa study cited above, 27 per cent of all birth anesthesia was given by such untrained R.N.s!)

Principle: You should discuss with your obstetrician the type of person who will administer anesthesia during your delivery.

If your doctor suggests that you undergo delivery with only a registered nurse for anesthesia, I would seek another source of obstetrical care. If you are a "high-risk" pregnancy and he suggests anything less than a Board-certified anesthesiologist (or anesthesia resident), I would likewise consider going elsewhere for care.

Indeed, if at all possible, you should try to have an anesthesiologist present at your delivery. The art and science of obstetrical anesthesia has made tremendous advances during the past decade; only a physician familiar with these advances can provide top-notch care.

What is "natural childbirth"?

I can remember, as a medical student in the sixties, attending women in labor at Boston's prestigious Lying-In Hospital. These women were all treated in the same fashion. They were placed in a darkened room. Their bed rails were raised and padded. The women were then given an injection of scopolamine, as well as a barbiturate.

The results were striking. In short order, a woman under the influence of "scope" would be thrashing about, totally delirious. She would have to be tied in bed, to prevent injury to herself. She would be as "out of it" as someone who had taken a healthy dose of LSD—and afterwards she would recall nothing of her labor or delivery.

The obstetricians defended this form of treatment by saying that women wanted to be "put to sleep," that they did not wish to remember their childbirth experience. For my part, I found this hard to believe. It seemed that the "scope" treatment was actually encouraged by the doctors, as much as the patients.

There are still, I am sure, hospitals where such treatment is used. But things are changing. Women are, more and more, insisting that they do not wish such methods. They are insisting that they want to be aware of their child's birth, that they want to rely as little as possible on drugs.

These women are insisting on "natural" childbirth.

Natural childbirth means different things to different people. In simplest terms, it is a system which attempts to avoid both drugs and the use of forceps or other aids, during labor and delivery.

There are actually several systems of natural childbirth. Best known, perhaps, is the Lamaze method. Lamaze classes start during the prenatal period. The expectant mother is taught the physiology of pregnancy, labor, and delivery. She learns what to expect when her labor begins. She is taught breathing and other exercises to aid her during the birth process.

Such classes would probably be beneficial for every woman. Women I know who have taken them are better prepared for childbirth. They have less fear. They are more confident. They are less likely to require pain-killing drugs, or the aid of forceps.

Principle: Every pregnant woman should strongly consider enrolling in a "natural" childbirth class.

You should discuss "natural" childbirth with your obstetrician early in pregnancy. You should question him as to his use of drugs and forceps. Needless to say, it will do you little good to enroll in a class if your doctor is unsympathetic.

It is, of course, unwise to expect that the classes will make the use of drugs and/or forceps unnecessary in any given case. Both are valid obstetrical aids, and must be used in certain situations. But your classes—plus a sympathetic physician—can go far towards minimizing the chance that you will have to rely on these aids.

You can get more information on "natural" childbirth from the following: American Society for Psychoprophylaxis in Obstetrics [Lamaze method], 1523 L St. N.W., Washington, D.C. 20005; International Childbirth Education Association [modified Lamaze], Box 5852, Milwaukee, Wisc. 53220.

What kind of care should your infant get at birth?

The moments following birth are probably the most crucial ones of your child's life. He must take his first breath and expand his lungs. His body temperature and circulation must begin to adapt to a new environment.

More and more mothers want to know what is going on during the time they are in the delivery room. They want to know what is being done to their infant in the first minutes after birth. They want to know what is considered good doctor and nursing practice (Table 34).

TABLE 34   Events During Infant's First Five Minutes of Life

0–1 mins.	Obstetrician delivers baby and immediately sucks out baby's mouth with rubber "bulb" syringe (baby usually takes first breath and cries at this time). Nurse notes exact time of birth. Obstetrician places baby in sterile sheet held by pediatrician. Obstetrician collects samples of cord blood for baby's blood type, Rh, and hematocrit. Pediatrician places baby on warmer table, and checks respiration, heart rate, and other vital signs. Pediatrician sucks out baby's mouth and throat, takes resuscitative measures, if needed (administers oxygen, positive pressure, etc.).[a]
1 min.	Pediatrician assigns one-minute Apgar score.
1–3 mins.	Pediatrician passes tube through both sides of infant's nose to check patency, passes tube through mouth into stomach, sucks out fluid and measures amount (usually only a few ccs.). Pediatrician re-checks vital signs.
3 mins.	Pediatrician assigns three-minute Apgar score.
3–5 mins.	Pediatrician does initial physical exam, looks for: prematurity, congenital malformations, birth injury (fractures, paralysis, forceps marks, etc.), anemia, infection. Nurse gives baby injection of vitamin K. Nurse instills two drops of silver nitrate or penicillin into baby's eyes (required by law to prevent gonococcal eye infection). Nurse takes baby's footprints and attaches ID bracelet.
5 mins.	Pediatrician assigns five-minute Apgar score. If infant's condition is stable, pediatrician gives approval for baby to leave delivery room. Pediatrician assigns baby to nursery (regular, special observation, intensive care, etc.).

[a] Resuscitative measures take precedence over everything else, if necessary.

Principle: One person, skilled in newborn resuscitation, and responsible only for the infant, should be present at the time of birth. A pediatrician should be present for all "high-risk" births.

Many women have their babies with only an obstetrician in attendance. This can be a dangerous practice. In the event that both you —and your baby—need quick attention, the obstetrician must make a rapid choice. This can happen, for example, if your baby does not breathe spontaneously and the doctor must attempt resuscitation— the initiation of respiration.

Just such a case is cited in a California study of maternal deaths. "In his efforts to establish respiration in the infant," the study states, "the physician overlooked the extent of lacerations in the mother, which resulted in her death from hemorrhage."

Very few infants (one estimate is about 6 per cent) need more than gentle sucking out of the mouth to start them breathing. But for those who do, it is a full-time job for one (and sometimes more than one) physician. Such an infant may need to have an "endotracheal" tube inserted into the windpipe, and breathing started for him by the doctor, before he will breathe on his own.

If you are having your baby in a medical school hospital, or other large teaching hospital, a pediatric resident or intern should be present to resuscitate your baby, if needed. This is one of the big advantages of such hospitals. When the Kienast quints were born, there were five pediatricians, all gowned and gloved, each ready to resuscitate one of the infants, if necessary.

If you have a private obstetrician or are delivering at a non-teaching hospital, you would do well to make sure that a pediatrician— whom you should select well before delivery—will be there *in the delivery room* when your baby is born. Resuscitation of your baby may just be his first "official duty."

In general, as with other types of doctors, a pediatrician who has recently finished his residency program at a large hospital is best. This doctor is most likely to be skilled at infant resuscitation. (You should also know—as a "fail-safe" measure—that most anesthesiologists who do obstetrical anesthesia are competent at this task.)

Personally, I would want to ask any doctor attending the birth of my child—first and foremost—about his resuscitation skill. I would want to ask him questions such as "Have you had recent experience at resuscitating infants?" and "Are you proficient at inserting an endotracheal tube?" While you might feel it awkward to ask these sorts of questions, they are ones whose answers could be all-important to your newborn child.

What does your infant's "Apgar score" mean?

The Apgar score (developed by anesthesiologist Virginia Apgar) should be the first measure of your newborn baby's health and vigor. The score is done in the delivery room, at exactly one, three, and five minutes after birth (this is why it's important for the nurse to note the exact moment of birth).

For the score, five functions—heart rate, breathing, color, tone, and irritability—are graded (0–2 points for each). Ten points is a perfect score. Babies who score 6 or less at 1 minute, or 8 or less at 3 (or 5) minutes have low scores.

Principle: You should make sure your pediatrician assesses (and tells you) your baby's Apgar scores.

There is, of course, more to a baby than its Apgar score. I have seen babies with high scores who subsequently developed serious problems. Conversely, a low score by no means signifies future trouble for your infant.

The score does, however, mean something. A high-scoring baby is likely to be in good condition, at least at the time of birth. A low scorer, on the other hand, is a baby who bears close observation in the immediate neonatal period.

Furthermore, the Apgar score is an indicator—for you—of the quality of medical care. High-grade pediatricians will not fail to score every infant. Likewise, the best obstetricians will take a serious interest in the baby's Apgar score. (You may hear your obstetrician ask, "What's the baby's score?", "What's the one-minute Apgar?", etc.)

If your baby is not scored—or if the scoring is done in an overly casual manner—it may mean you are not getting optimal infant care.

Which babies deserve special observation after birth?

Like mothers, there are "high-risk" babies. These are babies who stand a greater likelihood of developing problems. At Columbia-Presbyterian in New York, the following infants are considered "high-risk" and are given special observation:

(1) all infants of "high-risk" mothers
(2) all infants delivered by Cesarean section
(3) all breech (feet-first) deliveries
(4) all infants with "fetal distress" during labor (abnormal heart rate or blood acidosis or low oxygen content, as determined by fetal monitoring)
(5) all infants with low Apgar scores

In the case of infants of "high-risk" mothers, a number of conditions in the mother are associated with specific conditions in the baby (Table 35). For instance, if you are a diabetic mother, your infant is likely to suffer from low blood sugar (hypoglycemia). Such infants should have their blood sugar checked soon after birth and every two to three hours (or as often as needed) thereafter, until it is certain that the baby can maintain a normal blood sugar.

TABLE 35   Special Conditions in Pregnancy and Their Effects on the Infant

Condition during Pregnancy	Infant Should Be Observed/ Checked for
Excessive bleeding	anemia
Diabetes	low blood sugar (hypoglycemia)
Toxemia	low blood sugar
Tuberculosis	tuberculosis
Syphilis	syphilis
Drug addiction	drug withdrawal
Rh sensitivity	anemia, jaundice
Breech presentation	dislocated hips
Difficult or over-rapid delivery	bone fractures, facial or arm paralyses
Cesarean section	development of respiratory distress
Premature rupture of membranes ("bag of waters" ruptured more than 24 hrs. before delivery)	infection (pneumonia, meningitis, etc.)
Excessive amount of amniotic fluid	blockage in gastrointestinal tract
Too little amniotic fluid	abnormality of urinary tract

In some medical centers, all babies who are *low birth weight* (less than 2,000–2,500 grams) or whose birth weight is *inappropriate for their gestational age* (GA) are considered "high-risk." Such babies have a higher risk of neonatal death. They may also develop hypoglycemia, respiratory distress, and other problems.

Principle: You should make sure your pediatrician assesses (and tells you) your baby's gestational age (GA).

Your pediatrician should be able to estimate your baby's GA by doing a complete physical (including a neurologic) exam, with an error of only one to two weeks. You can also estimate your baby's GA by counting the weeks of your pregnancy (subtract two weeks from the time between your last menstrual period and birth). The obstetrician should be able to tell you this estimate.

A normal GA (a "term" pregnancy) is forty weeks. Table 36 shows which babies are at "high-risk" because of their abnormal birth weight and/or their gestational age. If your baby falls within the shaded zones it should receive special observation as a neonate and may require intensive care.

What is neonatal intensive care?

When the Kienast quints were born, they were rushed from the delivery room to a neonatal intensive care unit (ICU). There, each infant was placed in an "isolette"—a closed plexiglass box in which the temperature and oxygen content of the air can be controlled. To each baby's chest was attached an electrode which was connected to an "apnea monitor"—a machine that sounds an alarm if the baby's breathing stops or becomes erratic (a common problem in "high-risk" newborns).

Each of the quints had his or her blood tested several times a day for oxygen content, acidity (pH), electrolytes (salt content), and blood sugar. A careful record was kept of each baby's weight and how many ounces of feedings it took by mouth. If a baby failed to take an adequate amount, the rest was supplemented by intravenous feeding (special micro-pumps regulated the tiny amounts of fluids).

Finally, there were respirators standing by, just in case an infant required assisted breathing; equipment for blood transfusions; and cardiac pacemakers. Fortunately, none of this equipment was needed.

Principle: You should find out, before your baby is born, whether or not your hospital has a neonatal ICU. If not, you should ascertain the location of the nearest one.

Finding a neonatal ICU may not be easy. The American Hospital Association's *Guide Issue* indicates only hospitals which have a "pre-

TABLE 36

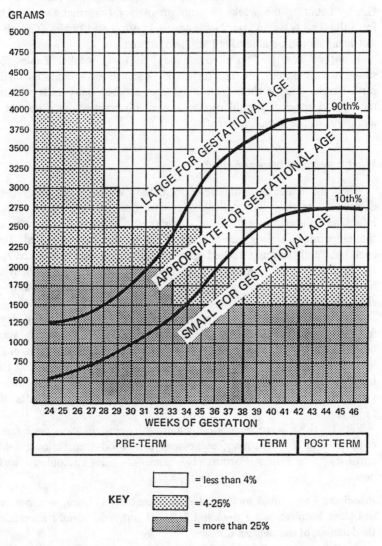

SOURCE: From Battaglia, F. C., and Lubchenco, L. O.: A practical classification of newborn infants by weight and gestational age, *Journal of Pediatrics,* 71: 159–63, 1967.

mature nursery." Usually, such a unit is merely one where low-weight babies are given careful observation. It is not necessarily an ICU.

"Many places say they're giving intensive care," warns Columbia's director of perinatology, Dr. Stanley James, "and not giving it. It's not even intensive observation."

A neonatal ICU should be run by a pediatrician who has had training in neonatology.* It should be staffed by other physicians similarly trained—a ratio of one doctor to every three to five patients. There should be specially trained nurses—one to every one to two patients.

The ICU should have the equipment mentioned above—ready for use and in good working order.

There is no doubt that neonatal ICUs work (Columbia's neonatal death rate is half that of the United States as a whole—even despite the hundreds of desperately ill infants referred for intensive care each year). You should know—and discuss with your pediatrician—where to obtain such care, in the event it is needed.

Should a baby be transferred to another hospital early in life?

Most people remember the infant boy born to John and Jacqueline Kennedy. This baby was delivered by Cesarean section at a military hospital on Cape Cod. The baby was born prematurely (before "term") and was low birth weight. A few hours after birth, this infant began to develop difficulty breathing—so-called "respiratory distress syndrome" (RDS). The doctors were faced with a decision: whether to try to care for the baby, or to transfer him to Boston, site of the nearest medical school hospital.

The infant was transferred. He made the one-hour drive, by ambulance, without incident (though he was subsequently to die).

Principle: Any sick infant should be promptly transferred to the hospital which is best suited to handle his problem.

More sick babies die because they are *not* transferred than because they are. Doctors—and parents—worry about the dangers of a baby's surviving the trip. They seldom worry about the dangers of leaving a deteriorating infant in a hospital which has no neonatal ICU or other special facilities.

* At present there is no Board certificate in pediatric neonatology. This situation will probably be remedied in the near future.

New York City has, for years, operated a transport service for sick newborns. Each year more than a thousand ill babies are transferred safely between hospitals.

During all the time I worked at a major medical center, I did not see a single infant die during transfer from another hospital.

If a baby is to be transferred, the transfer should be done, of course, with proper precaution. It should be done in an ambulance equipped with oxygen. The baby should be in an incubator. A nurse or physician, capable of assisting breathing, should accompany the infant.

Under these conditions, virtually all babies can be transferred to a major medical center for intensive care.

Can a newborn baby tolerate diagnostic tests or surgery?

This is a similar situation. Often parents (or doctors) are reluctant to subject a newborn infant to diagnostic tests. They may be concerned about the infant's ability to tolerate such procedures as a lumbar puncture (spinal tap) or phlebotomy (drawing blood).

While this may be a valid concern for some procedures (cardiac catheterization, for example) a baby's small size should in itself not be used as an excuse to defer needed tests.

Babies are, in general, able to withstand any test an adult can withstand (if it is done by properly trained pediatric personnel). A newborn will tolerate a lumbar puncture, for example, far more easily than you or I!

Principle: Your baby's size is not, in general, a reason to defer needed diagnostic tests.

Should you use an adult doctor for your child?

Adult doctors (internists and adult surgeons, for instance) are for adults. Infants and children deserve the benefit of doctors who are experienced in treating the diseases of children.

I remember one tiny infant who had congenital heart disease. This baby was in severe respiratory distress and near death. If nothing were done, there was no doubt that the baby had only a few hours to live.

This infant was placed on a respirator to assist his breathing, by a pediatric anesthesiologist. He underwent cardiac catheterization, done by a team of pediatric cardiologists. He then was operated upon by a pediatric surgeon (the entire operation was performed in only seven minutes!).

This infant was cured—and went on to live a normal life. But only because he received the attention of doctors who were accustomed to dealing with infants and children.

Principle: You should use a pediatrician and other pediatric specialists for all children under age fourteen.

You should not settle for an adult doctor to treat your children for any problem (except on-the-spot attention in an emergency). Infants and children are unique. They have diseases not found in adults. They require special doses of drugs and fluids.

I recall another child, almost not so lucky, who was operated on by an adult general surgeon. The operation was completed uneventfully. The surgeon then proceeded to write his post-op orders. Not being used to dealing with children, he vastly overestimated the amount of intravenous fluids required. Luckily, a more experienced anesthesiologist wandered by and picked up the error. Otherwise, the child would have been literally "drowned."

There are pediatric specialists in virtually every medical field. Though many are to be found only at the largest medical centers, you should seek out such specialists—if your child requires one (see Table 37).

TABLE 37   Selected Pediatric Specialties and Their Uses

SPECIALTY	COMMON USES
Pediatric allergy	treatment of asthma, "hay fever"; skin testing to determine sensitivity to plants, house dust, molds, animals, etc.
Pediatric cardiology	diagnosis and treatment of congenital heart disease; also rheumatic fever
Pediatric endocrinology	diagnosis and treatment of growth disorders (short stature, excessive tallness); also disorders of sexual development (precocious puberty, retarded puberty, ambiguous sexual development, etc.)

TABLE 37   Selected Pediatric Specialties and Their Uses

SPECIALTY	COMMON USES
Pediatric neurology	diagnosis and treatment of disorders of mental and motor development, including mental retardation, cerebral palsy, learning disabilities, etc.
Pediatric orthopedics	diagnosis and treatment of bone and joint disorders (flat feet, in- and out-toeing, congenital hip dislocation, etc.)
Pediatric (child) psychiatry	diagnosis and treatment of childhood mental and emotional conditions including schizophrenia and other psychoses, autism, school phobia, etc.

What is a complete pediatric physical exam?

In general, the infant or child exam follows the same format as the adult exam (see Chapter 4). As with your own exam, you should make sure that your child's doctor performs a complete exam.

Many doctors, unfortunately, fail to do a complete exam on infants and children.

In one recent survey, for instance, only 18 per cent of children examined had their vision tested. Only 3 per cent had a hearing test! In this same study, more than 75 per cent of all "solo" doctors admitted that they did not routinely test children for anemia.

You should remember, as already stressed, small size is no excuse for doing an incomplete exam. The smallest infant can have its blood pressure taken (with a small-size blood pressure cuff and a lot of patience). A newborn can have its eyes examined with an ophthalmoscope, though the process may take longer than with an adult.

There are a few items which are not generally done in children. In particular, the vaginal exam is usually omitted in pre-coital patients (a rectal exam alone will suffice).

Table 38 lists those items which should be included in the exam of infants and small children. This list includes items which are often omitted, and items which are peculiar to the infant-child exam.

TABLE 38   The Pediatric Physical Exam—Items Often Omitted
or Peculiar to Infants and Children

aBlood pressure
Head circumference (infants)
Measurement and palpation of fontanelles ("soft spots" in infant's skull)
aPalpation of skull for fractures, swellings (esp. newborn)
Transillumination of skull (M.D. holds flashlight to skull in dark closet)
aOphthalmoscope exam of eyes
aPalpation of ear cartilage (newborns)
Palpation of collarbones for fractures (newborns)
Observation of arms for paralysis (newborns)
Chest circumference (infants)
Palpation of nipples (newborns)
Identification of 3 blood vessels in umbilical cord (newborns)
Test for congenital hip dislocation (M.D. holds legs at knees, bends outwards)
aPalpation of groin for hernia
aPalpation of testes (males)
aObservation of vaginal orifice (females)
aRectal exam
Observation of creases of palms and soles (infants)
aObservation of skin turgor (M.D. picks up skin over abdomen, lets snap back)
Observation of posture and tone (infants)
Moro reflex (M.D. lifts up infant's head and shoulders, lets fall back onto crib
or hand)
Sucking reflex (M.D. places finger in infant's mouth)
Rooting reflex (M.D. places finger at corner of mouth)
Evaluation of cry (M.D. stimulates infant, observes volume and pitch)
Reaction to loud noise (M.D. claps hands, etc.)
Reaction to light (M.D. places light source near infant)

a Items marked are essentially the same as those in adult exam, but are frequently omitted in the pediatric examination by un-thorough examiners.

What is recommended well-child care?

Well-child, or preventive, care in the United States can only be described as a disaster. Some thirty-one million children under age
seventeen do not see a doctor once a year. Between one fourth to
one half of all preschool children are unimmunized against diseases
such as polio, measles, diphtheria, and others. Several million children have a chronic handicap which could have been prevented or
corrected with proper care.

Doctors themselves seem to be unaware of what constitutes decent
well-child care. In one survey, mothers of preschoolers reported that
large numbers of doctors did not encourage well-child visits.

Principle: Your child should be seen regularly by a pediatrician, even though s/he seems completely well.

The American Academy of Pediatrics urges the following schedule for well-baby care during the first year of life:

(1) the first visit should be made not later than six weeks (prematures and other "high-risk" infants should be seen earlier)

(2) one visit each month for the first six months

(3) one visit every other month for the next six months

After the first year, one visit every six months is usually adequate.

At each visit, there are *certain specific things* your doctor should do. He should, for instance, give the first DPT (diphtheria, whooping cough, tetanus) shot by six weeks of age (unless the child has a "cold" or other infection). He should do a hematocrit or hemoglobin as a "screening test" for anemia not later than six to seven months.

Many doctors, as I have noted, simply fail to provide these basic elements of well-child care. In one recent study, less than one quarter of all children who saw private physicians were screened for anemia, and only 10 per cent had a urinalysis.

TABLE 39 Child Care in the First 6 Years of Life

AGE	ITEMS AT VISIT
4–6 weeks	history and physical exam
	DPT #1
	Oral polio #1
10–12 weeks	ahistory and physical exam
	head circumference
	DPT #2
	Oral polio #2
4–5 months	ahistory and physical exam
	head circumference
	DPT #3
	Oral polio #3
	urinalysis
6–7 months	ahistory and physical exam
	head circumference
	anemia screening (hemoglobin or hematocrit)
	sickle-cell screening
9 months	history and physical exam
	TB skin test
12 months	ahistory and physical exam
	Measles vaccine

TABLE 39   Child Care in the First 6 Years of Life

Age	Items at Visit
	anemia screening
	sickle-cell screening
	lead poisoning screening
15–16 months	[a]history and physical exam
	German measles (Rubella) vaccine
	Smallpox vaccine
18–20 months	[a]history and physical exam
	DPT booster
	Oral polio booster
	TB skin test
2 years	history and physical exam
	Mumps vaccine
	anemia screening
	lead poisoning screening
2½ years	[a]history and physical exam
	TB skin test
3 years	[a]history and physical exam
	[b]vision screening
	[b]hearing screening
	anemia screening
	lead poisoning screening
3½ years	[a]history and physical exam
	TB skin test
4 years	[a]history and physical exam
	anemia screening
	lead poisoning screening
4½ years	[a]history and physical exam
	TB skin test
5 years	history and physical exam
	DPT booster
	Oral polio booster
	anemia screening
	lead poisoning screening
5½ years	[a]history and physical exam
	urinalysis
	TB skin test
6 years	[a]history and physical exam
	anemia screening
	lead poisoning screening

NOTE: All visits include measurement of height and weight, and assessment of development.

[a] May be done by a specially trained nurse or physician's assistant.

[b] Earliest time to attempt vision and hearing tests; should try again at next visit if unsuccessful.

Table 39 shows a suggested checklist for what your doctor should do during well-child visits. This is the checklist used at the Wagner Child Health Station—an experimental unit in New York City which emphasizes preventive care. The Wagner checklist is applicable, however, to all preschool children regardless of where they live or who their doctors are. It represents a minimal standard of well-child care.

Should you examine your own child?

There are many aspects of your child's growth and development that you can monitor. And in view of the present inadequate state of well-child care, this would seem like a good idea (though *not,* of course, as a substitute for well-child visits).

You should observe your infant or child. You should keep a record of anything that seems out of the ordinary and report it to your physician. From my own experience, I know that many early, subtle manifestations of serious disease are "picked up" by parents.

Tables for normal weight, height, and head circumference—as well as developmental milestones—may be found in many books, or obtained from your pediatrician (see Appendix for some references). You should use aids such as these to follow your own child's growth and development.

Which provider should you rely on for pediatric care?

Most people use a private pediatrician—either "solo" or in a group—for their child's primary care. For more specialized care they may use the OPD of a major medical school or teaching hospital.

There are also other "options" of which you should be aware.

Prepaid group practice plans have been shown to deliver a high level of primary child health care. One study showed a prepaid plan provided at least as good care as that given by medical school hospital OPDs.

The federal government's *Neighborhood Health Centers* have also been shown to provide a high level of care—again as high as (actually somewhat higher than) the medical school hospital.

Some local health departments operate child health clinics. In New York City, for instance, there is an extensive network of well-child stations, which, by and large, provide decent preventive care.

Possibly the best primary child health care is provided by the federal government's so-called *Children and Youth* (C and Y) *projects*. In one study these projects were shown to deliver a level of care *far better than any other source*. Most C and Y projects are run in conjunction with medical school hospitals. The projects have a limited enrollment. (Also, in one of the inexplicable ironies of federal health policy, many C and Y projects have been discontinued as an "economy" move!) If you can find such a project and manage to enroll your infant or child, you will receive high-caliber primary care.

Regardless of your source of child care, however, the principles in this chapter and the rest of the book still apply. You should try to utilize them, when appropriate, to judge the quality of the care your child receives.

11

The future: the need for reform

This has not been an easy book to write.

It is not easy to face the fact that members of one's own profession are not, in many instances, performing up to par. It is not easy to admit that many private physicians deliver sub-optimal care, or that sizable numbers of hospital patients get less than optimal attention.

As a physician I find these facts hard to face. They bother me because they mean that doctors have failed, as a profession, to keep their own house in order.

Are doctors concerned about the quality of medical care?

Most doctors, I believe, are concerned. They want to provide high-quality care. They want to do what is best for their patients.

But what about protecting the public against the poor care of other doctors?

Consider the case of John Nork. Nork, a California physician, performed spinal surgery on patients suffering from low back pain. Nork, it seems, was not only an eager surgeon, he was also a less than proficient one. The doctor lost several suits brought by patients who claimed that their conditions were actually made worse by his surgery. For nine years, summed up one trial judge, the physician "made a practice of performing unnecessary surgery, and performing it badly . . ."

But what about Nork's colleagues? Did not his errors come under scrutiny from his peers?

Apparently so. The hospital pathologist found pieces of spinal nerves in the surgeon's post-op specimens—clear evidence of poor surgical technique. Yet this physician did not mention the nerve fragments in "signing out" the specimens. He and another hospital physician testified that they did not know whose responsibility it was to bring the matter to the attention of the appropriate committee.

Other doctors saw patients who had been operated on by Nork. These patients were seen because they had persistent neurological or skeletal problems.

"Yet not once"—the words are from *The Lancet,* an English medical journal—"was any patient informed by a doctor that his or her condition was Nork's handiwork, although every consultant on the witness stand agreed that this was so . . ."

The case of John Nork is by no means unique. There are numerous other examples—most less blatantly horrendous—of doctors delivering poor-quality care. I wish, as a physician, I had confidence that these doctors were being scrutinized—and corrected—by their peers.

But, sadly, I have no such confidence.

Even in the best hospitals, doctors are pretty much autonomous. Their everyday performance is not closely scrutinized. One doctor is unlikely to criticize another's management.

Outside, in doctors' offices, the situation is even worse. Here— where most health care is delivered—there are virtually no checks whatever on quality. In fact, the medical profession seems to want to ignore the whole question of office quality.

There has never been a large-scale study of the office practices of American doctors. There is no data on how well they diagnose disease. On how appropriately they treat it.

"It is unfortunate," understates Mildred Morehead, professor of community health at Albert Einstein College of Medicine, "that so little is known about the general level of medical practice in solo practitioners' offices."

It *is* unfortunate. And the reason so little is known, plain and simple, is because the medical profession has not taken the trouble to look.

Even when serious quality problems are brought to light, the medical profession has failed to follow up on them. Consider, for example, the not so recent study of post-op death rates. This study was done under the auspices of the National Academy of Sciences. It revealed that some hospitals had ten times as many post-op deaths (after taking into account things such as patient age, type of operation, etc.) as others.

"Someone"—the study's authors said—should look into this problem further. "Quiet, unofficial, cooperatively oriented inquiries," should be made. What they called "indications of such importance" —ten times as many post-op deaths in some hospitals as in others —shouldn't, the authors agreed, "be swept under the rug."

Yet this is precisely what happened. The NAS study was done in the mid-sixties. There has been no follow-up. Undoubtedly, some hospitals still have excessively high death rates. And still no one can say why.

Doctors, then, are concerned about the quality of care. But it is a personal concern. It does not extend to a concern for their colleagues' care. Or for the care delivered by the profession as a whole.

Do any official bodies really police health care quality?

A few state and local health departments are active in policing the quality of health care. Most, unfortunately, are not. States and local governments are generally reluctant to discipline hospitals or nursing homes, even where clearly substandard care exists. Recently, Chicago's Mayor Daley closed a hospital for turning away an ill patient. The action was so rare it made the newspapers.

Official agencies have been just as reluctant to take steps against doctors. During the last five years, twenty states have taken no disciplinary action whatever against any physician practicing within their borders!

It took the state of California three months after Dr. John Nork's final malpractice conviction—the one that occasioned the most publicity—to revoke the surgeon's license. It has taken the state of New York more than a year to consider the case of Dr. Max Jacobson, who, by his own admission, habitually gave his patients injections of steroids, vitamins, and amphetamines.

The Joint Commission on Accreditation of Hospitals is a quasi-official body which is supposed to monitor hospital quality. The JCAH is a non-profit private agency run jointly (hence the name) by the AMA, the American Hospital Association, the American College of Physicians, and the College of Surgeons.

Yet the Joint Commission shies away from directly reviewing the quality of hospital care. In fact the commission's standards for hos-

pitals are deliberately designed to avoid looking at quality. Here
is how the commission's *Manual for Hospitals* describes these standards:

> The . . . standards are *free of all direct demands* upon the physician's
> clinical judgement and decision. . . . (and) relate entirely to the sup-
> porting elements of hospital life and the environment of medical prac-
> tice. [Italics mine.]

Needless to say, any effort to judge hospitals which avoid looking
at how well doctors make decisions is a questionable one, at best.
It seems a little like trying to determine the seaworthiness of a ship's
hull without looking below the waterline.

Lately, under prodding by the federal government, new types of
agencies have been set up to keep tabs on quality (see below).
Some of these agencies, financed by federal funds, are to be
run by local medical societies. It remains to be seen whether this
newest effort to get the medical profession to police itself will suc-
ceed. One can only note that, if the past is any guide, we can be less
than sanguine.

Have facts about health care quality been suppressed?

In 1958, Richard H. Blum did a study entitled "Hospitals and
Patient Dissatisfaction." The study was performed for the California
Medical Association. It scrutinized the caliber of care in several
California hospitals, as well as the amounts these hospitals paid for
malpractice insurance.

Some fifteen years later, in 1972, a Harvard professor wrote the
California Medical Association requesting a copy of the study for
teaching purposes. Here is the reply he got:

> Dear Dr. ———:
> I wish to acknowledge receipt of your letter of June 30 in which
> you request permission to utilize parts of a study by Richard H.
> Blum. . . . This study was never released publicity [sic]. . . . The
> CMA did not adopt the report and did not accept it as a valid piece
> of research. . . . Consequently *all copies have been destroyed* . . .
> [Italics mine.]

This is only one of many examples of suppression of facts about
the quality of care. In Massachusetts, the state went to court to

prevent the film *Titticut Follies,* a documentary on conditions in the Bridgewater State Hospital, from being publicly shown.

In New York City, that city's Health Insurance Plan refused to permit a study of its physicians to be published in a medical journal.

"The one thing they didn't want out," says the study's author, a professor of public health, "was the per cent of doctors who were unsatisfactory."

HIP informed the professor that the study could be published if —and only if—the facts were presented in such a fashion as to show *no* doctors to be performing unsatisfactorily!

A similar study of New York internists, done for the local society of internal medicine, was never made public for the same reason: the society did not want it publicized that any internists were providing substandard care.

This secrecy about the quality of care has reached epidemic proportions. The Joint Commission, charged by the government with approving hospitals for Medicare, conducts its hearings in secret. It refuses to release any of its reports. The JCAH is truly accountable to no one, least of all the nation's taxpayers or the aged whom it is supposed to serve.

In England the government publishes yearly data on hospital death rates. In the United States few hospitals even admit to keeping such information, let alone make it public. Blue Cross plans, which gather extensive data on hospitals, do not release this information to consumers.

In several states laws and professional sanctions have been used to prevent information on local doctors from reaching the public. When Ralph Nader tried to compile a consumer directory of doctors in Maryland's Prince Georges County, a Washington suburb, the county medical society warned doctors that the state's anti-advertising statute prohibited them from giving Nader's group anything but their names, specialties, and possibly their office hours.

The Federal government has also been guilty of concealing from the public data on quality. For some time the Uniform Financial and Statistical Reports of hospitals were held secret by the government. Finally, under pressure of a court suit, these reports were made public.

There is, in fact, a "conspiracy of silence" when it comes to the quality of health care. But this conspiracy is not, as some think, limited to one doctor's reluctance to criticize another. It extends to *any* attempt to judge *any* doctor or hospital. It is a conspiracy against telling the public any facts which would enable them to make more informed decisions about their own care.

Fortunately, not all health experts are part of this plot. Some, in fact, would like to see the public better informed. Harvard's Duncan Neuhauser talks about the problem of substandard hospitals:

There is a solution which is intriguing because it has never been tried. This is simply to make information about hospital performance available to the public through newspapers, public libraries, and other popular media and let the public pick the hospital . . . of their choice.

"Now," Neuhauser says, "their choice is comparatively blind. This way it would be more informed."

Harvard's Neuhauser is right. The public should be given the information they need to make informed choices. And not just about hospitals, either. The public deserves to know about each and every doctor practicing in their locale. About every nursing home, and other health facility.

What can government do about the quality of care?

Improving the quality of health care should be a national priority. It deserves at least as much attention as has been paid to the problem of financing care. It will not do us much good to have even the best health insurance system if we cannot obtain high-caliber care. It will not help a pregnant woman to have her pregnancy covered by health insurance if her obstetrician overlooks her high blood pressure. It will not help a forty-year-old executive to know that his checkup is covered by insurance if his physician overlooks his prostatic cancer.

Better-quality care is an acute national need. But the federal, state, and local governments are not likely to recognize it as such unless the public demands it.

What can government do?

I can think of several measures which, enacted by federal or state governments, would better the quality of care. Here are a few:

(1) Periodic re-licensure for doctors—Physicians (and perhaps nurses and other health professionals) should be required by law to take a competency exam every five years. This exam would

be like those now given new doctors by the National Board of Medical Examiners. Physicians who fail the exam would be placed on probation and given a chance to update their knowledge. Those who still could not pass would either have their license revoked, or would be subject to certain restrictions (much as automobile licenses are now handled).

This system of five-year exams is not a drastic measure. It is a fair and reasonable way to make sure physicians keep their medical knowledge up-to-date. It is, I think, far preferable to compulsory retirement.

(2) Medical audits of hospitals and doctors' offices—What goes on in a hospital or office should be checked periodically. By "what goes on" I mean the actual process of diagnosis and treatment. Non-physician observers can do this kind of checking quite well (see below). And there is no substitute for direct, firsthand observation of a doctor's examination and treatment techniques. As with (1) above, where substandard care is found, a probationary warning would be issued, followed by a second observer visit (and perhaps a third). If no improvement was detected, the doctor and/or hospital would be subject to license restriction or revocation.

(3) A national Scope of Practice law—This law would limit the scope of a doctor's practice, in line with his training. A doctor not Board-certified (or Board-eligible) in a surgical specialty, for instance, would not be allowed to perform surgery. Exceptions could be granted for areas of extreme doctor scarcity—but only after an examiner had satisfied himself that the physician in question would be able to perform outside his designated specialty.

(4) A national Hospital Quality Report—All hospitals would be required to report quality data each year. Such data would include: death rates, types of patients and illnesses treated, surgery performed and post-surgical complications, medical errors, infant and maternal deaths and complications, tissue and autopsy reports, recidivism rates, etc. Such a report could also, with benefit, be required for nursing homes and other health facilities as well.

(5) A U.S. Compendium of Medical Standards—This volume would be compiled by an appropriate government agency such as the Institute of Medicine of the National Academy of Sciences. The compendium would contain various quality standards agreed upon by medical experts. Many such standards have already been

promulgated, though most doctors are unaware that they exist. Examples are the recommended prenatal and well-baby regimens of the College of Obstetrics and Gynecology and the Academy of Pediatrics, the recommended diet of the National Nutrition Council, etc. Other examples might include standards for high-risk pregnancies, for cancer detection, and for disease prevention in general. The compendium would be sent free to every practicing U.S. physician for his own personal reference.

(6) A national Physician Practice Report—All licensed, practicing doctors would be required to file this yearly report, similar to that filed by hospitals. It would contain data on the numbers and types of patients treated during the year. It would state the numbers of patients referred to other physicians, hospitals, etc. It would include patient death and disability data, as well as data on drugs and other types of treatment prescribed.

These half dozen measures (or similar ones) should be mandated, I believe, by federal law. They would provide the facts needed to improve vastly the quality of medical care. They would allow officials to detect—and crack down on—health providers who engage in poor or questionable practices. And, on the more positive side, providers who are doing a superior job could be rewarded for their efforts.

Right now, to my knowledge, there is no plan—on the part of federal authorities—to take any of these badly needed steps. Such actions will happen only if the public demands and lobbies for them.

What can consumer groups do?

Consumer groups can be powerful forces in bettering the quality of health care. In New York State it was a group of parents, concerned about their retarded children, who first exposed the shocking conditions at Willowbrook, a state hospital. In other places, consumer groups have had similar beneficial effects in highlighting and changing health care practices.

The key thing to remember in forming a consumer group is that there are numerous ways in which you can have an impact on the quality of health care in your locale. Your group might, for instance, encourage local legislators to hold public hearings on the quality of care. You might lobby for changes in existing laws.

You might actually visit hospitals and other health institutions, perhaps with a local political leader, to see conditions firsthand. You might conduct interviews with "front-line" health workers such as interns, residents, nurses, and others.

Your group might wish to perform a study of the quality of care. You might wish, for instance, to conduct a "medical audit" of local physicians or hospitals, making use of the expertise and resources of a medical school.

Some consumer groups—in particular, women's groups—have compiled dossiers on local physicians, using their own members' experiences. These dossiers might contain the doctor's training, fees, office hours, as well as his attitudes toward certain medical issues such as abortion or "natural" childbirth.

Your group, if large enough, might consider hiring a health guide —someone who will help you cope with the intricacies of the health system. The guide could be a public health nurse who works part time. Or a retired hospital administrator. Or anyone with a knowledge of community health resources. The guide's job would be to aid local residents in finding high-caliber care.

Your group might try to use the resources of radio or television to help consumers obtain health services. This is a new method which shows great promise. Experiments are underway in several places to use these media to better inform consumers about health problems and where they can get care. Recently a Boston physician —Dr. Tim Johnson—initiated a television show called, appropriately enough, "House Call." In New York City, the Children's Television Workshop has begun an educational show for adult health problems. Your consumer group might pressure the local TV channels to carry such programs, either of their own or from other stations.

In which official agencies should consumers demand a voice?

There are a few "key" places, when it comes to bettering health care, where consumers should make sure their voice is heard. One such place is your local comprehensive health planning (CHP) agency. These agencies, funded by the federal government, have been set up in hundreds of locales and in all fifty state governments. Local CHP agencies are required, by law, to have a majority of consumer members.

Your group may wish to look into—or challenge—the consumer

membership of your local CHP agency. Or, if your area has no such agency, you may wish to form one. In any case, for more information, you should contact the Department of Health, Education and Welfare (HEW) in Washington, D.C.

The latest federal attempt to improve quality are the so-called Professional Standards Review Organizations (PSROs). The PSROs are supposed to monitor both the caliber and the appropriateness of care under the Medicare law (patients over sixty-five years). The PSROs are designed to be run by local medical societies or similar doctor-controlled groups, with some consumer input.

You should check on the status of your local PSRO. You should find out what steps it is taking to check on quality and to improve it. You should find out if consumers have any voice, and, if not, demand one. (In this regard, beware of local Blue Cross or hospital officials passing themselves off as "consumers"—make sure consumer input is from persons who will truly represent your interests.)

Another health quality forum are the visits of the Joint Commission on Accreditation of Hospitals to your local hospitals. The JCAH visits most hospitals every few years. Those which it has deemed to have problems are visited more often. These visits usually last a couple of days. They include interviews with hospital officials, examinations of hospital records, and a tour of the hospital.

Lately, for the first time, the JCAH has also been willing to hear the testimony of the public. How much weight such public testimony has in the JCAH's final decision of whether or not to "accredit" a hospital, I cannot say.

Nevertheless, at the present time, the JCAH is virtually the "only game in town" when it comes to conducting a periodic review of hospitals. It may be worthwhile, therefore, to try to participate in its visit. Your consumer group may wish to contact the JCAH in Chicago to find out when next your local hospitals are to be seen. You may wish to request an opportunity to make your feelings heard. You may even wish to demand an opportunity to tour the hospital with JCAH members in order to point out specific deficiencies.

Your consumer group might find it advantageous to establish a coalition with a group of hospital interns and residents, who usually have firsthand knowledge of hospital deficiencies. You might also wish to tip off the newspapers and local television stations about the impending accreditation visit, to guarantee press coverage and thus make it harder for the JCAH to sweep any deficiencies that exist under the rug. (These techniques are, of course, useful even in the absence of a JCAH visit; a "walking tour" of a local hospital for the television cameras, with interviews of interns and other hospital staff is a perfectly valid way of fighting for better-quality care.)

Finally, you should not forget your state and local health departments. Most, as we have seen, have been far from vigorous in the quality of care area. Many still adhere to a traditional view of public health, emphasizing such things as food and sanitary inspections.

You may discover, however, a sympathetic official—one who truly wants to do something about quality. You might, for example, find a local health commissioner who will let you form a health advisory council or other forum in which quality issues can be explored. You may find an official with whom you can work to get public or private funds for quality monitoring, such as the "medical audits" described above.

Whatever techniques your consumer group employs to assure better-quality care, you may not find the going smooth. You may run into opposition from the local medical society or from doctors who feel that you are stepping on their toes. You may find hospital officials unsympathetic to "outsiders" disturbing their institution. You may face outright hostility from those who believe that health care should be left to physicians and other "experts."

On the other hand, you may also find allies—often in unexpected places. A union leader concerned about the health of his members. A local businessman with a relative who has been the victim of poor care. A pharmacist with a firsthand knowledge of doctors' drug-prescribing errors. A hospital administrator who has been fighting his medical board to eliminate unneeded surgery.

In addition, there are several consumer-oriented national organizations you might contact for help or advice. These include the AFL-CIO, the United Auto Workers, and United Mine Workers unions, the American Public Health Association (APHA), the National Urban Coalition, the National Organization for Women (NOW), the National Urban League, the Congress of Racial Equality, the Health Policy Advisory Council (Health-PAC), and the Center for Study of Responsive Law. These organizations are a few of the more active fighters for consumer power in health, on the national level.

What can the individual consumer do?

As I said in the first chapter of this book, the individual consumer can be the most powerful force for bettering the quality of health care. More than any group or organization, when it comes to improving care, there is nothing to equal the force of millions of people.

Consumers must play a more active role in their own health care. They must challenge and question their doctors. They must realize that they—and not the physician—have the final say about decisions which concern their health.

This attitude is taking hold.

I spoke recently with one woman about her pregnancy. She had been emphatic in wanting as natural a childbirth as possible. I asked her if she had found any trouble in getting her obstetrician to go along.

"What could he say?" she replied, almost casually. "After all, it *was* our child."

I wish more patients had this attitude. It's too bad more people don't realize that they, and not the doctor, are in charge of their own and their family's health care.

It's too bad, I have often thought, there isn't some magic drug that would give people the self-confidence they need to deal with doctors and other providers. It's too bad there isn't a vaccine that could protect against the fear and trembling that seems to strike most people when they enter a physician's office, or a hospital.

Sadly, there is no such magic drug. There is only the protection that comes from knowledge, from being informed.

The battle for better-quality health care is just taking shape. The next ten years will see it grow. They will see the health professions forced to become more quality-conscious, as the public becomes more conscious of what top-notch health care really is.

This process is beginning. People are growing more reluctant to accept "on faith" the pronouncements of their doctors. They are demanding facts. They are demanding full, logical explanations. They are demanding second—and even third—opinions.

There is no doubt, in my mind, that all this is for the best.

I have no doubt that the caliber of our health care can be improved—but only if the public does its part. Only if people become more aggressive and less timorous. Only if, as individuals, we can all gain the knowledge—and the confidence—to begin to "talk back."

Appendix

Quality of care references

The following is a partial list of references on the quality of care. References marked with an asterisk (*) may be of special interest to consumers.

GENERAL

Battistella, R., and Southby, R. "Crisis in American Medicine," *The Lancet,* March 1968.

Bellin, L. E., and Kavaler, F. "Policing Publicly-Funded Health Care for Poor Quality, Overutilization, and Fraud," *Am. J. of Publ. H.,* May 1970.

* Donabedian, A. "An Evaluation of Prepaid Group Practice," *Inquiry,* September 1969.

* ———. "Promoting Quality through Evaluating the Process of Patient Care," *Medical Care,* May–June 1968.

Ellwood, P. M., and Herbert, M. E. "Health Care: Should Industry Buy It or Sell It?", *Harvard Business Review,* July–August 1973.

* "Facts on the Major Killing and Crippling Diseases in the United States." The National Health Education Committee, New York, 1971.

Guralnick, L., and Jackson, A. "An Index of Unnecessary Deaths," *Public H. Reports,* February 1967.

Morehead, M., et al. "The Quantity, Quality and Costs of Medical and Hospital Care Secured by a Sample of Teamster Families in the New York Area." Columbia University School of Public Health and Administrative Medicine, New York, 1964.

———. "Comparisons Between OEO Neighborhood Health Centers and Other Health Care Providers of Ratings of the Quality of Health Care," *Am. J. of Publ. H.,* July 1971.

National Health Insurance Resource Book, Committee on Ways and Means, House of Representatives, U. S. Government Printing Office, 1974.

Peterson, O., et al. "An Analytical Study of North Carolina General Practice," *J. of Med. Ed.,* December 1956.
* The Secretary's Commission on Medical Malpractice, U. S. Dept. of Health, Education and Welfare, Washington, 1972.
* Silverman, M., and Lee, P. R. *Pills, Profits, and Politics.* Berkeley: Univ. of California Press, 1974.
* Wilson, F. A., and Neuhauser, D. *Health Services in the United States,* Cambridge, Mass.: Ballinger 1974.

HOSPITALS AND NURSING HOMES

"Acute Myocardial Infarction: Death Rates in CCU's." Commission on Professional and Hospital Activities, *PAS Reporter,* vol. 8, no. 4, February 16, 1970.
* "Hospital Accreditation and the Role of the Consumer," *Consumer Commission on the Accreditation of Health Services Quarterly,* Fall 1973 (and also other Commission reports).
* Jacoby, S. "Waiting for the end: On nursing homes," *The New York Times Magazine,* March 31, 1974.
Neuhauser, D., and Turcotte, F. "Costs and Quality of Care in Different Types of Hospitals," *Annals of the Am. Acad. of Pol. and Soc. Sci.,* January 1972.
Pastore, J. O., et al. "Characteristics of Patients and Medical Care in New Haven Area Nursing Homes," *New Engl. J. of Med.,* vol. 279, 1968.
Pearson, R. J. C., et al. "Hospital Caseloads in Liverpool, New England, and Uppsala," *New Engl. J. of Med.,* vol. 279, 1968.
Rapoport, R. "A Candle for St. Greed's," *Harper's Magazine,* December 1972.
Roemer, M. I., et al. "A Proposed Hospital Quality Index: Hospital Death Rates Adjusted for Case Severity," *Health Services Research,* Summer 1968.
Tuck, J. N., et al. "A Consumer Guide to New York City Hospitals," *New York Magazine,* December 1972.
Tunley, Roul. "A Jury of Experts Picks America's 10 Best Hospitals," *Ladies' Home Journal,* February 1967.

SURGERY

Bunker, J. P. "Surgical Manpower: A comparison of operations and surgeons in the United States and in England and Wales," *New Engl. J. of Med.,* vol. 282, 1970.

————, and Wennberg, J. E. "Operation Rates, Mortality Statistics and the Quality of Life," *New Engl. J. of Med.*, editorial, vol. 289, 1973.

* Denenberg, H. S. "A Shopper's Guide to Hospitals." Commonwealth of Pennsylvania Insurance Department, July 1972.

Hughes, E. F. X., et al. "Surgical Workloads in a Community Practice," *Surgery,* March 1972.

————. "Operative Workloads in One Hospital's General Surgical Residency Program," *New Engl. J. of Med.*, vol. 289, 1973.

* McCarthy, E. G., and Widmer, G. W. "Effects of Screening by Consultants on Recommended Elective Surgical Procedures," *New Engl. J. of Med.*, vol. 291, 1974.

Moses, L. E., and Mosteller, F. "Institutional Differences in Postoperative Death Rates," *J. of the A. M. A.*, February 1968.

WOMEN, INFANTS, AND CHILDREN

* "Abortion: Questions and Answers." Pamphlet prepared by the National Abortion Rights Action League, New York, 1973 (and other publications by this group).

* "Assessment of Medical Care for Children." Institute of Medicine, National Academy of Sciences, Washington, D.C., 1974.

Graham, J. B., and Paloucek, F. P. "Where Should Cancer of the Cervix Be Treated?" *Am. J. of Obst. and Gyn.*, October 1963.

* "Infant Death: An Analysis by Maternal Risk and Health Care." Institute of Medicine, National Academy of Sciences, Washington, D.C., 1973.

* Jensen, E. D. *The Well Child's Problems,* Chicago: The Year Book Medical Publishers, Inc., 1962.

Keetel, W. C., et al. "An Appraisal of Maternity Care in Iowa." Chairman's address, Section on Obstetrics and Gynecology, Am. Publ. H. Ass. meeting, San Francisco, June 1968.

Mindlin, R. L., and Densen, P. M. "Medical Care of Urban Infants: Health Supervision," *Am. J. of Publ. H.*, April 1971.

Montgomery, T. A., and Lewis, A. "Maternal and Perinatal Deaths in California," *Calif. Med.*, November 1960.

Montgomery, T. A., et al. "Maternal Deaths in California, 1957–1962," *Calif. Med.*, June 1964.

* *Our Bodies, Ourselves.* By the Boston Women's Health Book Collective. New York: Simon & Schuster, 1973.

Peters, A. D. "Patterns of Health Care in Infancy in a Rural Southern County," *Am. J. of Publ. H.,* March 1967.
* Silver, H. K., Kempe, C. H., and Bruyn, H. *Handbook of Pediatrics,* Los Altos, California: Lange Medical Publishers, 1955.

Drug Information Sources

(1) The drug *package insert.* This is a slip of paper which, by federal requirement, must be inserted in each container sold. The
package insert has information on the particular drug's mechanism
of action, its indications and contra-indications, side effects and
adverse reactions, and dosage and route of administration. *Read
the package insert.* Many an alert patient has discovered that he
had a condition for which a drug was contra-indicated, or that his
physician has prescribed too high a dose, by reading this piece of
paper.

(2) The *U.S. Pharmacopeia* and the *National Formulary.* These
publications may be found in most libraries. Since they list drugs
by their official or generic names, you must know the generic name
for your drug. These volumes contain detailed information on all
aspects of a drug's pharmacology, including therapeutic value and
toxicity.

(3) *The New Handbook of Prescription Drugs,* by Richard Burack,
M.D. (New York: Ballantine, 1970). This 362-page paperback
is the consumer's best non-technical reference to date on drugs.

(4) *The Medical Letter.* This periodical sheet is the best source
for practicing physicians on drugs. It is also a good source for anyone. It is written in clear English. For example, this note on Librium, the nation's best-selling brand-name drug: "Even with doses
large enough to have sedative effects, no adequately controlled
study has shown Librium to be more effective in relieving anxiety
than other sedative drugs."

(5) Goodman, Louis, and Gilman, A., *Pharmacological Basis of
Therapeutics* (New York: Macmillan, 4th ed., 1970). A standard medical school pharmacology text, probably the best of its
kind. Tough reading for someone without a knowledge of basic
physiology, but probably comprehensible. Drugs are divided by
type, and generic names are used, though there are references to
brand names as well.

(6) *New and Non-official Remedies.* Drugs too new to be included

in the U.S.P or N.F. may be listed in this compendium, published
annually by the AMA.

(7) *Physicians' Desk Reference* (Oradell, New Jersey: Medical
Economics, Inc.). An industry-produced compendium of drugs,
listed by their brand names. Data on each drug is essentially the
same as that contained in the package insert. Entries are updated
periodically.

OF TENDONS AT POINT OF FRAC-
TURE.

XR LINE OF FRACTURE VISIBLE: OVER-
RIDING FRAGMENTS.

HAND, FRACTURE, PHALANGES 02 2206

ET CRUSHING INJURY OF FINGER.

SM EXTREME PAIN CAUSED BY EXTEN-
SION OF FINGERS.

SG SUBUNGUAL HEMORRHAGE; POS-
SIBLY DEFORMITY; UNBALANCED
MUSCLE ACTION; VOLAR ANGU-
LATION.

CM SECONDARY INFECTION.

XR LINE OF FRACTURE USUALLY VISI-
BLE.

PA FRACTURE OF DISTAL PHALANX:
USUALLY WITH CONTUSION OF
SOFT TISSUES; FREQUENTLY COM-
MINUTED. FRACTURE OF MIDDLE
PHALANX: FLEXION ANGULATION
OF DISTAL FRAGMENT, PHALANX;
OR FLEXION IF PROXIMAL FRAG-
MENT, DORSAL DISPLACEMENT OR
ANGULATION OF DISTAL FRAG-
MENT. FRACTURE OF PROXIMAL
PHALANX: FORWARD ANGULA-
TION; CONTRACTION OF LUM-
BRICALIS, INTEROSSEOUS MUS-
CLES.

**HAND, HEMATOMA, PAROXYSMAL SEE
ACHENBACH SYNDROME**

**HAND, MARFAN SYNDROME SEE
MARFAN SYNDROME**

**HAND, MILKER NODULES SEE MILKER
NODULES**

**HAND, OCCUPATIONAL CRAMP SEE
OCCUPATIONAL CRAMP**

**HAND-SCHUELLER-CHRISTIAN SYNDROME
00 3900**

SEE ALSO GRANULOMA, EOSINO-
PHILIC; LETTERER-SIWE DISEASE.

AT XANTHOMA, CRANIOHYPOPHY-
SIAL; XANTHOMATOSIS, IDIO-
PATHIC CHRONIC; SCHUELLER-
CHRISTIAN DISEASE.

ET UNKNOWN; POSSIBLY RECESSIVE
HEREDITY AS IN LETTERER-SIWE
DISEASE.

SG MOSTLY IN CHILDREN; POSSIBLY
PERSISTING INTO ADULT LIFE;
TRIAD OF EXOPHTHALMOS, DIA-
BETES INSIPIDUS, DEFECTS IN
MEMBRANOUS BONES, CHIEFLY
SCALP; RETARDATION OF
GROWTH, SEXUAL DEVELOPMENT;
POSSIBLY DWARFISM; OTITIS
MEDIA; SOFT NODULES OVERLY-
ING CRANIAL DEFECTS; YELLOW-
ISH XANTHOMAS OF SKIN; UL-
CERATIONS OF GUMS; LOSS OF
TEETH; POSSIBLY MODERATE EN-
LARGEMENT OF LIVER, SPLEEN,
LYMPH NODES. COURSE: GENER-
ALLY CHRONIC; RECOVERY IN
ONE THIRD OF CASES; IRRADIA-
TION, STEROID THERAPY HELPFUL
TO INDUCE PROLONGED REMIS-
SIONS; FATALITY IN 10–15 PER-
CENT.

LB ANEMIA USUALLY MILD; PANCY-
TOPENIA POSSIBLE; TISSUE CHO-
LESTEROL MANY TIMES NORMAL;
PLASMA CHOLESTEROL NORMAL.

XR AREAS OF RAREFACTION IN SKULL,
OTHER BONES; PULMONARY IN-
FILTRATION, BILATERAL, PERIHILAR,
OR CENTRAL, OR POSSIBLY DIF-
FUSE.

PA PUNCHED-OUT, GRANULOMA-
TOUS LESIONS IN SKULL, OTHER
BONES; PROLIFERATION OF RETIC-
ULOENDOTHELIAL TISSUES WITH
LIPOID CELL HYPERPLASIA, PROLIF-
ERATION OF HISTIOCYTES: GRAN-
ULOMATOUS CHANGES IN
SPLEEN; ACCUMULATION OF
XANTHOMATOUS TISSUE IN
RETRO-ORBITAL REGION.

HAND, SPLIT SEE SPLIT HAND DEFORMITY

**HAND, SYNDACTYLY SEE SYNDACTYLY;
SYNDACTYLY, TYPE IV**

**HAND, VIBRATION DISEASE SEE
VIBRATION DISEASE**

**HAND, VOLKMANN CONTRACTURE SEE
VOLKMANN CONTRACTURE**

**HANGMAN FRACTURE SEE SPINE,
FRACTURE, CERVICAL, HANGMAN
FRACTURE**

**HANHART DWARFISM SEE PITUITARY
DWARFISM II**

**HANOT SYNDROME SEE LIVER,
CIRRHOSIS, PRIMARY BILIARY**

**HANSEN DISEASE, BENIGN FORM SEE
LEPROSY, TUBERCULOID TYPE,
MINOR AND MAJOR**

**HANSEN DISEASE, MALIGNANT FORM
SEE LEPROSY, LEPROMATOUS**

**HARADA SYNDROME SEE VOGT-
KOYANAGI SYNDROME**

A Patient's Bill Of Rights*

1. The patient has the right to considerate and respectful care.

2. The patient has the right to obtain from his physician complete current information concerning his diagnosis, treatment, and prognosis in terms the patient can be reasonably expected to understand. When it is not medically advisable to give such information to the patient, the information should be made available to an appropriate person in his behalf. He has the right to know by name, the physician responsible for co-ordinating his care.

3. The patient has the right to receive from his physician information necessary to give informed consent prior to the start of any procedure and/or treatment. Except in emergencies, such information for informed consent should include but not necessarily be limited to the specific procedure and/or treatment, the medically significant risks involved, and the probable duration of incapacitation. Where medically significant alternatives for care or treatment exist, or when the patient requests information concerning medical alternatives, the patient has a right to such information. The patient also has the right to know the name of the person responsible for the procedures and/or treatment.

4. The patient has the right to refuse treatment to the extent permitted by law, and to be informed of the medical consequences of his action.

5. The patient has the right to every consideration of his privacy concerning his own medical care program. Case discussion, consultation, examination, and treatment are confidential and should be conducted discreetly. Those not directly involved in his care must have the permission of the patient to be present.

6. The patient has the right to expect that all communications and records pertaining to his care should be treated as confidential.

7. The patient has the right to expect that within its capacity a hospital must make reasonable response to the request of a patient for services. The hospital must provide evaluation, service, and/or referral as indicated by the urgency of the case. When medically permissible, a patient may be transferred to another facility

* Approved by the House of Delegates of the American Hospital Association, February 6, 1973. Reprinted with the permission of the American Hospital Association.

only after he has received complete information and explanation concerning the needs for and alternatives to such a transfer. The institution to which the patient is to be transferred must first have accepted the patient for transfer.

8. The patient has the right to obtain information as to any relationship of his hospital to other health care and educational institutions insofar as his care is concerned. The patient has the right to obtain information as to the existence of any professional relationships among individuals, by name, who are treating him.

9. The patient has the right to be advised if the hospital proposes to engage in or perform human experimentation affecting his care or treatment. The patient has the right to refuse to participate in such research projects.

10. The patient has the right to expect reasonable continuity of care. He has the right to know in advance what appointment times and physicians are available and where. The patient has the right to expect that the hospital will provide a mechanism whereby he is informed by his physician or a delegate of the physician of the patient's continuing health-care requirements following discharge.

11. The patient has the right to examine and receive an explanation of his bill regardless of source of payment.

12. The patient has the right to know what hospital rules and regulations apply to his conduct as a patient.

Index

240

Bunker, John, 158, 181
Burack, Richard, 99, 100, 186

California, 216–17, 218
California Medical Association, 219
Cancer, 3, 35, 74, 92
Cerebral angiography, 77
Chemistries, Table 12, 79–81; 85
Chest, 59, 88
Chicago hospitals, 122, 123, 218
Chief complaint, 49–51
Chief of service, hospital, 26–27
Childbirth (delivery), 194–96; natural, 199–201. *See also* Infants
Children, 4, 112, 154, 176; pediatric specialties for, Table 37, 209–10; physical exam for, 210, Table 38, 211; risk to from x-rays, 75; well-child care, 211–15, Table 39, 212–13
Children and Youth (C and Y) projects, 215
Children's Television Workshop, 224
Chromosome analysis (karyotyping), 88
Cine-angiograms (cines), 77
Clinical Judgment (Feinstein), 64
Clinical pharmacologist, 108
Clinics. *See* Outpatient departments (OPDs), Public health clinics
Collen, Morris, 90
Columbia hospital care studies, 17–18, 19, 122, Table 17, 125; 126, 127, 136, 161–62, 183n.
Columbia-Presbyterian Medical Center, 196, 197
Columbia University School of Public Health and Administrative Medicine, 125
Complete blood count (CBC), 62, 68, Table 9, 69–70
Comprehensive Health Planning (CHP) agency, 224–25
Connecticut nursing homes, 4, 156
Consent form, 147
Consumer groups for health care improvement, 223–26
Continuing education, doctor's, 21–22
Cooper, Irving, 96, 112
Cortisone, 82
Credentials, doctor's, 16–19
Cultures, 70–71; errors in use of, 72
Current Medical Information and

Terminology (CMIT), 42–43
Cystitis, 64–65
Cystoscopy, 92n.
Cytological tests, 87–88

Daley, Richard, 218
Deafness, 154
Death, 2, 4, 35; common causes of, Table 14, 93–95; in hospitals, 122, 123, 124, 220; and surgery, 158, 170, 217
Denenberg, Herbert, 132
Diabetes, 15, 82, 171, 204
Diagnosis, 28–44, 62; differential, 39–40; errors in, 31–37; follow-up of test results, 83–84; incomplete, 41–42; missing a diagnosis, 33–35; negative and positive findings, 40; for newborn infants, 208, 209; non-disease, 31–32; out-of-date or invented, 42–43; ruling out a disease, 29–30; and second opinion, 111–12
Diagnostic work-up, 37–38, 134; complete blood count (CBC), 68, Table 9, 69–70; lab tests, 64–70; and multiphasic screening, 89–92; TB skin test, 89; urinalysis (UA), 68, Table 9, 69–70; for women, 176–77
Diet, and lab tests, 82
Dietary counseling, 131
Directory of Approved Internships and Residencies, 13, 26, 126
Directory of Medical Specialists, 12, 13, 16, 19, 27, 162
Disability, 35; common causes of, Table 14, 93–95
Disease (illness). *See* under name of disease. *See also* various Tables throughout the book
Disease-oriented private organizations (associations, foundations, etc.), 121, 153–54
Disease process, 38
Diuretics, 98, 103
Doctors, 3–4, 6, 8–9, 24, 96, 177, 222, 223; age of, and performance, 14–15; assistants to, 23, 62–63; continuing education, 21–22; credentials, 16–19, 218; and diagnosis, 30–31, 111; family practice, 18, 24; GPs, 3, 17, 18, 100; hospital affiliation, 16–17, 133–34; initial visit to, 45–54, 62; and

Sweden, 157, 181
Symptoms, 29, 34–35, 37, 50

Teaching hospitals, 53, 125, 144–46,
161, 184, 214; chief of services in,
26–27; hierarchy in, Table 24, 144;
patients in, 142–43, 145
Television, health information on,
224
Thayer Hospital (Waterville, Me.),
129
Thoracentesis, 88
Thyroid radioactivity scan, 88
Tietze, C., 188
Titticut Follies (film), 220
Toxemia, 198
Tropical diseases, 121
Tubal ligation, 190–91
Tuberculosis, 2, 66, 73n., 89, 98, 100,
121
TB skin test, 62, 65, 66, 73n., 89
Tufts University Medical School,
165
Tumors, brain, 86

Uniform Financial and Statistical
Reports, 220
United Mine Workers, 161
Upper GI series, 77
Urinalysis (UA), 62, 65, 68, Table 9,
69–70
Urinary tract infection, 35, 77, 180–
81
Urologists, 191
U.S.: death rate, 2; health care
expenditure, 1; life expectancy,
Table 1, 3; suggested health care
measures, 221–23

U. S. Compendium of Medical
Standards, 222–23
U. S. Department of Health,
Education and Welfare, 3, 118,
154, 156
U. S. Pharmacopeia (U.S.P.), 103,
104

Vasectomy, 190–91
Venereal diseases, 121
Victim Is Always the Same, The
(Cooper), 112
Viruses, 71n.
Visiting Nurse Association, 151–52
Visual acuity, 4, 35
Vital signs, 57–58

Wagner Child Health Station, 214
Ward patients, 142–43, 145; and
surgery, 171–72, 173, 174
Willowbrook (New York state
hospital), 223
Woman's Day, 6
Women, 24n., 92, 176; diagnostic
work-up for, 176–77; as doctors,
183–84; drug treatment for, 179–81;
emotional illness diagnosis, 178–79;
and hysterectomies, 181–83;
physical exam for, 176, 180; risk to
from x-rays, 75; and self-
examination, 184–85; surgery for,
Table 29, 181. *See also* Abortion;
Childbirth; Pregnancy
Women doctors, 183–84

X-rays, 73–79; contrast, 77, Table 11,
78–79; dosage, Table 10, 75